A Guide to
Medieval Sites
in Britain

By the same authors

A Guide to Anglo-Saxon Sites
A Guide to Norman Sites in Britain

A Guide to Medieval Sites in Britain

NIGEL AND MARY KERR

PALADIN
GRAFTON BOOKS
A Division of the Collins Publishing Group

LONDON GLASGOW
TORONTO SYDNEY AUCKLAND

Grafton Books
A Division of the Collins Publishing Group
8 Grafton Street, London W1X 3LA

First published in Great Britain by Grafton Books 1988
Published in Paladin Books 1989

British Library Cataloguing in Publication Data
Kerr, Nigel
    A guide to medieval sites in Britain.
    1. Great Britain – History – Medieval
    period 1200–1485   2. Great Britain –
    Antiquities
    I. Title
    914.1'003'21   DA175
ISBN 0-246-12470-9
ISBN 0-586-08496-7 (paper covers)

Photoset by Rowland Phototypesetting Ltd
Bury St Edmunds, Suffolk
Printed in Great Britain by
Butler & Tanner Ltd, Frome, Somerset

CONTENTS

ACKNOWLEDGEMENTS

Many people have helped us in the preparation of this book, both friends and scholars alike, as well as numerous incumbents of churches, custodians and others. We could not afford to write a guide of this sort without a comprehensive network of friends with whom we can stay. They include Peter Warner, Adam Welfare, Jack and Jandy Stevenson, the Greenhalves, Blaise Vyner, Yvonne Copeland, David Dawson, Ian Flett and Don Benson among many others. They and other friends and colleagues have contributed much valuable advice as well as trenchant criticisms on occasion. We would also like to mention assistance given in the choice of sites by John Lewis of the National Museum of Wales and the Sites and Monuments staff of most of the English archaeological trusts and units. We thank Roger Mockford and Angela for processing the photographs (previously done in our kitchen sink!), Douglas Jeal and Stephen Norton for help with the illustrations and the Pagets for looking after the cats during our numerous absences. Last, but by no means least, we thank Uncle Guy for his understanding.

INTRODUCTION

This guide is concerned with the physical remains of the Middle Ages in Britain. The period begins and ends rather arbitrarily with the dates of 1200 and 1485. The first date marks the time of the general change from Romanesque to Gothic in the field of architecture, and the second is, of course, the date of the Battle of Bosworth which marked the accession of the Tudors. Although it deals with a historical period, it is not a 'history book'; it aims to provide basic information and comment about the sites it contains, together with clear directions as to how they can best be reached. It is a guide book, and as such is not intended as a comprehensive reference work for a whole subject, but merely to be a source of information and enlightenment for the traveller.

The illustrations which complement the text are designed to give a foretaste of the delights in store. Most of the photographs are our own work, and many of the drawings were actually made on site. The drawings seek to reproduce the vigour and quality of the original compositions rather than to reflect the evidence of time and damage which have befallen the objects since they were made. By comparing our illustrations with the objects 'in the flesh' the visitor will perceive not only the design as the artist intended it to be seen, but also the traces of wear and tear which add to an appreciation of the antiquity of the material. Like a piece of fine antique furniture, it is both the original design and the patina of age which delight the eye.

The 160 entries in this book – many of which are grouped entries of related sites, bringing the total to well over 200 – are not by any means a complete catalogue of medieval remains in Britain. If such a compendium were ever assembled, it would run to thousands of entries since many churches contain medieval workmanship in their fabrics; and when castles, monasteries, houses, towns and villages and other field monuments are added, the sheer weight of evidence is staggering. During the three centuries covered by this book, much was done to change the face of England.

We have divided the country into geographical regions, and we have tried to choose a range of sites reflecting the attributes of each area. As with our previous books, the criteria within these regionally based selections depend upon sites being good examples of particular types of monuments, or having strong historical or other associations, or else that they have fine settings; many have all three. In eastern England, for example, there are many churches worthy of inclusion on the basis of their quality and interest, but we have included only a selection. Again in Wales, castles are the most dramatic medieval legacy, but we have included other types of site as well in order to balance the view of medieval Welsh society. Inevitably, however, with such a rich field of study as the Middle Ages, much has been omitted, and it is hoped that the visitor will use this book as a starting point for other journeys round medieval Britain, for it is a fascinating and stimulating place, alive with the qualities of faith, endeavour and humanity.

Medieval Britain

After the Norman Conquest, there was a general increase in wealth and prosperity, coupled with a rising population. New towns and villages were established, as we illustrated in our *Norman Guide*, and although wealth tended to be concentrated in the upper echelons of society, there is much evidence of expansion and growth. This success was shortlived, however, and in the years after 1300 we can detect signs of economic instability including levels of inflation which sound decidedly modern. These difficulties, coupled with overbearing kings and increased taxation, led to widespread discontent and eventually rebellion. As if this were not enough, the fourteenth century also saw a deteriorating climate, troubles in France and the Black Death. By the fifteenth century signs of economic failure, brought on by political as well as economic factors, were all about and the promise of the early Middle Ages remained unfulfilled.

Yet if the period covered by this book was ultimately one of economic reverse, we can extract much that is positive from the experience. For one thing, the failure of the medieval economy paradoxically had little discernible effect upon building programmes and standards of individual comfort among at least the upper ranks of society. By contrast with social development, art and architecture made tremendous strides during those 'Gothic' centuries, culminating in the Perpendicular Style which England made her own. Secular buildings also fail to mirror the decline in fortunes, and comfortable fifteenth-century yeoman houses can be set beside the castles and manors of the gentry to show that at least the upper ranks of the peasantry enjoyed a good standard of living.

If we look more closely at medieval Britain, we find three great divisions recognized at the time and which are still helpful. Society was composed of those who worked, those who fought and those who prayed, broadly known as peasants, knights and clerics. To take the peasants first, we find that it was this class which probably enjoyed the greatest change in its fortunes. In the early Middle Ages, they were bound to the soil of their manor and enjoyed few freedoms under the law. But gradually new rights and privileges were obtained and the development of the monetary economy combined with the shortage of labour after the Black Death raised living standards and increased their independence. Later, wealthy merchants became a powerful force in the realm, and they laid the foundations of the new age which dawned with the Tudors.

This was the reverse of the fortunes enjoyed by the knightly class. Individual families encountered financial difficulties by the thirteenth century, and the proliferation of quarrels at home as well as overseas service and wars with Scotland and Wales made the knightly calling difficult and expensive. The bloody carnage of the Wars of the Roses had little effect on the country at large, but for the families and retainers involved it was frequently a ruinous experience. These difficulties were exacerbated by the high and rising taxation needed to finance wars at home and abroad. Yet through all this, some great magnates did well enough, increasing their holdings and displaying their wealth by building lavishly appointed houses and endowing religious foundations.

The fortunes of the Church followed those of society at large. During the early Middle Ages there was a tide of monastic foundations, spurred on by the proliferation of new Orders and an ample supply of marginal land for endowments. In later times, however, kings and laymen alike resented the power of the Church. The arrival of the friars early in the thirteenth century triggered further foundations, but the great days of monastic expansion were over. If men no longer chose to endow religious houses, it did not stop them from enlarging and beautifying parish churches. Although many had been rebuilt or extended in Norman times, most were altered later. After the Black Death in particular, individuals and guilds made munificent contributions to church fabric funds. The proliferation of chantry chapels, provided to ease the founder's sojourn in Purgatory, demonstrated the motivation for this reawakened piety.

Yet what was life like in medieval Britain? How would we react to it today? The popular view probably falls somewhere between Chaucer's jolly pilgrims summoning up a vision of 'Merrie England', and the darker undertones of the word 'medieval' when used pejoratively to invoke images of violence and ignorance. Again the Middle Ages was an 'age of faith', and certainly a tremendous amount of effort was expended in the construction and elaboration of churches. A further factor was the regionalism mentioned earlier; medieval Britain was a large and complex place showing many variations and differences. Unsatisfactory communications and varying settlement patterns, coupled with local industries like Cotswold wool, tin-mining in Cornwall or salt-making in the east of England, produced a picture as varied as it is today.

The answer to the question, 'What was medieval Britain like?' is that it was so varied, large and fascinating that it is up to the visitor to decide from the evidence available. We found the medieval scene by turns profoundly moving, as for example when we stood in the ravaged ruins of Coventry Cathedral; comfortingly familiar in the case of the still used field systems at Braunton and Laxton; and amusing, as with the 'giant' funeral effigies at Aldworth. Our travels around medieval Britain were never dull, and we hope that you will derive as much pleasure and enlightenment from your journeys as we have from ours.

How to Use This Book

We have divided the mainland of Britain into eight geographical regions which reflect most satisfactorily the pattern of medieval settlement. Each region forms the basis of a separate section of the book, and each is prefaced by a brief outline of its history. A key map showing the modern county boundaries will also be found at the beginning of each section, and the numbers on it correspond with the consecutive descriptions in the text. If you wish to look up a particular site, consult the index at the end of the book in order to find its page number.

Each site is located in detail, and a six-figure Ordnance Survey grid reference is provided. An Ordnance Survey 1:50,000 metric map, which has replaced the old one-inch survey, is a valuable tool when visiting sites and our map directions refer to this series, but if you don't have the relevant map the directions can be followed quite easily from a good road atlas. Most of the sites lie in villages or towns, but any which are particularly difficult to find have been located by a small map showing nearest major roads and other features as well as a verbal description. Where appropriate, nearest towns and villages are indicated, together with their distances from the site.

Some of the sites in this book are on private land, and their inclusion implies no right of access. Nevertheless, owners are generally very co-operative, and are pleased to allow genuinely interested people access to sites on their land. Many of the sites are churches, and it is hoped that visitors will behave in a suitable manner; a contribution to the fabric fund is not only courteous but also helps to ensure the survival of the very sites which the visitor sees. When in the countryside please follow the Country Code, and *never*, in any circumstances, dig into a site. This is a very complicated business which archaeologists spend a lot of time learning about!

Certain of the sites are in the guardianship of the Historic Buildings and Monuments Commission (English Heritage), the Scottish Development Department or the Welsh Office and this is indicated under the relevant entries. Some are open at all reasonable times without charge, others have special opening hours which are indicated in the entries, while most are open during standard hours, which are in England:

	Weekdays	*Sundays*
16 October to 14 March	9.30–4	2–4
15 March to 15 October	9.30–6.30	2–6.30

And in Scotland:

	Weekdays	*Sundays*
Winter: 4 January–31 March		
1 October–31 December	9.30–4.20	12.30–3.35
Summer: 1 April–30 September	9.30–5.15	10.30–4.45

A list of medieval kings and a glossary of unfamiliar terms will be found at the back of the book.

THE
MIDLANDS

EASTERN
ENGLAND

GREATER
LONDON

17 ♦ Reading 16 ♦
BERKSHIRE   15 ♦

14 ♦

KENT   ♦ 1

12 ♦   4 ♦
                                              Canterbury
Basingstoke •   • Guildford 13 ♦   Tonbridge
                         SURREY   5 ♦   ♦ 3 Ashford   ♦ 2
HAMPSHIRE   6 ♦   Dover •
18 ♦ Winchester   7 ♦ ♦ 8
                         ♦ 11   9 ♦
Southampton ♦ 19   WEST SUSSEX   EAST SUSSEX
                                        6 ♦ ♦ 8
                • Chichester   Lewes •   Hastings
                                    10 ♦
                Portsmouth
        IOW
        ♦ 20

0   10   20   30 Miles
|___|___|___|___|

0 10 20 30 40 50 Km

SOUTH-EASTERN
ENGLAND

SOUTH-EASTERN ENGLAND

Introduction

The south-east of England achieved early economic and social dominance over the rest of the country with London and the Thames Valley becoming a favoured haunt of kings. In this part of England we see a concentration of sites and buildings associated with the highest echelons of medieval society. Windsor and Eltham Palace are superb buildings commissioned by kings for their own use. Windsor was always much more than just a stronghold; it was a celebration of monarchy in stone, with St George's Chapel, closely associated with the exalted Order of the Garter, adding the finishing touch to the complex. Eltham, by contrast, was not a defended site and is now less well preserved, but the Great Hall is a magnificent building, the roof of which alone is finer by far than many a church elsewhere.

Where kings led, the leading commoners of the later Middle Ages followed. The castles of Bodiam and Herstmonceux were built less as serious fortresses than as demonstrations of their owners' rank, wealth and status. Bodiam is on a scale to resist an army of conquest rather than the feared French raids, and Herstmonceux belongs to the heady days of the early fifteenth century when dash and display were the guiding stars of many a modish gentleman. A different expression of prestige is visible at Penshurst Place; this great hall was built by a leading London merchant, and well illustrates the gathering power of his class during the fourteenth century. Although not on the scale of Eltham, Penshurst is still impressive, and the generous proportions of the house demonstrated the owner's prominence just as effectively as walls and battlements elsewhere.

Further down the scale are the houses of the yeomen and lesser gentry with which Kent is particularly well blessed. Here in the 'Garden of England' we find the sort of houses of which English dreams are made: comfortable, well matured and fashioned in the materials and styles of the country which made them. Old Soar Manor is without doubt one of the best examples of an early manor house to be seen anywhere: simple, secure and yet affording an acceptable degree of comfort for an undemanding owner. At Pattyndene, Eyhorne and the Priest's House at Alfriston, we see the robust timber-framed houses of the more prosperous farmers and priests. These 'Wealden' houses embodied the idea of a central open hall with a hearth on the floor and the smoke finding its own way out through a hole in the roof. At either end of the hall were chambers on two floors, and doubtless these houses worked well enough, although the presence of sweet-smelling melilot at Eyhorne reminded us of the drawbacks of communal life!

Of towns we find several important examples in the south-east. South-ampton continued as a major trading port until the end of the Middle Ages and, despite the French raid in 1338, its citizens continued to roam the seas of the known world. There may be seen merchants' houses, the town walls and even a medieval warehouse built originally for the all-important wool trade. Canterbury was always dominated by its Cathedral and the pilgrims to St Thomas's tomb. Chaucer has ensured undying fame for this great shrine of medieval Christendom, and what visitor can walk its streets today without some sense of wonder at the continuity shared with pilgrims of the past? Finally at Winchester we see again the quality of buildings commissioned by medieval monarchs. The Castle Hall there is a triumph of the builder's art, with slender clustered columns, a mighty roof and a most imposing scale. Here was a fit setting for a royal feast, and the presence of the Round Table reminds us of the mystical ideals of chivalry and courtliness to which those kings aspired.

Also at Winchester is the splendid Cathedral, essentially the great church built by the Normans to replace the Saxon shrine and rallying point which stood next door. But the cathedrals of Winchester and Canterbury are supported by an interesting group of religious monuments in this region. Bayham and Michelham are two unusual monasteries, the first because it is fortified, and the second because an otherwise obscure house contains architectural work of the highest quality. Bayham, now replete with an imaginative Physic Garden reminding us of the monks' skill with healing herbs, was provided with a moat and gatehouse against the French, and still enjoys a secluded setting untrammelled by modernity.

As to the parish churches, Stoke d'Abernon has the earliest memorial brass in England and at Etchingham is an excellent example of a four-teenth-century chantry, complete with collegiate stalls, founders' brasses and contemporary architecture. Trotton takes the story a stage further for there, apart from the splendid brass to Lord Camoys, Garter Knight and hero of Agincourt, are ethereal wall-paintings reminding the living of the inevitability of judgement. Henry VI's collegiate foundation at Eton was also conceived partly as a chantry, sharing a common inspiration with Etchingham and Trotton. As befitted a royal foundation, it was conceived on a lavish scale, but the early demise of the founder resulted in a much reduced building programme.

There are sites in the south-east which call forth a response deeper than mere curiosity, however. We found Winchelsea, grave of urban ambition, peculiarly moving with the bones of its huge projected church and forlorn lanes which should have been thronged with people. But most affecting of all is the crypt of bones at Hythe, where we meet our medieval forebears 'face to face', divided from them and their world by a wink of time and the warmth of flesh. In regarding these remnants of an earlier England, we should resist thoughts of superiority, and temper our intrusion with compassion.

1
CANTERBURY, Kent

City of pilgrims

The story of the venerable city of Canterbury, goal of Chaucer's pilgrims, has been charted in our Anglo-Saxon and Norman guides. By the opening of our period, the cult of the 'Holy Blissful Martyr' was well established and Canterbury Cathedral remained popular throughout our period. Many miracles are recorded at the tomb and one such, the story of Sir John FitzEisulf of Pontefract, is recorded in the stained glass of the Trinity Chapel whence his body was translated in 1220. The pilgrims came from far and wide and, although many hoped to be cured of ailments, others came to obtain forgiveness or to do penance. A further potent reason was the desire to shorten the trials of Purgatory, and later the wealthy often paid a priest to go in their stead after death.

There are many descriptions of the wonders of Becket's tomb, of how it stood about a man's height, the upper parts entirely covered with plates of pure gold that were hardly visible beneath the precious stones with which it was studded – sapphires, diamonds, rubies and emeralds. The gold was carved with beautiful designs and set with agates, jaspers and cornelians and a remarkable ruby. Prudence dictated that the wooden cover which was lowered over the shrine had bells attached to it in case of burglars!

The shrine was swept away in the Reformation; on 10 April 1538 twenty-six cartloads of treasure were taken away, and the bones of the martyr mysteriously vanished. We are left with a magnificent church which, although largely Norman, has important later work. The nave in particular had its Romanesque piers encased in Gothic mouldings by the King's master mason Henry Yevele early in the fifteenth century, and now

Map Reference Canterbury: TR 155579, Map 179
Cathedral is open Sun 7.30–6; weekdays (summer) 7.30–7; (winter) 7.30–6.30 (Sat 5).

View of the lacy fan-vaulting of 'Bell Harry' above the crossing at Canterbury. John Wastell was the master mason of this great tower, which was completed in 1503. (Photo courtesy Peter Burton/Harland Walshall.)

affords one of the best Gothic vistas in England. An echo of the majesty of Becket's tomb is provided by that of Edward, Prince of Wales, the Black Prince. The glowing effigy of the 'chief flower of chivalry of all the world', as the Chronicler Froissart called him, lies surrounded by the symbols of his knightly prowess.

The city of Canterbury retains many early buildings, including its walls and the famous Mercery Lane, a street of medieval narrowness on the west side of which lay the Chequers Inn, originally built to house pilgrims. The centre of the city has much of its medieval scale, and timber-framed houses lurk behind many façades. England has many medieval towns, but only one shrine of Canterbury's celebrity; we must leave the last word to Geoffrey Chaucer, who gave us that warm and spirited picture of the fourteenth-century pilgrims. Can we not ride with them along the lanes of our imagination?

> When the sweet showers of April fall and shoot
> Down through the drought of March to pierce the root,
> Bathing every vein in liquid power
> From which there springs the engendering of the flower . . .
> Then people long to go on pilgrimages . . .

2
HYTHE CHURCH, Kent

The crypt of bones
Hythe – the name means 'landing place' – was one of the original Cinque Ports, which provided the chief part of the English navy and in return enjoyed favoured trading status. This points to an early prosperity which is borne out by an examination of its splendid church of St Leonard. The

Map Reference Hythe: TR 161349, Map 189
Nearest Town Folkestone
Church is on the cliff above the town, approached via narrow lanes and steep steps. Crypt is reached from the south porch. Open daily, small entrance charge.

The medieval inhabitants of Hythe, awaiting the last trump.

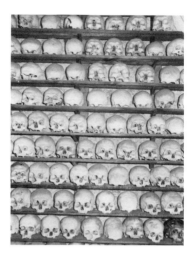

Some of the 2,000 skulls in the crypt.

thirteenth century saw the apogee of Hythe's fortunes, and the chancel, rebuilt about 1230, is a stunning monument to that period, replete with carvings, clustered Bethersden marble shafts and luxuriant fittings. It has a full three-storeyed elevation, and the whole was intended to be vaulted in stone. But it is what happened beneath this chancel that provides the chief interest. A processional way was contrived right round the east end at churchyard level, and the sanctuary raised up above a vaulted passage. This lends drama to the interior, with a precipitous flight of steps up from the nave, and far below is a bizarre chamber, filled with bones.

Hythe Church is situated on a shelf half-way up a steep cliff. Space round the church must always have been at a premium, and the digging of graves in the rocky subsoil a demanding task. It was probably these factors which led to the assembling of the great collection of bones in the chamber beneath the sanctuary. As new burials were made, old ones were taken up and the remains reverently placed in the chamber. There are 8,000 thigh bones and 2,000 skulls, and they were probably all put here before 1540. At Hythe we enjoy a unique opportunity of 'meeting' its medieval inhabitants.

The Hythe bones are disarticulated, so the scope for detailed examination is limited, but they seem to conform broadly with the somewhat gloomy results of recent work elsewhere. At Wharram Percy and York, it has been calculated that fewer than ten per cent of people lived beyond the ages of fifty and sixty respectively. The life expectancy from birth was only 18.7 years, with twenty-seven per cent at York dying in childhood. The average lifespan for males at Wharram was 35.3 years, and for females only 31.3, the reverse of modern patterns. These statistics are depressing, and for all the fascination we might derive from our study of the Middle Ages, there is much to be said for the twentieth century!

3
PATTYNDENE AND EYHORNE, Kent

Two Wealden houses

Map Reference Pattyndene: TQ 720366, Map 188
Nearest Town Tunbridge Wells
About 12 miles (19 km) east of Tunbridge Wells. In Goudhurst on the A262 turn south down the B2079 towards Bedgebury Pinetum, by the village pond. The house is on the west side of the road near a hump-backed bridge. It is a private home, open to the public on Sun afternoons in Aug and Sept, and by arrangement throughout the year.

These houses are excellent examples of the 'Wealden' type, which, as the name suggests, is particularly common in the Weald of Kent. Houses of this general pattern occur in many parts of lowland England, however, and were particularly favoured in the fifteenth century, when these two were built. They have a hall open to the roof as their main element which, in imitation of higher-status houses like Penshurst, formed the central bar of an H-shaped plan. At either end are two-storey ranges containing a parlour at the high end and services at the lower, both with chambers over.

The upper chambers are jettied, a symbol of status, and it is this feature which gives the Wealden house its distinctive form of a central hall recessed behind projecting flanking wings.

Pattyndene is a particularly clear example of this pattern, and the front retains the larger central ground-floor window which lit the hall. The angle posts of the frame are elaborately carved, and the deep hipped roof preserves the steep pitch required for thatch. Today, there is a chimney on the roof ridge instead of the pottery or wooden smoke louvre which would have been there when the house was built. This was the whole point of the open hall: to diminish the fire risk posed by an open hearth in the centre of the floor before the widespread use of chimneys. During the sixteenth century open halls were, as in the case of Pattyndene, normally floored in, and a fireplace with chimney was built to replace the open hearth. A rare example of an unfloored small hall can be seen at Alfriston.

At Eyhorne, the fifteenth-century house was extended at the rear during the seventeenth century giving an L-shaped plan. Here hang bunches of melilot, a herb used to sweeten the atmosphere of these early houses, and in the bedrooms are roots of elecampane, used to dispel evil spirits. These two houses are important reminders of the agreeable possibilities of medieval life, and their cheerful comfort should be borne in mind when we visit many a cold ruin or unheated 'museum' elsewhere.

Both these houses are good examples of timber frames, where the basic structure is composed of oak beams jointed together to form a strong construction which, with adequate maintenance, should last for another five centuries. The buildings were prefabricated, with all the joints being cut and fitted before they were raised. The resulting timber skeleton then

Map Reference Eyhorne: TQ 832547, Map 188
Nearest Town Maidstone
5 miles (8 km) east of Maidstone, just off the A20 on the B2163. Shortly after a turning off the main road, the house is up a lane to the left. It is a private house, no longer open, but the exterior can be seen from the road.

BELOW LEFT: *Pattyndene is a delectable timber-framed Wealden house.*

BELOW: *The structure exposed. The open hall is flanked by two-storey wings.*

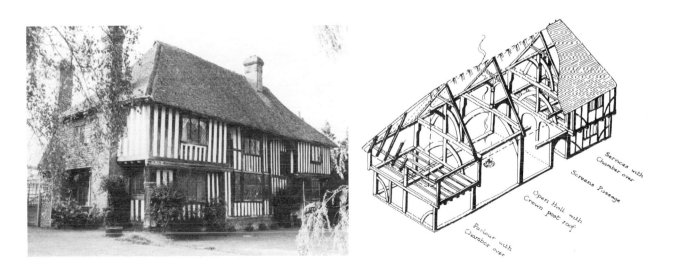

had the panels of its walls filled with clay and chopped straw, finished with a coat of lime plaster and the roof covered with thatch. Much skill was required in the making of these buildings, and the details of the carpentry, such as the Roman numerals used to identify the different frames and timbers, repay careful examination.

4
OLD SOAR AND IGHTHAM MOTE, Kent

Map Reference Old Soar Manor, Plaxtol: TQ 619541, Map 188 *Nearest Town* Sevenoaks 7 miles (11 km) south-east of Sevenoaks, 1 mile east of Plaxtol, on the east side of the A227. Owned by the National Trust, in guardianship of the HBMCE, and open during the summer season, standard hours. There is an exhibition by the Plaxtol Local History Group of some of the late medieval timber frames in the village, with a map of how to get to them.

Map Reference Ightham Mote, Plaxtol: TQ 583534, Map 188 *Nearest Town* Sevenoaks 6 miles (9.5 km) south-east of Sevenoaks on the west side of the A227, down Mote Lane. It has recently been taken over by the National Trust. Tel Lamberhurst 810378 for opening times.

Both sites are well signposted.

Two manor houses

These two houses provide an opportunity to see the homes of lesser knights, the sort of men who always formed the bulk of the chivalry at the great medieval battles and who followed their feudal lords, bound by bonds of fealty and devotion. Old Soar is the earlier of the two, and preserves a late-thirteenth-century solar block. The hall to which it was attached stood on the site of the adjacent eighteenth-century house. Old Soar continues the early medieval tradition of first-floor accommodation, since the Great Chamber with its fine crownpost roof is raised over a vaulted undercroft. The room appears somewhat spartan now but with its painted plaster and hangings, furs or rugs on the floor and a fire in the hearth, it would have been comfortable enough. Apart from the Great Chamber, there is a chapel and a small closet with garderobe. This manor, granted to the Culpeppers by the Archbishop of Canterbury, stood on the edge of the great forest of the Weald. We can imagine the days of its owner taken up with hunting as well as the ordering of the estate and the occasional blast of war.

Ightham Mote has, as its name suggests, a moat around it. This feature immediately distinguishes it from Old Soar, and correctly suggests that it is rather higher up the social scale. The earliest owner to have left an architectural mark on the house is Sir Thomas Cawne, a knight who fought with the Black Prince in France and who built the hall at Ightham in about 1340. It is interesting to compare this hall with Pulteney's at nearby Penshurst. Scale was an indication of rank: Penshurst is almost exactly twice as big. Likewise, although Ightham has traceried stone windows, they are smaller and less fine.

Old Soar, Ightham and Penshurst together provide a clear impression of differing standards of living in fourteenth-century England for, although Soar was built earlier, the modest fortunes of the family evidently did not extend to modernizing their house. Each has its quotient of fascination – Penshurst with its splendid hall, Ightham with its idyllic setting – yet of the three, Soar is in some ways the best, for it preserves most faithfully the simplicity of its medieval past.

Ightham Mote was the home of Sir Thomas Cawne, who fought with the Black Prince in France.

The crown post roof of the Great Chamber at Old Soar.

5

PENSHURST PLACE, Kent

A great merchant's house

At Penshurst can be seen the most complete fourteenth-century manor house in England. It was originally built for Sir John de Pulteney, who died of the plague in 1349. Pulteney was a prominent London merchant and financier, mayor four times and, after he bought the manor of Penshurst in 1338, a country gentleman. The house had an H-plan, with a magnificent

Map Reference Penshurst Place: TQ 527439, Map 188
Nearest Town Tonbridge
3 miles (5 km) west of Tonbridge. In the village on the B2176. Open every afternoon except Mon from 1 April to 6 Oct 1–5.30. Tearoom. The church at the south-west corner of the park also has some medieval work including nave and aisles.

Great Hall linking two ranges containing chambers and services. As originally built, the house had no defences, but by 1392 Sir John Devereux, a later owner, added a stone wall with towers at the angles, parts of which remain. But the major medieval fabric at Penshurst belongs to the mid fourteenth century, and it shows us something of the standard of living which a very wealthy man could afford.

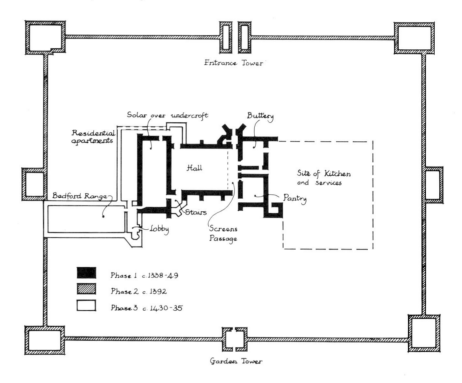

Penshurst was a fitting rural seat for a Lord Mayor of London and conveys something of the drama of medieval domestic architecture.

The Great Hall is the principal survival, since the flanking ranges (although largely intact) were altered and incorporated into the later house, which was the home of the sixteenth-century *literatus* Sir Philip Sidney. This hall would have been the centre of the household, where Sir John and his lady would have taken meals with their family, friends and retainers. It is a magnificent chamber wonderfully preserved, even down to the central hearth, although the roof louvre – through which the smoke would have passed – has gone.

The side walls have tall paired lights with embattled transoms and cusped tracery. The richly decorated wooden screens are actually sixteenth-century, but they reflect the original arrangement, baffling the draughts from the opposed entrance doors at the lower end. Some of the trestle tables are medieval, however, and are exceptionally rare. We can imagine rows of such tables in the body of the hall, stretching down from

the dais end. It is the roof which is the most impressive survival. This has a span of over sixty feet, and is of kingpost construction. The ties are supported on great curved braces which rest on wooden corbels carved as human figures, said to represent people who worked on the manor. The roof is made of chestnut, an unusual wood for such a purpose, and it glows with an agreeable pale colour, much livelier than the usual oak.

Standing in this hall, there is little difficulty in conjuring scenes of medieval feasting and jollity, but soon after it was built the fashion for communal dining began to decline. This was lamented only twenty years later in Langland's *Vision of Piers Plowman*:

> Wretched is the hall . . . each day in the week
> There the lord and lady liketh not to sit.
> Now have the rich a rule to eat by themselves
> In a privy parlour . . . for poor men's sake,
> Or in a chamber with a chimney, and leave the chief hall
> That was made for meals, for men to eat in.

The Great Hall still dominates the house, and the addition of defences reflects the uncertainties of the later fourteenth century.

6

BAYHAM AND MICHELHAM, East Sussex

Map Reference Bayham: TQ 651366,
Map 188
Nearest Town Tunbridge Wells
5 miles (8 km) east of Tunbridge
Wells, up minor roads north of
B2169. It is in guardianship of the
HBMCE and open standard hours,
summer season only.

Map Reference Michelham: TQ
558093, Map 199
Nearest Town Hailsham
2 miles (3 km) east of Hailsham on
minor road off the A22. Owned by
the Sussex Archaeological Society,
open Easter–Oct daily, 11–5.30.
The extensively moated site is in
the Cuckmere Valley.

RIGHT: *Romantic Bayham, a feast of
architecture and landscape.*

Two Sussex monasteries

These two sites, although their origins and histories differ, were never in
the forefront of affairs and are chiefly memorable because of their delightful
settings. Bayham Abbey in particular, sometimes described as 'the Fountains of the South', lies in a late-eighteenth-century landscape of delight,
and its ruins doubtless provided an agreeably Gothick air. The abbey was a
Premonstratensian house and was founded by 1211 as the result of an
amalgamation of two ailing houses at Otham and Brockley. Although
never a wealthy house, Bayham surprises the visitor by the richness and
quality of the masonry in the eastern parts of the church.

*Michelham Priory was moated against
the French late in the thirteenth
century.*

Late in the thirteenth century an ambitious building programme was
initiated, beginning with a large new choir and presbytery. The masonry is
in the latest style, following the pattern used by Henry III at Westminster,
but the circumstances of its execution are entirely unknown, as is the
identity of the designer. Here are found luxuriant groves of stiff leaf foliage,
carved heads, free-standing shafts and an overall sculptural quality which
marks it out as an innovative masterpiece. Whether there was an anony-
mous patron, or the canons of this somewhat remote and uncelebrated
house were seized by the same passion for building as had earlier infected
the king himself, we will almost certainly never know. Yet here in this
idyllic setting we find the additional bonus of splendid architecture.

Michelham Priory, by contrast, is not architecturally distinguished but has other compensations. It is best known as an example of a defended monastery, since it was moated late in the thirteenth century perhaps in anticipation of French attack, and the extant gatetower was added. Of the monastic buildings, elements of the claustral ranges survive above ground, mostly incorporated into the later house on the site. The site is owned by the Sussex Archaeological Society, which has interpreted the remains with admirable lucidity and transformed Michelham into something of a heritage centre. Apart from such noteworthy features as the Physic Garden, which reminds us of the importance of herbs in medieval times, there are displays of Sussex historical collections as well as the welcome facility of a coffee shop.

7
ETCHINGHAM CHURCH, East Sussex

A fourteenth-century gem

Sussex is not a county renowned for its churches, but it has a few gems, one of which is here at Etchingham. For one thing, the church appears to be moated, a highly unusual feature and one which is so far unexplained. Secondly, it is overwhelmingly a church of one period and one patron, Sir William de Echyngham who, as his brass in the chancel declares, 'caused this church to be rebuilt anew'. Sir William died in 1388, and his church had been constructed about twenty years before since a contract dated 1369 records arrangements for five windows, including one of three lights,

Map Reference Etchingham: TQ 713262, Map 199
Nearest Town Hastings
14 miles (22.5 km) north of Hastings, 1 mile (1.6 km) west of Hurst Green on the A265. Key obtainable from local shop.

The large chancel at Etchingham church reflects the centrality of its function as a chantry.

A detail of the hands on the brass to Sir William de Echyngham, d. 1388.

Reynard the cunning fox preaches to his trusting flock of geese on a misericord.

Map Reference Bodiam: TQ 782256, Map 199
Nearest Town Hastings
12 miles (19 km) north of Hastings, 1 mile (1.6 km) east of the A229. Owned by the National Trust, open April–end Oct every day, 10–6; Nov–end March, Mon–Sat, 10–sunset. Car park and admissions charge. Museum with models and exhibits. Tearoom.

which is perhaps the existing west nave window. The church is tall and handsome, with a crossing tower and elegant flowing traceried lights, but it is the chancel which attracts our principal interest.

Here is an almost uniquely well-preserved collegiate chancel, retaining its screen and, more importantly, the pews used by the members of the college, complete with misericords. Prominent in the chancel are the brasses of the founder and his family, a physical reminder of the purpose of the institution. Collegiate churches became common enough in the later Middle Ages. A benefactor built a church with, as here, a capacious chancel and left money to pay a 'college' of priests whose sole charge was to say masses for his soul and those of his family.

The Etchingham college was obviously quite large and may have been similar to that at Tormarton (Gloucestershire), which had a complement of a warden (who was the rector), a staff of four chaplains, two clerks (who were a deacon and subdeacon) and three choristers. They had to maintain an elaborate series of services, observing the anniversaries of the deaths of the founder and his kin, apart from the great festivals of the church. The parish church of Etchingham therefore became a sort of shrine to its most munificent benefactor, wherein power and riches were deployed in a determined attempt to assist the soul of the departed.

8

BODIAM AND HERSTMONCEUX, East Sussex

Two 'picture-book' castles

Bodiam was built by Sir Edward Dalyngrigge after he received a licence to crenellate in 1385. It belongs to the troubled times after the French raid on nearby Winchelsea in 1380, and was intended to provide a strongpoint to

Bodiam floats like a great warship in the midst of its broad moat.

The trim brickwork and embattled towers of Herstmonceux mark it out as a sophisticated essay in late Medieval military planning.

discourage further depredations. But Bodiam is more than a mere strongpoint: it is built in a grand style which proclaimed its owner's intention to cut a dash as much as to deter the enemy. It is surely the quintessence of the chivalric stronghold, serene within its moat, the mighty drum towers topped by battlements and the lord's comfortable accommodation lurking within its walls.

But despite the obvious comfort and elaboration of the castle, Bodiam is a cunningly designed and businesslike fortress. Frenchmen sailing up the River Rother would find it squarely blocking their advance. The rectangular plan, strong and approved by contemporary military science, was further strengthened by a complex approach via three drawbridges and a barbican before the main entrance was even reached. A further refinement was dictated by the necessary evil of housing mercenary – and therefore potentially unreliable – soldiers. As a result, the lord and his family directly controlled three of the four angle towers, as well as both entrances. The retainers' hall is self-contained, and thus an uneasy relationship was underpinned by a defence within the defence, as at Raglan.

Herstmonceux, built of brick like its northern counterparts at Caister and Tattershall, is a product of the 1440s and is on a much larger scale than Bodiam. It too is a product of the Hundred Years War, and of the lessons in defensive strategy learned there. The wide wet moat, tall gatehouses bristling with loops and battlements, and the appearance of gun ports are the hallmarks of the most advanced military technology. Its builder, Sir Roger Fiennes, was a prominent grandee and Treasurer of the King's household. As at Bodiam, the castle is an expression of the owner's prestige as well as a serious fortification, an impression made manifest by the proud display of heraldry over their main entrances. Apart from the French, Fiennes was wise to secure his own safety behind high walls; his younger brother James was to be murdered by Jack Cade's insurgents in 1450, and the Wars of the Roses were about to begin.

Map Reference Herstmonceux: TQ 646104, Map 199
Nearest Town Hailsham
5 miles (8 km) east of Hailsham on the A271. Castle is 2 miles (3 km) south on minor hedged lanes and is currently the Royal Greenwich Observatory. Grounds are open Good Friday–30 Sept, Mon–Sun, 10.30–5.30, with admission charge. Castle closed to the public but the exterior can be viewed; the interior was much altered in 1912–20 and in 1930. Exhibition Hall shows early photographs of the castle before alterations. The church opposite the park gate has a brass of William Fiennes (d 1402), father of Sir Roger Fiennes, and the Dacre Chapel (c 1450), also in brick. Tea is available in the Castle Tea Shop.

9

WINCHELSEA, East Sussex

Map Reference Winchelsea: TQ
905175, Map 189
Nearest Town Hastings
7 miles (11 km) north-east of
Hastings on the A259. Church
stands in a large square at the centre
of the town. In the church is a large
plan showing how the town was
originally laid out according to a
rent roll of 1292. On the north side
of the church in the High Street is
the Court Hall, now a museum. By
turning down the minor road to
Winchelsea Beach south of the
town you can see how it has been
marooned from the sea, and fields
now stand beneath the cliffs.

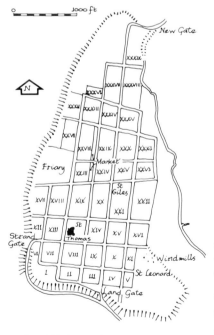

*By 1292 the royal new town of
Winchelsea had thirty-nine quarters
divided by a grid of rectilinear streets
and a sumptuous parish church.*

A new town

The matter of new towns was touched on in our *Norman Guide*, and the processes of planning, replanning and replacing towns were important activities in the later period too, as the story of Salisbury reminds us. Here at Winchelsea, the situation was rather different. There was an earlier site, 'Old' Winchelsea, one of the Cinque Ports, at the mouth of the River Brede which was progressively eroded after storms in 1244 until, in 1287, the sea finally destroyed it. Before this time, Edward I had begun a replacement town on a site above the estuary, which he laid out in a regular manner, and to which he encouraged the inhabitants of the threatened town to repair. Human nature is not so easily directed, however, and it was not until after the final disaster of 1287 that 'New' Winchelsea became populous. This story is interesting enough, but the importance of the site lies in the fact that the sea, with cruel irony, then silted up the Brede, ruining the trade of the town. At Winchelsea we can therefore see the layout of a medieval new town with remarkable clarity.

The new town was on a level site, laid out in a regular manner. In a survey of 1292, the plan consisted of a series of streets, 'strata', set approximately at right angles to form thirty-nine quarters, 'quarteria', which varied in size from one to three acres. Some were allocated to public uses like the market-place, the three churches of the town and the Franciscan friary which occupied a four-acre site on the east side. Other quarters were developed with houses, shops and yards, but the predominant feeling at Winchelsea today is one of emptiness; it is a village rather than a town. For apart from the silting of the river, Winchelsea fell prey to the economic difficulties of the fourteenth century, which included the French raid in 1380.

As well as the pattern of broad regular streets, it is possible to see the Strand Gate with its drum towers at the north-east corner of the town, and the New Gate to the south. Remains of houses largely consist of undercrofts, as in the house called Manna Platt, but the Court House retains much fourteenth-century work. It is, however, the parish church of St Thomas which provides the most dramatic evidence of Winchelsea's curious history. It was conceived on a grand scale in a lavish Decorated Gothic style. Only the chancel remains of what was evidently a mighty composition, either unfinished or destroyed by the French. Inside, among the clustered shafts and moulded arches, are found a sumptuous group of tombs, the resting places of knights and their ladies and, above all, of Gervase de Alard, first Admiral of the Cinque Ports, who died in 1310.

The superlative decoration of this tomb with its proud heraldry bears witness to the high endeavour attendant upon the foundation of this town, and of the bitterness of its fall; it should have been a second Salisbury.

ABOVE: *This head of Edward II appears on one of the splendid tombs in the north aisle.*

LEFT: *It is doubtful whether the great church at Winchelsea was ever finished, but what remains is impressive enough.*

10
ALFRISTON, East Sussex

Priest's house

The Clergy House at Alfriston is a fine example of a small fourteenth-century timber-framed residence, which embodies similar features to the Wealden houses discussed on page 19. It is a 'doubled-ended' house, having a central hall open to the roof with two storeyed ranges at either end. The hall retains its central hearth and fine crown post roof; the timbers are smoke-blackened, the telltale sign of the former existence of an open hall in which the smoke found its own way out through the roof. The hall floor is of the traditional Kentish type, consisting of chalk lumps tamped down and sealed with sour milk. The frame is of oak, the panels being filled with laths covered in daub and limewashed.

This house was obviously of fairly high status, as indicated by the occupation of its owner and such minor decorative details as the carved doorheads, moulded principal beams and a carved oak leaf chamfer stop in the north-east corner of the hall. But it stands as a rare survival of a lesser house, and one which retains its open central hall. There must have been many such houses in lowland England, and a visit to the adjacent church of

Map Reference Alfriston: TQ 521029, Map 189
Nearest Town Eastbourne 9 miles (14.4 km) north-west of Eastbourne, 1 mile (1.6 km) south of A27. In the village beside St Andrew's Church. This was the National Trust's first property. Exhibition room, cottage garden. Open April–end Oct, every day, 11–6. Note also the Star Inn of 15th-century date in the village and the fine church, called the 'cathedral of the South Downs', containing much 14th-century work contemporary with the Clergy House; fine sedilia and piscina.

The timber-framed clergy house at Alfriston, the first National Trust property in England.

St Andrew shows a building handsome enough, but which would not excite particular comment in many parts of England. The importance of Alfriston lies precisely in the fact that its church and house must always have been fairly unexceptional, and that is why this house, set in its lovely garden beside a wide valley, is such a priceless survival.

11

TROTTON CHURCH, West Sussex

Map Reference Trotton: SU 836225, Map 197

Nearest Town Midhurst

4 miles (6.4 km) west of Midhurst on A272. The medieval bridge, on the east side of the village, is controlled by traffic lights. Immediately after the bridge turn right and park by the church gates. Church stands in a pleasant churchyard and has a Sussex wood shingled cap to the tower. A framed diagram on the wall of the church gives the biblical texts for the wall-paintings.

A feast of paintings and brass

The idea of the Four Last Things – Death, Judgement, Heaven and Hell – seized the minds of men with peculiar ferocity late in the fourteenth century. An age which had seen economic decline, plague, riots and famines had had many reminders of mortality, and it is therefore unsurprising that lurid representations of the inevitable should be found in churches of the time. Here at Trotton the west wall of the nave of this otherwise unprepossessing church has been used as a vast canvas upon which the didactic medieval painters had free rein.

Above it all God sits in judgement, seated upon a rainbow and flanked by angels who regard a just and an unjust man respectively. Beneath God's feet are Moses and the Tablets of the Law; to either side are larger than life-size representations of the Carnal Man surrounded by images of the Seven Deadly Sins and the Spiritual Man with the Seven Works of Mercy. The scene of Gluttony on the left is both clear and lively, depicting a man draining a large flagon. On the right the naked are clothed, the hungry fed, the stranger welcomed and so on. The paintings are a unique scheme and of high quality, as befitted their patron. Although worn, restoration is in progress and more of the original scheme is being uncovered.

But this does not exhaust the interest of Trotton; for this place, like Etchingham, is as much a mortuary chapel as a parish church. In the chancel are brasses of the Camoys family. The earliest is that of Margaret, and at 1310 it is the oldest female brass in England. The lady wears a long loose cote hardie, the short sleeves of which reveal the tight-buttoned sleeves of her kirtle. A wimple covers her throat and a veil falls to her shoulders.

ABOVE: *'Visiting the Sick', as prescribed in Matthew Ch 25, v 26.*

LEFT: *The Seven Works of Mercy on the west wall of Trotton church.*

Most famous of all, however, is the magnificent monument to Sir Thomas, 1st Baron Camoys, who died in 1419, and his wife Elizabeth. He commanded the left wing at Agincourt and was a Garter Knight, as the insignia on his left leg makes plain. He wears full armour and the SS collar of the House of Lancaster. The figures are contained within an elaborate architectural border beneath cusped and crocketed ogee canopies. This is one of the largest, most richly carved and best preserved brasses in England and, despite the perspex that now covers it, it is a matchless example of medieval craftsmanship.

12

STOKE D'ABERNON, Surrey

The earliest brass in England

Here at Stoke d'Abernon is the earliest surviving and one of the most famous of the English brasses. It is dated to 1277 and is very finely worked, with each link of the chain mail being accurately represented. It depicts Sir John D'Aubernon, life-sized, fully armed with his sword, shield and lance, his feet resting on a lion, symbol of courage. We will now describe his armour and accoutrements, together with their names, which are all Norman French. He wears a chain mail shirt (hauberk), close cap (coif), stockings (chausses) and gloves as well as knee guards made of steel or stiff boiled leather (cuir boulli) strapped over the mail. His loose-fitting surcoat, introduced to ward off the sun during the Crusades, reaches below the knee and is fastened by a cord at the waist. It is open back and front to facilitate riding.

The shield is of the 'heater' form, that is, shaped like an old-fashioned flat iron, and bears Sir John's arms in coloured enamels: a gold chevron on a blue ground, or 'azure, a chevron or' as he would have described it. It hangs by a belt (gigue) over the right shoulder, which is ornamented with swastikas and roses. The sword is long and tapers slightly; it has a decorated circular pommel and hangs diagonally in front of the body, held in two places by a decorated sword belt. Short prick spurs tied to the feet complete this splendid equipage.

Monumental brasses, cheaper than stone effigies, became very popular after their introduction, probably from the Low Countries, in the thirteenth century. The 'brass' was actually a metal called latten, an alloy of copper and tin with some lead. The earliest brasses, like the one here at Stoke d'Abernon, are bold and life-sized, and usually depict knights or occasionally priests. From the mid fourteenth century they include more civilians and particularly merchants, while after about 1450 the designs

The brass to Sir John D'Aubernon, d. 1277, the earliest surviving example in England.

Map Reference TQ 129585, Map 187
Nearest Town Leatherhead
Set in north Surrey suburbia, Stoke d'Abernon is 4 miles (6.4 km) north-west of Leatherhead, on the A245. Turn into the drive of Parkside School, in open country just before the village is reached. St Mary's Church is located in the grounds – a flint church, much restored in Victorian times. Open Sat and Sun afternoons 2.30–4.30, Nov–March; and 2–6, April–Oct, or by special appointment with the verger.

tend to be smaller, more conventionalized and of lesser quality. Brasses are important for the details they provide of costume and armour, but it should be remembered that manufacturers sometimes reused older designs.

13
LIMPSFIELD, Surrey

A hidden house

It is easy to form the impression that medieval houses are much rarer than they actually are, simply because many of them are 'hidden'. People haven't changed that much over the past 500 years, and many were keen to

Map Reference TQ 405530, Map 187
Nearest Town Oxted
Adjacent to Oxted on the east side, signposted off the A25. Detillens is on the corner of Detillens Lane and the High Street, by the Bull Inn. A private house, open May and June, Sat; July–Sept, Wed and Sat, 2–5.

Exterior of the house called 'Detillens' showing a Georgian front on the medieval rear.

keep up with changing fashions but often didn't have a deep enough pocket! The easiest and cheapest option, therefore, was to alter the appearance of a house without actually going to the expense of rebuilding the whole structure. This process results in houses being hidden behind later façades, and it is often difficult to spot them.

The house called 'Detillens' at Limpsfield is an excellent example of this process: behind an elegant eighteenth-century front lurks a familiar fifteenth-century timber-framed house, of the type seen at Eyhorne and elsewhere in this book. A casual glance discloses nothing untoward, but if you look 'round the back' the situation is clear enough. It is worth watching out for this sort of evidence when building works are in progress, or if you get an opportunity to look at the backs of houses. The sort of clues to watch out for are irregular patterns of windows, brick walls that bow or bulge, and above all steep roofs, which were designed for thatch and which went out of use in most parts of England with the introduction of pantiles early in the eighteenth century.

14
ELTHAM, London

Map Reference TQ 424740, Map 177
Take the A20 south-east out of central London. Turn north up Court Road (A208) by the Royal Tavern towards Eltham. Go past Mottingham Station until the Tilt Yard approach is reached and turn up the Tilt Yard to the Palace. The Great Hall is used as a mess hall for the Royal Army Education Corps, and is normally open 1–6 Thurs and Sun in summer and 11–4 in winter. It is advisable to check with the RAEC (01–859 2112) in advance. Foundations of other buildings can be seen; the moat and the park setting survive.

Royal palace

Eltham first came into Crown possession in 1305 when Bishop Anthony Bek of Durham presented it to Edward II, then Prince of Wales. Edward's Queen Isabella spent much time here, and Bek's original manor house was much extended. Edward III spent most of his youth here, and between 1350 and 1359 paid over £2,000 for new works. It was at Eltham that his Garter Knights, discussed under the entry for Windsor, first wore their insignia in the New Year of 1348, and many of them jousted before the King. Edward IV, who began the construction of St George's Chapel at Windsor, contributed the main surviving structure at Eltham, however. He built the Great Hall, which was finished by 1480, and probably the bridge by which the Inner Court is entered.

The palace was laid out, as was customary with major medieval residences, in two courts, the Inner and the Outer. This plan provided both privacy and security: the services and lesser lodgings were relegated to the Outer Court, while the Inner Court was reserved for the King, his family and close retainers. Apart from the Great Hall, which is the principal survival at Eltham, we know there was a chapel as well as a great mass of other high-status accommodation, including separate suites of rooms for the King and Queen.

The Great Hall is essentially a brick building, although its north front is

The smoke louvre at the centre of the Great Hall of Eltham Palace.

ashlar faced, and that to the south is of ragstone. There has been considerable restoration of the exterior and some of the carved detail, particularly of the parapet, has been lost. The side walls are lit by pairs of cinquefoil headed lights, except for the western end or 'high' end which has square full height bay windows. At the lower end of the hall are two opposed doorways leading into the screens passage.

Inside, the size of the hall is very impressive, and in truth it would have made an excellent barn (for which purpose it was actually used after Eltham fell from royal favour!). The roof is by far the most impressive feature; it is an example of the 'hammerbeam' type used at the Pilgrims' Hall at Winchester. But here, instead of the hammer posts (which are the vertical members above the pendants), resting on the shorter horizontal hammer beams, they are actually tenoned into the sides of the posts.

The roof timbers are elaborately moulded and the great four centred arched collar beams have pierced trefoil spandrels. Above, the spaces between the collars and the ridge contain delicate pierced traceried lights, giving the whole a decidedly 'architectural' appearance. The curved braces below the hammer beams are supported on embattled octagonal corbels and the pendants beneath the hammer posts are panelled in the manner of the lanterns at Astbury in Cheshire.

15

WINDSOR CASTLE AND ST GEORGE'S CHAPEL,
Berkshire

Map Reference SU 970770, Map 176
St George's Chapel is open 10.45–3.45 daily, 2–3.40 Sun. Admission charge. Note the king's-head frescos in the cloister and the galilee porch.

Another misericord depicting a city gateway with curiously inscrutable inhabitants.

This finely carved windmill with cheeky sparrows stealing grain is on a misericord in St George's Chapel.

A castle was first built at Windsor by the Conqueror, and it soon became a favoured royal resort. The basic plan of his castle, a motte with a bailey on the east side, is fossilized in the later plan. The buildings were substantial from the first, but in 1175 Henry II refurbished the defences, improved the accommodation and added a further bailey to the west. Further works were instituted by Henry III, but it is to the middle of the fourteenth century and the reign of Edward III that the next major phase of the castle's history belongs.

His works here were so extensive that after the Black Death in 1349, 'almost all the masons and carpenters throughout the whole of England were brought to that building, so that hardly anyone could have any good mason or carpenter except in secret'. Edward lavished £50,000 on Windsor, making it the largest individual Crown building project during the whole of the Middle Ages. Sadly, much is hidden behind later façades, but this expenditure must be seen as an attempt by the English Crown to vie with France in architectural as well as military affairs.

Edward III was grandson to Edward I and, like him, a great warrior. His reign was marked by the bloody struggle with France – the epic battles of Crécy and Poitiers, where the English arrows fell 'with such force and quickness it seemed as if it snowed', were fought during his reign. Against a background of crisis in the wool trade, the Black Death and Scottish unrest, Edward and his knights elevated the matter of chivalry to a cult, and covered themselves with glory. Edward founded the 'Order of the Blue Garter', which we know as the 'Most Noble Order of the Garter', and at Windsor is that shrine of kings and warriors called St George's Chapel, wherein its traditions are still observed.

The Order was apparently founded after the king retrieved a garter lost by Joan of Kent while dancing at Calais; he reproved his smiling courtiers with the words 'Honi soit qui mal y pense', meaning 'Evil to him who evil thinks'. The membership always includes the Prince of Wales, since he is descended from the Black Prince. It is sad to relate that this model of chivalry, named from the colour of his armour, was less than chivalrous in the treatment of his enemies, and that his father, the King, died sadly and alone, his rings torn from his fingers by his mistress.

The College of St George was established in 1348 with a complement of priests dedicated to prayer for the sovereign and all faithful people. Work was not actually begun on the Chapel, which was also the spiritual centre of the Order of the Garter, until 1475, and it was not finished until the reign of Henry VIII. It is a spectacular example of the English Perpendicular style and the Garter stalls, carved between 1478 and 1485, shimmer with regal red and gold. Here are the tombs of kings, some of whom, like Henry VI buried near the high altar, were credited with miracle-working after death. There are so many resonances and associations from our period that we are at a loss to conjure them. King Edward's own address to his knights before the victory at Poitiers must suffice:

'I therefore entreat of you to exert yourselves, and combat manfully; for, if it please God and St George, you shall see me this day act like a true knight.'

16

ETON COLLEGE, Berkshire

A Royal school

Henry VI founded 'The King's College of Our Lady of Eton beside Windsor' in 1440. Henry, who also founded King's College, Cambridge, modelled his colleges on William of Wykeham's foundations at Winchester and New College, Oxford. The second half of the fifteenth century saw notable strides in education, and the collegiate structure, which had the useful benefit of commemorating the founder after death, was much favoured. The large foundation at Eton included a community of ten secular priests, and Henry stipulated that masses should be offered for the repose of his soul.

It is fitting that the Chapel is the dominant element of the College buildings, for apart from the customary endowments of land Henry also provided a comprehensive collection of relics, which included fragments of the True Cross. In addition, Eton was afforded a privilege unique in England of granting indulgences to penitents on the Feast of the Assumption, which takes place in August. These marks of favour were intended to ensure the foundation a secure income, and the Chapel was the goal of many pilgrims.

All did not go smoothly, however, and the Chapel is only the choir of what was conceived as a huge pilgrimage church. Henry was deposed in 1461 and the College was almost closed, but it managed to survive although on a considerably reduced scale. In the early 1470s the choir stood roofless and work on the nave had not begun. Bishop William Waynflete arranged the roofing of the structure in wood, rather than the intended stone vault, and built the ante chapel at the west end. This is substantially the chapel as we see it today.

The greatest medieval treasure of the College are the wall paintings in

Map Reference SU 967779, Map 175
Open daily April—early Oct, 2–5, and from 10.30 in the summer holidays. Ordinary admission gives access to School Yard, College Chapel, Cloister Court and Museum of Eton Life. For an additional fee an extended tour gives access to Upper School and College Hall.

View across the School Yard. The Chapel is on the right and the gateway in Lupton's Tower gives access to the Cloisters beyond.

the Chapel. They are the work of at least four masters who, with assistance, took eight years to complete them in 1479–87. The paintings are of an exquisite quality, and were designed as a *trompe-l'oeil*, to give the impression of aisles in the otherwise rather narrow space. In a bold Flemish style, the pictures breathe life and sophistication. They depict the Miracles of the Virgin Mary and the story of a mythical empress who is rescued from various misfortunes by the intervention of the Virgin.

Apart from the Chapel, the cloisters, originally built to house the clergy who officiated in the Chapel, were built in the 1440s, as was the College Hall, which has a fine timber roof. The Lower School on the north side of the School Yard beside the Chapel was completed in about 1443, and is probably the oldest continually used classroom in the world. Above is a large dormitory called the Long Chamber. These ancillary buildings are all of red brick with stone dressings, only the Chapel is entirely of stone. Even though Henry VI's grandiose plans were never fully realized, the College is an impressive tribute to his initiative, and its fame has endured in a manner which fully justifies the founder's zeal.

17
ALDWORTH CHURCH, Berkshire

The 'Giants'

St Mary's Church has a celebrated collection of funerary effigies to members of the de la Beche family. There are nine in all, and they completely dominate the interior of this agreeable little church. The south aisle, which contains three of the tombs, was added in 1330–40 by Lord Nicholas de la Beche, and has fine reticulated windows and squat octagonal capitals with grotesque heads. But these tombs with their splendid cusped canopies are late in a series which begins on the north side with Sir Robert, who was knighted by Edward I in 1278.

Next comes Sir Philip, the largest of the effigies, and depicted awkwardly lying on his side, as if he had been crammed by Procrustean methods into his last resting place. He wears a surcoat over his armour and by his feet, in place of the more usual lion or dog, is a dwarf. He apparently took the dwarf with him to court in order to show off his considerable height to better advantage! Sir Philip's son John is next in sequence with his wife Isabella; he was guardian to the young Black Prince, and occupied a high place in royal favour before his death in 1348.

The other monuments are less impressive individually, but together they make a group unparalleled in any other church of comparable size to this, which seems more like a mortuary chapel than a parish church. That the tombs made a deep impression on the inhabitants is clear from the folklore they have engendered. When Elizabeth I visited the church in company with the Earl of Leicester, she was regaled with stories of the 'Giants' called John Strong, John Long and John Never Afraid, but the last John, called 'Ever Afraid', has vanished from his tomb in the south wall. He was apparently buried there because he 'gave his soule to ye Divil if ever he was buried either in Church or churchyard, so he was buried under the Church Wall under an Arche'.

Map Reference SU 554794, Map 174
Nearest Town Goring
3 miles (4.5 km) west of Goring on the B4009. Church is in the village, just off main road on the north side.

The effigy of Sir Philip de la Beche, who looks most uncomfortable!

18
WINCHESTER, Hampshire

Map Reference SU 482292,
Map 185
Castle is open daily 10–5, and close
by is the Westgate Museum, once
one of the main gateways into the
city, open Sat 10–5, Sun 2–5, and
Mon during summer. In the
Cathedral Close is the 13th-century
Pilgrims' Hall, open daily; the ruins
of the Bishop's Palace are in
guardianship of the HBMCE and
open standard hours in the summer
season. Note also the 15th-century
High Cross in the town centre and
the 15th-century timber-framed
Chesil Rectory on the east side of
the town by Bridge Street.

Ancient capital of England

Winchester, called Venta Belgarum by the Romans, was capital of
England under the kings of Wessex before the Norman Conquest, and
even afterwards it rivalled Westminster as a seat of government. During
our period it was a major wool trading centre, and the fair on St Giles Hill
attracted merchants from all over Europe. The city has a remarkable legacy
of medieval buildings, and the fifteenth-century Market Cross in High
Street and the Westgate, which is basically of the thirteenth century,
remind us of its early prosperity. But at the heart of the city are its two most
famous buildings: the Castle Hall and the Cathedral.

The first castle was built soon after the Conquest; it was extended and
modernized on several occasions, though much was destroyed during the
Civil War. Miraculously, the Great Hall built by Henry III in 1222–35 has
survived. This splendid construction is of the finest quality, as might be
expected under royal patronage, and is second only to Westminster. It was
the centrepiece of a strong castle, the excavated circular north-east tower
of which, with built-in sally ports, can be seen nearby.

The hall has an aisled plan of five bays, and is divided by two rows of
slender Purbeck marble columns into a broad central nave and flanking
aisles. The columns are formed of eight clustered shafts with annular
capitals from which spring chamfered and rolled arches. The large two-
light windows in the side walls are original, but the aisles were raised and
reroofed in the fourteenth century, and the round windows moved to their

*The enigmatic Round Table in the
Great Hall of Winchester Castle has
recently been dated to the reign of
Edward I.*

present positions. The hall is now entered through a central nineteenth-century doorway, but originally there was a screens passage with opposed doorways at the east end, where traces of the openings can still be seen. The dais was at the west end, where the elaborate doorway led to the royal apartments. The famous Round Table hanging on the west wall reminds us of the courtly life which took place here. Recently dated to the reign of Edward I, this unique survival demonstrates the importance of the Arthurian legends to medieval kings, which found its ultimate expression in St George's Chapel, Windsor.

Winchester Cathedral is the longest Gothic church in Europe and, while the twelve bays of the nave are basically Norman, they were cunningly reworked in the Perpendicular style in 1367–1404. The retro choir is of the earliest Gothic, and has the most extensive area of medieval floor tiles in England. The paintings of c 1225 in the Chapel of the Holy Sepulchre are both the best and most dramatic of the three sets remaining. In the choir is a good set of misericords; of the tombs, the chantry of William of Wykeham, the cathedral's greatest benefactor, is appropriately the finest.

At the feet of the Bishop's effigy are three diminutive figures, probably representing secretaries, which remind us of his great learning. This found practical expression in the foundation of a college in 1382 to train seventy scholars for the Church. New College, Oxford, was part of the same foundation, an arrangement which prefigured Henry VI's joint foundation at Eton and King's College, Cambridge. The College buildings survive substantially intact, and were planned round two courtyards and a cloister.

19
SOUTHAMPTON, Hampshire

Port and town
The early medieval history of Southampton has been outlined in our *Norman Guide*, but it was such a wealthy and significant town throughout the Middle Ages that we must chart something of its later development. It was an invasion base against France, and fell victim to the famous French raid in 1338 which signalled the beginning of the Hundred Years War. But, more importantly, it was a port of trade where English cloth, coal, tin and lead were exchanged for the riches of the Mediterranean and the Baltic. Figs, raisins and rice, spices and wine, as well as timber and rarer merchandise like glass and silks, came to this great market-place. As a result, there is a legacy of town houses with capacious cellars, town walls, towers and a great wool warehouse.

Map Reference SU 420110, Map 196
The Wool House is on the Quay side by Bugle Street and is now a maritime museum open Tues–Sat, 10–1 and 2–5, and Sun, 2–5. A new acquisition of the HBMCE is a late-13th-century merchant's house and shop on the inner ring road near the Quay, at 58 French Street. Open standard hours, summer season.

The Wool House at Southampton was probably built by the Abbey of Beaulieu during the fourteenth century.

The town defences, though less complete than Chester and York, are visually more impressive, the only missing element being the important royal castle. The defences were begun early in the thirteenth century but took over 200 years to complete. They demonstrate an early familiarity with artillery, and gunports were incorporated in the western walls before 1338. Three medieval gateways survive – the Bargate, the Westgate and God's House Tower – and mural towers can be seen along several remaining lengths of wall.

Of the town houses, No 58 French Street, currently being renovated prior to public opening, is one of the most complete early-fourteenth-century houses in the country. It was built over a stone vault and had an open central hall with two-storey chamber blocks back and front, the latter containing a shop. The house is timber-framed, and its attenuated site illustrates the long narrow tenement plots which maximized the vital street frontage space. The cellars beneath such houses could often be well detailed and even provided with fireplaces, suggesting that they should perhaps be seen as 'show rooms' or counting houses rather than simple storeplaces. Such refinements can be seen in 'The Undercroft', Simnel Street.

Last but by no means least in this brief survey comes the fourteenth-century Wool House. It has a fine arched collar brace roof, and was probably built by Beaulieu Abbey. This may have been the building leased by Thomas Middleton, a prosperous merchant and thrice mayor, in 1407. The warehouse is located close to the Town Quay, on a prime site. Its substantial rubble walls have withstood the chances of trade and the fury of enemy action. They stand today as an enduring reminder of this city's proud medieval past, when it was a hub of trade for the known world.

20

CHALE, Isle of Wight

A medieval lighthouse

Lighthouses are known to have existed at fifteen places on the coast of England during our period, and there were almost certainly many more. As with bridges and other structures associated with communications, the Church played a major part in their establishment and maintenance. Here at Chale, on St Catherine's Down high above the waters of the Channel, a light still stands which was erected early in the fourteenth century. The story of the origin of this light is interesting, since it arose out of the loss of a ship called the *St Marie of Bayonne* which was laden with wine belonging to a monastery in Picardy in 1314. The cargo was salvaged and sold to the islanders, but the owners were awarded damages in court and the receivers of the wine, including Walter de Godeton, a local squire, were heavily fined. This was not the end of the matter, since the case went up to Rome, and de Godeton was deemed to have committed sacrilege in accepting the wine. As a result, he was required to endow a chapel and to maintain a priest there to pray for the souls of shipwrecked mariners. He also had to build a lighthouse to prevent further disasters, and it is this tower which survives at Chale.

The lighthouse has four stages beneath an eight-sided pyramidal roof, and is octagonal on plan. In the fourth stage are tall slits through which the light shone. Given the absence of reflectors, lenses and the other accoutrements of later lights, we cannot imagine that this arrangement was very effective. Perhaps the prayers offered up in the adjoining oratory, the foundations of which remain, were more efficacious!

Map Reference SZ 494773, Map 196
Nearest Town Ventnor
The lighthouse known as St Catherine's Oratory is 6 miles (9.5 km) west of Ventnor on the A3055, ¾ mile (1 km) north-west of Niton. In guardianship of the HBMCE, open at any reasonable time.

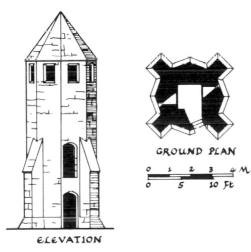

GROUND PLAN

0   1   2   3   4 M
0   5   10 Ft

ELEVATION

Elevation and plan of St Catherine's Lighthouse at Chale.

WALES

Gloucester
GLOUCESTERSHIRE

♦27 ♦26
♦28 ♦25

AVON
Swindon

♦29
Bristol
Bath ♦23
♦24
♦30 ♦22
WILTSHIRE
♦32
Bridgewater ♦33 31
♦31
21
Salisbury

38
Barnstaple .... 34 SOMERSET
Taunton

39

DEVON
DORSET
Dorchester
♦36
♦35

Exeter
Launceston
37 ♦
40 ♦
CORNWALL ♦ 41
Plymouth

♦ 42
Truro

Penzance

0   10   20   30 Miles
|—|—|—|—|—|—|
0 10 20 30 40 50 Km

SOUTH~WESTERN
ENGLAND

SOUTH-WESTERN ENGLAND

Introduction

The south-west of England has a wealth of medieval monuments of all types. It was generally a prosperous region with large flocks of sheep and valuable natural resources. Apart from national upheavals like the Wars of the Roses, the area was generally peaceful during the Middle Ages. There were some castles, of course, notably those at Nunney and Old Wardour, but they were built late in our period by soldiers returning from the French wars. These 'castles' were in reality tower houses in the latest Continental fashion, their tall walls and battlements being designed less for defence than for display, as their generous planning and large windows indicate.

Most people lived without defences of any kind, however, as the delightful manor house at Great Chalfield reminds us. The house of William Grevel, the great wool merchant of Chipping Campden, for example, is an essentially similar type of house moved into a town. It sprawls along the side of the main street, its very bulk an advertisement of its owner's prestige. Lesser men required lesser houses, and at Tewkesbury we see a fascinating row of houses and shops built as a speculation by the abbey there. These shop 'units' as they might be called today were comfortable enough, built of framed timber with plastered panels, and retaining the open hall with central hearth characteristic of the principal room of a medieval household. At Gloucester and Norton St Phillip we also see inns which offered the same standards of comfort to the stranger as the householder enjoyed for himself.

Economic life is also well represented in the region, with one element, the tin mines of Cornwall, being unique to this part of England. The Duchy of Cornwall regulated these activities, and an important source of revenue they were too. At Lostwithiel we can see the remains of the Duchy Palace, but it was in the villages beyond the town that the precious metal was won, and where we can still see the evidence of the laborious excavations. At Braunton, labours of another type are brought to mind. At the Great Field there is a remarkable instance of medieval agricultural practice, and it provides one of the most authentic and informative landscapes to have come down to us from the whole of medieval England.

When we come to the towns, we find a rich field for our attention. Wells could be a time capsule of medieval life. At its centre are the jewel-like Cathedral, the rows of priests' houses, the Bishop's Palace and the Market-Place, combining all the elements of an ancient English ecclesiastical city while retaining a medieval scale. Gloucester is less cohesive as a medieval town, but the cloister of its Cathedral prefigures the glories of the English Perpendicular Gothic style, and the Blackfriars elsewhere in the city is an important survival.

Meanwhile at Bristol, at the heart of that thriving and yet still beautiful metropolis, we find the matchless pearl of St Mary Redcliffe. This church is of the first quality, a lively reminder of Bristol's *fons et origo* in the paths of international trade. This was also the calling of the church's greatest benefactor, William Canynges, a man who was by turns capitalist, benefactor, priest and penitent, and whose example shames attempts to belittle the breadth and aspirations of the period.

In considering other churches, we find, for example, the incomparable and varied towers of Somerset, originally inspired by the work at Wells. At Edington is a precocious example of Perpendicular austerity. Restraint is also evident in the churches at Northleach and Chipping Campden built by the Cotswold wool barons. Theirs was not any common or vulgar taste for they were in touch with the channels of wider European influence. They experimented inside their churches at least with light and space rather than over-elaborate decoration.

Let us now turn from these measured creations to atmospheric churches elsewhere. Beyond the gates of Hailes Abbey is a small shrine to medieval faith, replete with tiles and glowing paintings. At Whitchurch Canonicorum can be seen the shrine of an enigmatic female saint. The flowers of the periwinkle are still locally called 'St Candida's Eyes' in commemoration of the miracles of healing which she performed here.

This sense of mystery and the numinous exists at many of the ecclesiastical sites of the remoter west. Hartland Church, associated with St Nectan, is a superb example of the Devon style, with a richly painted screen alive with delicate carving. Beyond again we come to the enigmatic holy well at Linkinhorne and the playing place called St Piran's Round. Here we are brought up sharp by Celtic traditions already ancient before the Middle Ages began. From at least the tenth century the Church attempted to forbid the worship of wells and streams, but in Cornwall it made no difference and the Church had to accept what it could not change. As to Piran's Round, the use of such circles of earth originated in the remotest ages of antiquity. It would be a bold person indeed who could define the motives of the medieval players.

We are on firmer ground once more with the monastic sites, of course.

At Hailes Abbey is a delightful Cistercian house superbly built of mellow Cotswold stone with decorative carving of the highest quality. These attributes are coupled with a memorable setting and a wealth of historical associations stemming from its function as a pilgrimage place after it received the gift of the Holy Blood. At Abbotsbury the site of an important Benedictine house is marked by the remains of a huge tithe barn, an eloquent testimonial to the resources of an Order untroubled by considerations of asceticism. A similar reminder is provided by the Bradford-on-Avon barn: a fine structure affording an unrivalled opportunity to study the intricacies of medieval carpentry at close quarters.

Finally, two of our favourite south-western medieval gems must be mentioned. Salisbury is the queen of medieval cities all, with at its heart an uplifting cathedral, homogenous in style, felicitous in design, and around it are the measured 'chequers' of the thirteenth-century town plan. Here, if we close one eye, we can still imbibe the sense of a large town by medieval standards, and one which retains many of its early buildings behind later façades. At Salisbury we experience a medieval town, while at Hound Tor on Dartmoor we avail ourselves of an opposite sensation. This place is silent and deserted now, a haunt of wild creatures. Yet once it supported a community of men who eked a difficult living from the thin soil and took what comfort they could from their Spartan surroundings. Hound Tor is part of the medieval Britain which we see, like gods, perceiving the failures as well as the successes of our forebears, and seeking to learn from both.

21
SALISBURY, Wiltshire

New Sarum

Late in the twelfth century the momentous decision was made to move the Cathedral at Old Sarum (for which see our *Norman Guide*) to a new site in the valley below, 'New' Sarum. Thus Salisbury, as the city is now called, is an example of a medieval new town. In its regular plan and the ample space around its splendid Cathedral, it demonstrates the advantages of a 'green field' site. Bishop Poore laid the foundation stone of the Cathedral in 1220, and it seems to have taken some forty years to build, although the famous spire was not added until the mid fourteenth century. The result is a uniquely integrated major church executed in a precisely detailed Early English style with dark Purbeck marble being used against a background of white Chilmark limestone. The cloisters and octagonal chapter house were begun late in the thirteenth century, and are in an altogether more festive early Decorated Gothic style with Geometric tracery.

Map Reference Cathedral: SU 143295, Map 184
St Thomas's Church: SU 143299
The Museum in the Close has good displays, near the east end of the Cathedral in the King's House. It is open daily and has a refreshment room. St Thomas's Church is just off the High Street in St Thomas's Square, and is usually open. The Poultry Cross is nearby in Market Square.

The largest cloister in England, and perhaps also the finest, Salisbury provides a textbook exposition of the early Decorated style.

At the heart of the new town, laid out on a grid plan in a series of 'chequers', we find the Poultry Cross, first mentioned in 1335 but fifteenth-century in its present form. This stood at the centre of the bustling medieval city, which waxed mightily on the profits from the wool clip of Salisbury Plain. There are many fifteenth-century houses and other buildings surviving in the town, and the scale is still largely medieval. In Queen Street, for example, is the house of John a Port, wool merchant; built in about 1450, it has the jetties and timber-framed construction typical of town houses of the period. Behind the cinema in the street called New Canal is wondrously preserved the late-fifteenth-century hall of John Halle, a wool merchant and leading citizen, notorious for his foul mouth and overbearing manner. Between the Cathedral Close and the town stands the High Street Gate licensed in 1327 on account of frictions between the townspeople and their ecclesiastical landlords.

In the midst of so many buildings and objects which claim our attention, we will mention just two others here. The first is the Salisbury Giant, now preserved in the Museum in the Close, and his familiar called Hob Nob. Such large figures, carried in processions on high days and holidays, are known from documents in many medieval towns. Gog and Magog in the London Guildhall are two such, but Salisbury is fortunate indeed to have preserved these trophies. Wool was, of course, the key to the city's prosperity, and the Guild of Tailors was very powerful. The Giant was their symbol, appropriately clad in yards of the best red cloth. But the Giant and his strange companion also hark back to far earlier times as well, and they remind us of the rich folk traditions of our medieval forebears.

Finally, in the Church of St Thomas à Becket in the middle of the city, is a great treasure from the late fifteenth century. Over the chancel arch is painted a fearsome 'Doom', a depiction of the Four Last Things: Death, Judgement, Heaven and Hell. This too belongs to that disturbing imaginative substructure of medieval society. Doubtless such images, alive with devils, fires and other horrors, were needed to instil fear in such as the haughty John Halle, who certainly feared no man, bolstered as he was by the vast wealth grown on sheep's backs.

22
EDINGTON CHURCH, Wiltshire

The Perpendicular style

Edington Church is of the greatest interest to the study of medieval architecture, for it shows the use of Decorated and Perpendicular Gothic motifs in the same building. But before looking at it in detail, we must say something of its origins. A glance at the exterior of the building shows that it is not a normal parish church. It has a decidedly domestic air, with embattled parapets and a generally rather 'low-rise' aspect, all of which makes it look more like a collegiate building than a parish church *per se*. This impression is an accurate one for in 1351 William of Edington, Bishop of Winchester, decided to build a college here at his birthplace, rather like the arrangements at Higham Ferrers, Northants. The church was accordingly rebuilt in a grand manner – and in a short space of time, for it was consecrated in 1361.

Map Reference ST 926534, Map 184
Nearest Town Trowbridge
5 miles (8 km) south-east of Trowbridge on the B3098. The church is in the village, off the main road on the north side, looking up to the steep edge of Edington Hill.

The Perpendicular west window is one of the earliest examples of the 'English style'.

When medieval churches were built work normally started at the east end, and Edington is no exception. The chancel is in a Decorated Gothic style, albeit with some vertical lines indicating Perpendicular influence. The prevailing impression here is still one of curves and cusps, however, an impression strengthened by the pinnacles surmounting the battlements and the lavish figure sculpture. Moving further west, the change from Decorated to Perpendicular, with its emphasis on straight lines and restrained decoration, is manifest. Triple windows under cambered arches already exhibit the rectangular form which became so familiar later, and in the west front the eight-light window is entirely Perpendicular in style. The Edington masons may have earlier worked at Gloucester Cathedral, where the Perpendicular Gothic style was born, but here we see a perfect small-scale example of the origins of the English style.

23
BRADFORD-ON-AVON TITHE BARN, Wiltshire

Map Reference ST 824604, Map 173 The barn is ¼ mile (0.4 km) south of the town centre. It is in the guardianship of the HBMCE and open at reasonable times. It stands in a country park with Barton Farm and granary nearby; they also contain medieval work, but unfortunately are now in poor condition. A short walk by the River Avon takes you to the 14th-century Barton Bridge.

Bradford is, of course, chiefly famous for the Chapel of St Laurence, for which see our *Saxon Guide*, but we return now on account of its majestic fourteenth-century tithe barn, which belonged to the great abbey of Shaftesbury. The barn is the principal remnant of the medieval grange farm called Barton on the outskirts of the town. It is a vast structure indeed, of churchlike proportions, and provided with two gabled entrances. The roof has collar beams supported on arch braces, and is strengthened by three tiers of windbraces. Unusually, the principal trusses are formed of crucks, the bases of which spring from the upper parts of the side walls. Bradford is a good place to study this technique of construction in which pairs of naturally shaped timbers were used. The examples here

The Great Tithe Barn at Bradford-on-Avon, a symbol of monastic endeavour and agricultural success.

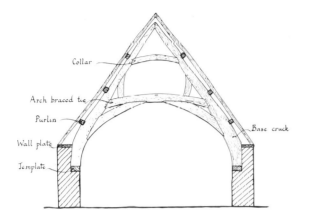

Collar
Arch braced tie
Purlin
Wall plate
Template
Base cruck

The base crucks were formed from great oak trees, which were carefully selected for their natural shape.

are called 'base crucks', since they only reach about half-way up to the roof, whereas a 'true' cruck goes from the wall right up to the apex. The floor is of earth, except where it is paved at the entrances to form threshing floors, arranged so that the dust and chaff would blow out through the open doors.

24
GREAT CHALFIELD MANOR AND CHURCH, Wiltshire

Great Chalfield Manor was built in about 1480 on the site of an earlier house by Thomas Tropnell, a merchant and landowner who did well out of the Wars of the Roses. It is one of the best late medieval manor houses in England and, with the church and farm buildings, forms a delightful group of buildings. The house is approached by a bridge across the moat and a gatehouse, the upper parts of which have been rebuilt. The central element of the house is a hall, but here it was ceiled from the first rather than being open to the roof, and its larger windows provide the central focus of an unusually balanced front, rare for the time. The hall block is recessed behind two gables with oriels at right angles, forming the H-plan seen at Penshurst and elsewhere, and in the angles are lesser gables containing the hall bay and entrance porch.

The hall is entered through a vaulted porch which retains the original door. Inside, the hall ceiling has moulded principals with bosses, and is lit by two-light windows with plain Y-tracery. The fireplace, with its elaborate moulding and decorated spandrels, is original, and marks another departure from the classical medieval arrangement. The exuberance of the fireplace and the strange masked spyholes in the upper walls are in sharp contrast with the very restrained uncusped window lights throughout the house, which are an advanced feature.

Map Reference ST 860630, Map 173
Nearest Town Melksham
From Melksham take the B3107 towards Holt and Bradford-on-Avon. Turn right (west) down the first minor road, over the railway, through the minor settlement of Broughton Common, and then turn left (south) to Great Chalfield. In all a journey of about 5 miles (8 km). The house stands next to the parish church; it belongs to the National Trust and is open April–end Oct, Tues–Thurs 12–1, 2–5.

These engaging essays in Medieval humour allowed the Master to covertly look down into the hall if the party got out of hand.

At the upper end of the hall is a vaulted room with small windows which may have been a strongroom or counting house. On the upper floor is the Great Chamber, approached by a spiral staircase, the roof of which is copied from the surviving chamber over the service end. At the lower end of the hall is the usual arrangement of a screens passage, but beyond is a separate dining-room before the kitchen is reached. This contains a rare mural painting of Tropnell, seated in a chair, and is a further un-medieval touch. The house hovers on the brink of the new: many features, including the Tudoresque windows and the ceiled hall are innovatory, while the provision of a dining-room points the way towards future separation of functions between different rooms.

The little church of All Saints is within the manorial moat, and is basically of the thirteenth century. Tropnell altered it, however, and added the south chapel with its fine pierced stone screen featuring the arms of his second wife. On the walls of the chapel are sadly mutilated paintings depicting scenes from the life of St Catherine, and he must have provided the wooden screen between the chancel and organ chamber.

25

THE COTSWOLD WOOL TOWNS, Gloucestershire

Map Reference Northleach: SP 112147, Map 163
Chipping Campden: SP 154395, Map 151
Northleach, on the A40 Oxford to Cheltenham road, has recently been bypassed and consequently greatly improved. Chipping Campden is on the B4035, some 4 miles (6 km) east of Broadway; William Grevel's house on the High Street is now a doctor's residence. There is also a Woolpack Museum nearby, open March–Sept, 11–6.

Throughout this book repeated reference is made to wool and sheep, and nowhere is the debt owed by medieval man to these creatures more apparent than in the Cotswolds, for it was said at the time:

> In Europe the best wool is English,
> In England, the best wool is the Cotswold.

The breeders of the Lincolnshire longwools might have disagreed, and Herefordshire wool actually commanded a higher price, but there can be no doubt about the general accuracy of the statement; for sheer quantity, the Cotswolds held the palm by the later Middle Ages. Wool had been important in Anglo-Saxon times, as the name 'Cotswold' from *cote* (or sheep fold) and *wold* (a bare hill) indicates. But during the twelfth and thirteenth centuries lay and ecclesiastical owners vastly increased their flocks. Some villagers even had larger flocks than their lords – at South Domerham (Wiltshire), for example, the villagers had 3,760 head as against the landlords, Glastonbury Abbey, who had only 570.

As with the Cornish tin industry, the Crown saw an opportunity to levy taxes, and as early as 1191 entire clips from several monasteries were confiscated to pay Richard I's ransom. Eventually, a system of 'Staple' towns was evolved at which wool was assessed for duty. This led to the formation of a company of monopolistic English merchants 'of the Staple' who handled all shipments of English wool. By the early fourteenth century there were between three and four hundred such merchants, and some of the greatest 'wool gatherers' lived in the Cotswold towns of Northleach and Chipping Campden.

Northleach lies near the centre of the Cotswold sheepwalks, and during the fifteenth and early sixteenth centuries the families of Midwinter, Fortey, Taylor and Bush were the principal merchants of the town. They rebuilt the church during the fifteenth century in the elaborate Perpendicular style characteristic of the wool towns, and their resplendent brasses call them individually to memory. When we approach the church from the east we see an elevation lit by large traceried windows, with a large one even tucked into the east wall of the nave. Windows and the glass that went in them were symbols of prestige, and no opportunity was lost at Northleach. The effect is splendid from outside, with fascinating patterns of tracery trapping the sunlight on the warm Cotswold stone, but internally the church, in common with others in the area, is somewhat austere. We must, however, imagine the walls and glass glowing with colour, like a jewel box.

The Northleach brasses are one of the best collections in England. The earliest, of about 1400, in the north aisle shows an unknown merchant, his

The boldly traceried exterior of Northleach Church, complete with a contented sheep, a reminder of the church's origins.

Detail from the brass of John Taylour in Northleach Church. Notice his woolmark of a cross formed from two shepherds' crooks.

William Grevel, 'flower of all the wool merchants of all England'.

feet on a woolsack, and his wife. Next comes a triple brass to Agnes with her two husbands – William Scors, a tailor, shown with his scissors, and Thomas Fortey, woolman. In the margins are charming figures of animals and birds, and the figures appear under elaborate canopies. Then comes John Fortey, died 1458, who rebuilt most of the church; he is appropriately shown with one foot on a woolsack and the other on a sheep which has the slender neck and long wool of the Cotswold breed. There follows a procession of other woolmen, displaying their distinctive woolmarks as proudly as any knightly heraldry.

Chipping Campden tells a similar tale: a fine Perpendicular church, brasses and – a rare survival – some of the costly vestments and altar hangings with which these same merchants beautified the church. The altar frontal in particular, showing the Blessed Virgin Mary surrounded by angels, is a wonderful creation, and reminds us once more of the sumptuous interiors of these late medieval churches.

But the story is amplified here by the evidence of one merchant in particular, William Grevel. His brass, the finest in the church, lies in the chancel and a Latin inscription relates, 'Here lies William Grevel of Campden, formerly a citizen of London and flower of all the wool merchants of all England, who died on the first day of October, 1401.' In the High Street, which also contains the Market-Place, you can still see his house, set eaves on to the street in complete disregard of considerations of space on the frontage, and provided with a fine canted bay window and an original pointed and moulded entrance door. The original plan probably consisted of a parlour or counting house to the left and a hall to the right, the services being located through the archway beyond. Grevel's house is but one of many fine examples of early buildings in the town, and these Cotswold towns still exude an air of quiet prosperity which has its roots deep in the Middle Ages.

26
HAILES, Gloucestershire

The Holy Blood

The Cistercian house at Hailes was founded in 1246 by Richard, Earl of Cornwall, brother of Henry III, in fulfilment of a vow he made after narrowly escaping shipwreck. It has an idyllic setting on the edge of the Cotswold scarp and is a place of happy recollection for the present writer, since he excavated the cloister here. The house was a late foundation, and from the first a magnificent one, as the superbly carved vaulting bosses and richly patterned tiled floors attest. The King, Queen, thirteen bishops and a great party of nobles attended the consecration in 1251, but this early success was short-lived.

The early building programme was ruinously expensive and, despite the abbey's large flocks of sheep, we know that by 1270 the house was in decline. It was in that year, however, that the founder's son Edmund came to the abbey's rescue by donating a phial containing a few drops of the Blood of Christ. The relic's authenticity was guaranteed by the Patriarch of Jerusalem, and Hailes became one of the greatest pilgrimage centres of medieval England. To accommodate so venerable a relic, the east end of the church was rebuilt, the traditional Cistercian square end being replaced by an innovative design called a 'chevet'. Chevets were a French development consisting of an apse with a coronet of radiating chapels, and were always rare in England. The use of such a daring architectural form accords well with the earlier grandeur of the buildings, and marks a further step away from the early Cistercian tenets of austerity and simplicity.

Although ruined, the remains of the abbey are full of interest, and the foundations of the chevet, which would have allowed a free passage for pilgrims, are clearly marked out on the ground. The cloisters were rebuilt in their present form during the fifteenth century, indicating the later prosperity of the house. In the museum are many wonderful tiles from the church floor, bearing the arms of the founder, his family and supporters, as well as foliage, birds and beasts both real and imagined. Similar designs are also visible on the walls of the nearby parish church which was owned by the abbey. Here is a display of tiles, painting and woodcarving seldom seen in so small a building. We can perhaps imagine pilgrims praying here before entering the abbey precincts; this delightful building sets the seal on one of the most delectable sites in this book.

Map Reference SP 051301, Map 150
Nearest Town Winchcombe
Follow the A46 north-east through Winchcombe. Hailes Abbey is signposted off to the left about 3 miles (4.5 km) from the town. It is owned by the National Trust but is also in guardianship of the HBMCE and open standard hours. There is a site museum and exhibition of tiles and sculpture plus an excellent custodian. Visit also the small parish church nearby which has fine medieval wall paintings.
At Buckland (SP 082360), north-east of Hailes, just off the A46, is a 15th-century rectory open May–Sept, Mon 11–4, admission free.

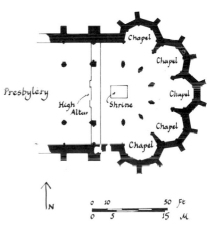

Plan of the chevet with radiating chapels and the base of the Shrine of the Holy Blood at the centre.

27

TEWKESBURY, Gloucestershire

Map Reference SO 890324, Map 150
The battle site is on the west side of the A38, south of the town centre. The Abbey Cottages in Church Street on the north side of the abbey contain the Little Museum, open during daylight hours, and the John Moore Museum at No 41.

An early example of speculative building

One of the decisive battles of the Wars of the Roses, the rout of the Lancastrians, happened about half a mile to the south of Tewkesbury on 4 May 1471. A housing estate covers a good deal of the site, but a model of the battle can be seen in the Museum in Barton Street. Fighting actually spilled over into the abbey, and the month which it took to arrange its reconsecration is the only gap in the history of worship here since its foundation in 1121 (for which see our *Norman Guide*). Edward, Prince of Wales, was killed in the battle, and a brass plate in the floor of the choir marks his grave. A further interesting detail is that the door to the sacristy, where the abbey plate was kept, is reinforced with pieces of armour gleaned from the battlefield. There are some excellent monuments in the church; the best are probably the unique tomb of Edward Despenser, who died in 1375, showing him kneeling before the high altar, and the incomparable Beauchamp Chapel, begun in 1422 and currently being restored to expose its original dazzling livery of blue, red and gold.

Our purpose in coming to Tewkesbury is not so much to look at the abbey itself, however, as to ponder its early economic activity. The phenomenon of 'speculative' building is generally thought to be a product of the later expansion of our larger cities, but it has a long history, part of which is illustrated here. In Church Street are the Abbey Cottages, an impressive row of timber-framed shops and houses built as a speculation late in the fifteenth century by the monks of Tewkesbury. Monastic

The Abbey Cottages, an instance of fifteenth-century speculative building.

enterprise has been seen elsewhere – the inns at Gloucester and Norton St Phillip, and the wool warehouse at Southampton – but here we see a further aspect of enterprise.

Originally, there were twenty-four individual units, arranged on two storeys with a jetty to the first. One unit, called the 'Little Museum', has been restored to its medieval condition, and shows the early arrangement very clearly. On the ground floor is a shop on the frontage with a hall and kitchen behind; a stair leads to the first floor and above the open hall is a smoke void to the roof. Many of the details are fascinating: the unglazed windows covered by shutters, the open fireplace in the hall with the smoke-blackened beams above, and a busy garden behind with a view of the abbey. The house has basic furniture, and upstairs the bedroom is open to the roof. Abbey Cottages provided a uniquely comprehensive impression of a medieval townscape, but this by-law of late medieval Gloucester reminds us that not all was sweetness and light:

> Item that all inhabitantes within this toune make clene byfore ther soyles the strete and so dayly kepe it clene and cause it to be caried awey and not to stryke it doune by the chanell.

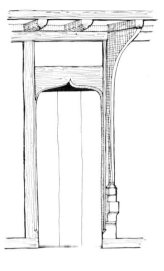

Ogee arched doorway from one of the Cottages.

28
GLOUCESTER

The English style

At the centre of the city is the great Cathedral, half Norman and half the earliest major Perpendicular Gothic work in England. The late prosperity came because the abbot was farsighted enough to procure the burial in the church of King Edward II, who was foully done to death at nearby Berkeley Castle in 1327. It was the fact of his murder which led to his spontaneous popularity, and his tomb rapidly became a pilgrimage place, with the financial rewards which that engendered. It was this revenue which enabled work to begin on the south transept in 1331, and which financed the twenty-year programme of renewal that followed.

The eastern parts of Gloucester Cathedral were conceived as a great 'cage' of masonry, with prominent vertical lines, but also with a considerable horizontal emphasis which was in its way even more innovatory. The effect is undeniably stark and the great east window, the largest in England, has more than a little of the greenhouse about it. Here all art of sculpture and detail are sublimated in a desire to achieve clean lines and a dizzying sense of height; the effects are spectacular but, in the end, mechanical. Yet this was to be the dominant style in England until the end

Map Reference SO 830186, Map 162 Cathedral has a fine close with 13th-century St Mary's Gate. The Treasury has an exhibition of medieval glaziers and tile-makers. The New Inn is a fine eating house in the centre of the town, well worth visiting. Blackfriars is in Ladybellgate Street off Southgate Street, in guardianship of the HBMCE and open standard hours in the summer season. 6 miles (9.6 km) north of Gloucester is Ashleworth (SO 818252, Map 162). Here are a church, a 15th-century rectory and a tithe barn, parts of the manor of the Augustinian Canons of Bristol. The tithe barn is owned by the National Trust. This rectorial group is south-east of Ashleworth village down the tree-lined road signposted 'Ashleworth Quay'.

ABOVE: *Rich fan vaulting in the cloister at Gloucester.*

BELOW: *The head of an unhappy king; the effigy of Edward II in Gloucester Cathedral.*

of the Middle Ages and beyond. It was a distinctive national innovation, and in the incomparable cloisters at Gloucester we see an important example of its later development in which fan vaults make an early appearance.

The City of Gloucester has a number of medieval buildings, but pride of place must go to the New Inn, built by the Abbey, reputedly for pilgrims, in the mid fifteenth century. It is an exceptionally well-preserved example of the courtyard type, in which the buildings were ranged round a yard set back from the road. The building is timber-framed and of three storeys, having galleries at first- and second-floor levels with chambers opening off them. The courtyard must have looked very much as it does today, and it is an agreeable place to visit. The other major survival of medieval Gloucester is the Blackfriars, one of a handful of friaries to survive relatively intact, and the subject of much recent repair. The church was consecrated in 1284 and it, together with the refectory and the dormitory with its spectacular scissor-braced roof, are well worth seeing.

29
ST MARY REDCLIFFE, BRISTOL, Avon

Queen Elizabeth described St Mary Redcliffe as 'the fairest, goodliest and most famous parish church in England', and this description, fulsome as it is, is entirely justified. It is a testament in stone to the power of the merchants of medieval Bristol, which was by the fifteenth century one of the largest ports in the land, and from which John Cabot set sail to the New World in 1497. One of the greatest of these merchant princes was William Canynges; his tomb is in the church, and he was one of its major benefactors.

Canynges, born in 1400, had a most interesting career: he was five times mayor of the city and twice its member of parliament. He owned a fleet of ten ships and built a fine house nearby, but eight years after his wife's death in 1460 he was ordained priest, and celebrated his first Mass here at St Mary Redcliffe on Whit Sunday that year. In 1445 the steeple had been struck by lightning, and Canynges had largely paid for the necessary repairs as well as the clerestorey and vaults. In 1483 a town record describes him as 'renovator and as it were in other respects founder and among others a very special benefactor of the church of Redcliffe'.

The most distinctive feature of the exterior of the church, apart from the tower, is the north porch of 1320–30. It is hexagonal, which is extraordinary enough, but the outer arch is composed of a series of concave arches swinging up into points and has a distinctly Oriental flavour. Could someone have been inspired by a visit to India? It is possible in view of Bristol's far-flung mercantile connections. Inside, it is the view down the nave, with its attenuated mouldings, wall shafts and Canynges's great clerestorey windows, that causes visitors to stop in their tracks. This prospect has been well likened to the interior of a cathedral, and the effect is enhanced by the superb gilded vaulting bosses, over 1,200 altogether, regilded in the eighteenth century when prominent citizens donated trinkets to be melted down for the purpose. The nave, transepts and chancel are all of a piece, and comprise one of the grandest late medieval compositions in England.

Map Reference ST 591723, Map 172
The setting of this fine church has been rendered desolate by the inner ring road, and yet it still stands majestically by the dual carriageway just south of the city centre in the direction of Bath and Wells. The small isolated Georgian house opposite, birthplace of the tragic poet Thomas Chatterton, gives a slight idea of the type of housing which once surrounded this wonderful church before town and traffic planners had their way. Visit also the Cathedral to see the magnificent 14th-century choir.

The tomb of William Canynges, who was by turns a merchant prince, Lord Mayor and ultimately a priest.

30
THE GEORGE INN, NORTON ST PHILLIP, Somerset

Map Reference ST 772558, Map 172
Nearest Town Trowbridge
Norton St Phillip, an old cloth town, lies 5 miles (8 km) west of Trowbridge on the A366 in the Radstock direction. The inn is at the busy road junction at the centre of the village. The interior is simply and traditionally furnished and gives a good flavour of a medieval inn.

Medieval inns were built for a variety of purposes: for pilgrims, as at the New Inn, Gloucester; for the accommodation of students or others; and the town houses of important merchants could be called 'inns'. The George at Norton St Phillip was built late in the fourteenth century by the Carthusian monastery at Hinton, which owned the manor. It was apparently intended both to accommodate merchants and to trade in the monastery's produce of cloth and cattle at the two annual fairs which were held here. The inn is of the block or gatehouse type also seen at the Angel at Grantham, in which the principal accommodation is contained in a range directly beside the street, rather than being arranged round a courtyard as at Gloucester.

The front range has a stone ground floor, and a four-centred archway with shields in the spandrels leads to the later courtyard at the rear. To the left of the archway were probably the hall with a parlour beyond, both lit by two-light rectangular bay windows. To the right of the archway were two service rooms, probably the buttery and cellar; the kitchen was presumably at the rear and possibly detached. The upper floors are timber-framed with broad panels and curving braces; both are jettied, except over the archway, which is slightly advanced. There seem to have been large chambers on the first floor, which are now lit by oriel windows. The George is a splendid example of a medieval inn, and is a rare delight to visit, fulfilling the requirements of conviviality and research!

The George at Norton St Phillip, which has maintained a tradition of hospitality for the last 600 years.

31
NUNNEY AND OLD WARDOUR, Somerset and Wiltshire

Two fourteenth-century tower houses

These two 'castles', both built late in the fourteenth century, reflect the experiences of their builders gained during the wars in France. They are essentially fortified manor houses, with the accommodation stacked vertically rather than in the more normal horizontal grouping to be seen at Penshurst in Kent and elsewhere. This 'high-rise' planning followed French originals, and lent dignity to the owner; perhaps the noblest English example is the great Percy keep at Warkworth in Northumberland.

At Nunney, Sir John de la Mare, reputedly enriched by the spoils of France, obtained a licence to crenellate in 1373. He built a strong moated fortress, rectangular in plan, with four drum towers at the angles. The accommodation was arranged on four storeys and the whole was well provided with machicolations to discourage assault. The lord's hall was, unusually, on the second floor, since the first floor was taken up with a common hall for retainers. This continued the late medieval practice of social distinctions being enshrined in the planning of buildings seen, for example, at Bodiam. On the topmost floor was a solar and the chambers were contained in the angle towers.

Map Reference Nunney (Somerset): ST 737457, Map 183
Nearest Town Frome
3½ miles (5.6 km) south-west of Frome off the A361 to Shepton Mallet. In guardianship of the HBMCE, open at any reasonable time. Church contains an effigy of Sir John de la Mare in the north transept.

Map Reference Old Wardour (Wiltshire): ST 939263, Map 184
Nearest Town Shaftesbury
3½ miles (5.6 km), north-east of Shaftesbury. Take the A30 in the direction of Salisbury, turn north towards Donhead St Andrew, through the village and east towards Tisbury. Wardour Castle is signposted down a minor dead-end road to the south. Site is in guardianship of the HBMCE and open 15 March–15 Oct, standard hours; 16 Oct–14 March, Sat 9.30–4, Sun 2–4. Site exhibitions.

The tall drum towers of Nunney, built by Sir John de la Mare on his return from the French wars.

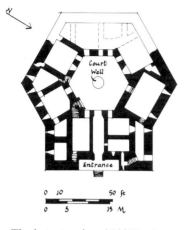

The distinctive plan of Old Wardour with its five-sided tower, central courtyard and entrance block supporting a first-floor hall.

Map Reference ST 551459, Map 182
2 medieval gateways, built by Bishop Bekynton in the 15th century, lead from the Market-Place to the Cathedral Green. On the north side of the Cathedral is the 15th-century Old Deanery, now the Diocesan Office, and the former Chancellor's House, now Wells Museum, open daily. Beyond these buildings is a covered bridge called Chain Gate which connects the Cathedral to the Vicars' Close. The bridge leads from the north transept to the hall, kitchen and treasury of the Vicars' Close. You can walk up this medieval street to the Vicars' Chapel and library. Notice as you pass the Cathedral the medieval clock on the north transept wall. The Bishop's Palace is on the south side of the Cathedral and is still the home of the Bishop of Bath and Wells. The house, chapel and grounds are open from Easter to 31 Oct, Thurs, Sun, 2–6; 1 May–25 Sept, Wed, 11–6. Every day in August and Bank Holidays. The moated site with its collection of water fowl and swans is well worth visiting. While in Wells, see also St Cuthbert's Church which appears in the entry on the *Somerset Towers*.

Old Wardour shows a similar pattern, though on a yet grander scale. Its builder, John, Lord Lovel, took advantage of a lull in the French wars to create a tower house following the style of his enemies. The plan form here follows the more exotic precepts of Warkworth, and features a five-sided tower around a central courtyard, the sixth side being closed by a large entrance block supporting a lavish first-floor hall. This hall lends the castle a decidedly unmilitary aspect, since it was well provided with tall two-light windows on the outer wall as well as the inner. Although the tops of the walls were garnished with machicolations and a strong drawbridge lent some air of military purpose, there can be little doubt that the high walls of Wardour were intended to communicate the owner's prestige as much as his might.

32
WELLS, Somerset

The incomparable city

At many sites in the West of England the early religious importance of water is clear enough; we think of the holy wells of Cornwall and St Nectan's Well at Hartland, Devon, and the City of Wells manifests this connection in its name. Recent excavations have disclosed a Romano-British origin for the importance of Wells, and there was a late Saxon cathedral here. Today, Wells has one of the most beautiful cathedrals in England, which has recently been subject to an imaginative and controversial restoration. The west front in particular is a gem of English architecture, and the crossing tower provided the inspiration for many of the famous Somerset towers, one of the finest of which can be seen at St Cuthbert's Church in the city. Inside, there is a magnificent display of fourteenth-century glass in the east end, and the contemporary misericords are of the finest quality. But the highest place should perhaps be reserved for the exquisite octagonal Chapter House, finished by 1306 – a place of the sublimest Gothic grandeur.

Apart from the Cathedral, Wells has important domestic evidence deriving from the medieval church. The Bishop's Palace is a most agreeable place and retains much early fabric, although rather heavily handled in the Romantic styles of later ages. The Palace is surrounded by its mid-fourteenth-century walls and gatehouse, and is essentially a great medieval house of a pattern indistinguishable from secular buildings elsewhere. The present accommodation originated in the time of Bishop Jocelyn in about 1230, and his fine vaulted hall with a spectacular fifteenth-century fireplace can still be seen. It was, however, Bishop

One of the handsome two-light windows of Bishop Burnell's late thirteenth-century hall.

Burnell, Chancellor of England under Edward I, and responsible for the innovative house at Acton Burnell, who aggrandized these early arrangements. He added the now ruined hall at right angles to the earlier block, and built the memorable vaulted chapel in the angle between the two ranges.

While bishops were the chief residents of cathedral cities there were, of course, considerable numbers of lesser clergy. These priests were celibate and their domestic arrangements were generally communally organized – often, as here, on a collegiate basis. The Vicars' Close at Wells, which is a planned medieval street, provides a unique insight into this organization. It was established in 1348 and the houses, although somewhat altered, retain much of their original appearance. Each house had a hall and chamber and was well detailed with paired pointed lights to the upper and lower floors. The most prominent features are the chimney stacks bearing shields of arms and surmounted by delicate pierced polygonal louvres. At the north end of the street is a chapel which, although an original feature, was remodelled late in the fifteenth century as a result of a bequest by Bishop Bekynton. At that time, the upper library chamber was added, and provided with the existing paired upper lights and battlements.

At the southern end of the street is the Chain Bridge, built in 1459 by Bishop Bekynton, and linking the Vicars' Court with the Cathedral. This is a finely finished structure, the lower part of which forms a gateway with a four-centred vehicle arch flanked by pedestrian entrances. The walls are panelled, matching the crossing tower. At the north end of the bridge is the Vicars' Hall or refectory, part of the fourteenth-century collegiate plan. It is a readily recognizable first-floor hall with a later fireplace but with the distinctive ecclesiastical feature of a pulpit in the thickness of the wall from which the Steward could read holy scripture during meals, just like a monastic refectory. The pointed waggon roof is original, as are the wooden figures representing the Annunciation on the west wall; at Wells, they would be!

The Vicars' Court at Wells, a model of Medieval domesticity.

33

GLASTONBURY AND MEARE, Somerset

Glastonbury, ancient in legend, has had a monastery since the seventh century or before; here can still be seen the Chalice Well and the Holy Thorn, which supposedly blossomed forth from the staff of St Joseph of Arimathea when he came here in AD 60. These and other delights, such as the reputed site of King Arthur's grave conveniently discovered by the monks during the twelfth century, assured the Benedictine Monastery here a wealthy pilgrim trade, and it was the richest house in the country at the time of its Dissolution in 1539. This is reflected by the magnificence of the surviving monastic buildings, although they were ruthlessly pillaged after the Dissolution. A further relic of the trade is the (St) George Inn with its fine moulded and panelled front, built late in the fifteenth century as accommodation for high-status pilgrims.

If the ruins of the church and conventual buildings at Glastonbury are not particularly impressive, the deficiency is remedied by the unusual interest which attaches to certain of its domestic arrangements. The most famous survival is the wonderful fourteenth-century kitchen, but there is also a good tithe barn and a rare fish house at nearby Meare. These structures together shed light on the economic basis of this wealthy community. The kitchen bespeaks the higher standard of food and comfort espoused by the Benedictine Order; the tithe barn directs our attention towards one aspect of its revenues; and the Fish House reminds us of the central importance of fish to the medieval diet, and of the fact that it could be a major product in its own right.

The kitchen is square on plan, with a steeply pitched octagonal roof crowned by an elaborate louvre through which the heat and smoke would have dissipated. This represents a rare survival of a feature once common in halls and other domestic buildings during the Middle Ages. Most of the important halls would have had louvres along the lines of the one here at Glastonbury, and lower status would have been reflected by pottery or wood being used for its construction rather than stone as here. It should also be pointed out that a considerable degree of skill has gone into the design of this building, with its sloping roof and tall louvre helping to disperse the fumes more efficiently. Inside, there are four broad fireplaces across the angles of the chamber, reminiscent of St Hugh's kitchen at Lincoln. The place was doubtless a hell of noise and heat when in use, and we can only speculate upon the lavish dainties which were prepared here.

In a Catholic country fish was an important staple of the diet, and had the advantage of being easily salted, smoked or dried to provide protein during the winter. At Meare (the name gives the game away) we find a

Map Reference Glastonbury: ST 499390, Map 182
Meare: ST 458418, Map 182
Abbey is administered by the Glastonbury Abbey Trust, and is open daily. In the kitchen is an interesting exhibition of the life and work of the Abbey. The High Street has the George Inn (where refreshments and accommodation can still be obtained as in the days of pilgrimages), the Tribunal, and the 15th-century Abbey courthouse which was altered in the 16th century. The fine tithe barn, dating from c 1420, has a granger's loft and good architectural details. It is a rural life museum open 10–5 weekdays, and 2–6.30 at weekends.

Meare is 4 miles (6.5 km) north-west of Glastonbury on the B3151. The Fish House is set back from the road in a field on the north side, full of earthworks. The site is in HBMCE guardianship and is open at any reasonable time. The key has to be obtained from the Manor House beside the church. This affords the visitor the chance to study the outside of the Manor which was built by Abbot Mornington in the mid 14th century as a summerhouse. Evidence of medieval fenestration can be seen, although the house was altered in the 17th century.

The central louvre from inside.

structure apparently dedicated to this important commodity. It stands back from the road, and beyond the ground shelves away to the edge of the great Meare Pool, a lake five miles in circumference which was in early times boiling with fish. The lake was drained during the eighteenth century and is now good farmland, but its extent is clear enough on the ground. This was a great natural fishpond, the vast counterpart of many an artificial stew elsewhere.

The Fish House seems to have been a regular first-floor hall with an external stair, and is well appointed with chamfered doors and windows, probably the work of Adam de Sodbury who was Abbot between 1322 and 1355. On the ground floor are rooms apparently devoted to the care of the fishing nets and tackle, and to the processing of the catch. However, we felt that the accommodation would be inadequate for such a task, and that the smell would have been indescribable. Perhaps the abbey's fishermen banished these unwholesome tasks to the buildings whose foundations can be seen nearby!

The fourteenth-century kitchen at Glastonbury, a notable architectural tribute to the culinary art.

34
THE SOMERSET TOWERS, Somerset

Somerset is justly famous for its glittering array of late medieval church towers. They are indeed a fine body of buildings, of which those mentioned are probably the best – an invidious choice! The inspiration of the towers derived from the central tower at Wells Cathedral, which was begun in 1322 and slightly altered in 1440. This established the architectural importance of the tower, and pioneered some of the particular design features of the Somerset group. Specifically, it had three two-light belfry openings which were continued downwards as blank panels, carved figures on the buttresses, and was surmounted by a forest of pinnacles.

These features were taken up with violent enthusiasm by the masons of Somerset, and they used the copious local supplies of good and easily worked oolitic limestone to produce a wealth of variations on the basic themes. This stone also permitted the distinctive local device of perforated stone belfry lights, rather than the more common wooden louvres. The designs of the towers are frequently eclectic, borrowing their details from elsewhere and recombining them. The result is a collection of over sixty major towers, which have largely defied repeated attempts at classification. They provide a fascinating puzzle for the architectural student, and are a source of delight to the visitor.

The Somerset towers can be divided into two basic groups by the presence or absence of external horizontal divisions. In the first case, the tower was conceived as a single unit, following the great tower at Wells, whereas in the second, the more usual division into a series of structural storeys was followed. Of the towers without horizontal divisions, the Church of St Cuthbert at Wells itself is one of the best examples. This demonstrates the soaring vertical lines of this type to perfection, as does the marvellous Perpendicular Gothic tracery in the rest of the church. Wrington and Evercreech – the latter in particular is delightfully chaste – are further examples of the type.

Towers with horizontal divisions are much more numerous, and there are many good examples. The towers at Huish and Kingsbury Episcopi (the names reflect their ownership by the See of Wells) have three stages divided by quatrefoil friezes. The setback buttresses have crocketed pinnacles matching those on the oversailing embattled parapets. Isle Abbots is similar but with a more restrained and pierced parapet. The carvings are well preserved here and, as rebuilding during the last century was carried out in a sensitive fashion, it has much original detail. The grandest of these towers is undoubtedly the very late example at St Mary Magdalene, Taunton. It was actually rebuilt during the last century but

Map Reference Batcombe: ST 690390, Map 183
Evercreech: ST 649387, Map 183
Huish Episcopi: ST 427266, Map 193
Isle Abbots: ST 353209, Map 193
Kingsbury Episcopi: ST 437210, Map 193
Kingston St Mary: ST 222297, Map 193
Leigh on Mendip: ST 693473, Map 183
North Petherton: ST 290330, Map 182
Staple Fitzpaine: ST 263182, Map 193
Taunton, St Mary Magdalene: ST 229245, Map 193
Wells, St Cuthbert: ST 546456, Map 183
Wrington: ST 468628, Map 182
Nearest Town Taunton
All these churches are easily found in village or town centres.

The tower of Isle Abbots Church demonstrates that lofty stateliness which is the chief distinction of the Somerset towers.

retains its erstwhile appearance. This has four stages, with paired triple lights to the upper three. The pinnacles here are large and panelled, and the whole effect is reminiscent of a spectacular attenuated wedding cake. The view of the tower up Hammet Street is unforgettable.

35

ABBOTSBURY TITHE BARN, CHAPEL AND
SWANNERY, Dorset

A Benedictine monastery was founded in this delightful place during the eleventh century and it remained in use throughout the Middle Ages, although little now remains above ground. There are two other ecclesiastical monuments which demand our attention, however, the first of which is the early-fifteenth-century monastic tithe barn. This was a prodigious structure, one of the largest in England, and provided with two entrances. Time has used it harshly, however, and less than half the original structure is now roofed, though the west end retains a fine gable niche. It is now used as a store for the thatching reeds which are grown in the adjacent pond, an interesting survival of traditional practices.

Nearby is St Catherine's Chapel, at the top of a grassy hill looking out towards the sea, and reputedly the site of a beacon. The dedication is interesting, and reflects the popularity of this saint in the West Country, where over sixty dedications are recorded. The siting of her chapel on a hill might relate to the traditional story of her body having been transported after death by angels to the summit of Mount Sinai. The Chapel is of early-fifteenth-century date and is distinguished by a splendid panelled stone vault with cusped ogee decorations. This highly unusual construction can best be paralleled at such northern sites as Boltongate (Cumbria). As you approach the chapel, notice the good set of lynchets on the slopes below. They are probably medieval in their present form, but may represent remodelled Iron Age fields.

Map Reference St Catherine's Chapel: SY 572848, Map 194
Abbey: SY 578852
Nearest Town Weymouth
Chapel is ½ mile (0.8 km) south of the village by a pedestrian track off the B3157. It is in HBMCE guardianship and open at any reasonable time. The Abbey remains, beside the churchyard, are also in guardianship and open at any reasonable time. The tithe barn can be viewed from the outside, but it is not open because of its use as a reed store. The Swannery is open during the summer months and has well-interpreted landscape features.

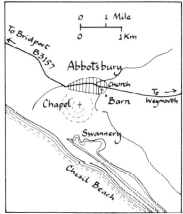

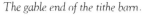

The gable end of the tithe barn.

Finally at Abbotsbury, which has so many engaging delights in addition to its fine setting, we must mention the Swannery. This place, first mentioned in 1393, consists of a squarish pond carved out of the low-lying ground near Chesil Beach. It is unique in still being used for its original purpose, and is a breeding place for mute swans. Swans were, of course, closely associated with royalty and chivalry in early times, and are still owned by the Queen, with the exception of those belonging to the London livery companies on the Thames. The landscape around the Swannery is as historically interesting as the pond itself, with pollarded trees and more thatching reeds.

36
WHITCHURCH CANONICORUM, Dorset

Map Reference ST 394955, Map 193
Nearest Town Bridport
Take the A35 west from Bridport in the direction of Lyme Regis. After 3 miles (4.5 km) turn north up minor roads to Whitchurch Canonicorum. The village is beautifully set in the Marchwood Valley and the church is on the slope of a hill slightly above the village.

The Shrine of St Candida

The Church of St Candida and Holy Cross is unique among English parish churches because it contains the shrine of the saint to whom it is dedicated. The career of St Candida (Latin for 'shiny white'), otherwise known as St 'Whyte', is more than usually obscure. At least three different origins have been advanced, including one which suggests that 'she' was a 'he' called Albinus, martyred with Archbishop Boniface in Germany during the eighth century. Whatever the truth of the matter, the shrine in the church here has been venerated since early times, and the discovery of Roman material on the site together with the 'white church' name could indicate a very early origin indeed.

During the eleventh century the church was presented to the Abbey of St Wandrille in Normandy, and in the twelfth it was evidently rebuilt on an ambitious scale, as the existing nave arcades indicate. In the thirteenth century further extensive works were undertaken, and the saint's shrine constructed in its present form. The shrine is in the north transept and consists of a tomb chest with three mandorla-shaped openings surmounted by a Purbeck marble slab. When the tomb was opened in 1900 the bones of a small woman were found in a lead casket inscribed HIC. REQESCT. RELIQE. SCE. WITE – 'here lie the relics of St Wite'. But whether these bones were original or not must remain uncertain. The trade in relics was brisk throughout the Middle Ages, and the tomb showed signs of having been opened previously.

The healing properties of the saint were well known in the area during our period, and pilgrims came hoping to be cured of a variety of ailments. It seems that eye ailments were particularly favoured, since the pale blue flowers of the periwinkle are still known locally as 'St Candida's Eyes' and

St Candida's shrine; prayers and offerings are still placed in the holes in the front.

her well at Morcombelake was efficacious for sore eyes. Offerings were placed in the holes in the front of the tomb, and we were delighted to discover that this practice is yet continuing, and there were many written prayers and invocations there when we visited.

37
HOUND TOR, Devon

A deserted village

Dartmoor, upon which Hound Tor is located, is a place of ancient mystery and fascination. For the archaeologist it is a palimpsest of many periods, bearing traces of varied activities from prehistoric and later times. New discoveries are constantly being made, and many of its features are found to be unimaginably old, their antiquity being measured in millennia rather than mere centuries. At Postbridge is the enigmatic clapper bridge, which some have claimed as being fifteenth-century. Its megalithic construction renders certainty impossible; it could as easily be Bronze Age, but if it is medieval it may have been associated with the exploitation of tin which is described in more detail under the entry for Lostwithiel.

Hound Tor is a classical example of a deserted settlement, although it is an 'upland' village, having a somewhat haphazard clutch of houses with barns and small garden plots. The earlier houses, which dated to the eleventh and twelfth centuries, had thick walls of turf blocks stabilized by wattles. During the thirteenth century roughly coursed granite blocks replaced turf as the normal building material, possibly reflecting some deterioration in climatic conditions. It is the ruined walls of these buildings which can still be seen on the site.

They are of three main types: houses, barns and corn-drying kilns. The dwellings were of the 'longhouse' type in which men and animals shared the same roof and a single doorway in a side wall. For obvious reasons, the houses are built against slopes with the byres at the lower end! Architectural refinements were few; some houses had porches, and all were found to have postholes for wooden door frames when excavated. Central hearths heated the houses, some with wattle and daub chimney hoods; there were also cooking pits in which pots could be placed on a bed of hot ash. The smaller rectangular barns probably had hipped roofs, since they are rounded at the corners. Three of them contained corn-drying kilns, one of which yielded charred oat grains. These ovens were doubtless a necessity as the climate worsened towards the end of the village's life in the fourteenth century.

The economy of the village depended on mixed farming; the longhouses

Map Reference SX 748796, Map 191
Nearest Town Newton Abbot
The village site is 10 miles (16 km) north-west of Newton Abbot. Take the road to Bovey Tracey and from there the B3344 to Manaton. The site is 1½ miles (2.5 km) south of the village off the B road. Above the village are the medieval fields and beyond these the bracken-covered open moorland. In the guardianship of the HBMCE, and open at any reasonable time. In summer there are guided walks of the area available from the Dartmoor National Park car park at Hound Tor (SX 741792), lasting 1½ hours. For further information telephone Bovey Tracey 832093. Postbridge is at SX 648789.

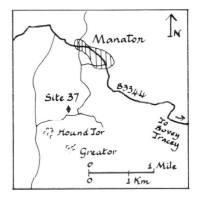

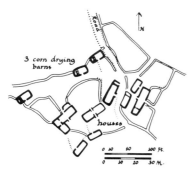

Hound Tor provides a good example of the informality encountered in many an upland village.

3 corn drying barns

houses

provide evidence of animals and, on the slopes above the village, faint corrugations indicate the existence of arable farming. The irregular outlines of the fields can still be descried, and we can only wonder at the sheer brute effort needed to clear these mean fields of boulders and to turn their thin soil. As at Wharram Percy, it appears that the villagers of Hound Tor fared badly during the troubled times of the fourteenth century. As the climate worsened, winter fodder would have become difficult to obtain, and their precious supply of grain would have become undependable. Oats, with their higher tolerance of moisture and cold, as well as their nutritious straw, were an obvious choice of crop, but their efforts were apparently unavailing. Some time in the fourteenth century the villagers gave up their one-sided struggle and Hound Tor became a place of ghosts and memories, in which condition it remains.

38
BRAUNTON GREAT FIELD, Devon

Map Reference SS 475360, Map 180
Nearest Town Barnstaple
Braunton is 5 miles (8 km) north-west of Barnstaple on the A31 to Ilfracombe. To find the open fields take the B3231 to Staunton. At the edge of Braunton village take the first turn left; this road runs round the open field system and divides it from the Braunton Burrows salt marshes. Take the hedge-lined track on to the open field; look across the open field to the village and see the former open common pasture on the hills above and the woodland which provided pannage for the pigs. The church is in the centre of the village on the east side. In the churchyard is a museum with a model of the open field system. Open mid May–mid Sept, 10.30–12, 2–4, Tues–Sat.

Another good site displaying open fields is at Forrabury Stitches near Boscastle, Cornwall (SX 095910, Map 190).

Braunton, which emerges into history during the ninth century with the significant name of 'Brannocminster', was a large and prosperous royal manor at the time of Domesday. It was nurtured by the rich alluvial arable land around the Taw–Torridge estuary and remained an agricultural community until the twentieth century, when it began to develop as a tourist centre. The parish church of St Brannoc is endowed with excellent fifteenth-century woodwork and waggon roofs. A fragment of Saxon carving reused as a window lintel in the west wall of the tower hints at its pre-Conquest origins. But it is, of course, Braunton's renowned 'Great Field' which demands our closest attention.

It was long thought that this famous open field was of comparatively recent origin, since it was held to be a late example of land apportionment after draining the marshes there. Research has revealed that the strips can be traced back to at least the early fourteenth century, and they are of the greatest interest. Braunton, like other lowland villages, had more than one open field of course, and traces of them, including lynchets, survive on West Hill and Braunton Down elsewhere in the parish.

Here we see what is in essence a medieval arable landscape, caught like a fly in amber, a challenge to our imagination. There have been changes, of course, for repeated cultivation is bound to take its toll of the fragile boundaries and other features, but field systems like these must always have responded to differing patterns of use and husbandry. The overwhelming impression, as in the fields of Laugharne (Dyfed), is one of the openness, an absence of walls and hedges. The boundaries are marked instead by the

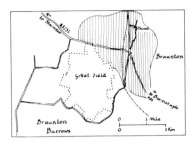

narrowest of unploughed ridges, kept to a minimum to avoid loss of cultivable land. Some consolidation of strips has occurred, and there are now only twenty owners, two of them having just one strip each.

When walking over the field, it is still possible to follow the thick outer boundary hedges on the south, east and west sides. The individual furlongs, which are the larger blocks of land containing the strips, can easily be detected since they are still reached by the tracks which also formed the communal headlands where the plough was turned. Within the furlongs, the strips or 'lands' can be seen, many displaying the curving reversed S shapes which are characteristic of medieval ploughlands. Some of the ends of the narrow grassy baulks, 'landsherds', are sometimes marked with large pebbles called 'bond stones', and they are also used to mark the corners of the furlongs.

The field is still very much in use and is some of the best land in the area, yielding large crops of vegetables like leeks, cabbages and cauliflowers, as well as cereals and fodder. Change has obviously altered some of the earlier patterns; cattle graze the field only occasionally, and seaweed from the nearby beach is no longer used as fertilizer. But the timeless continuity of this intricate husbandry has been maintained, and the farmers of Braunton are to be congratulated. It is to be hoped that they will continue to resist the blandishments of large machines and correspondingly larger fields which have so transformed the countryside elsewhere.

Braunton Great Field showing one of the dividing baulks in the left foreground with further strips in the distance. The picture illustrates the openness of the Medieval arable landscape, lending a curiously contemporary air to this hedgeless scene.

39
HARTLAND CHURCH, Devon

Map Reference SS 235248, Map 190
Nearest Town Bideford
12 miles (19 km) west of Bideford, signposted off the A39 (T). As you approach the village you will see the church standing proud against the sea. Go through the village and follow the signs to Stoke and Hartland Quay. Church is about 1 mile (1.6 km) outside the village at Stoke.

Other fine Devon rood screens can be seen at:
Ottery St Mary: SY 099956, Map 192
Bovey Tracey: SX 821786, Map 191
Halberton: ST 005129, Map 181
Uffculme: ST 069127, Map 181

Hartland Church is dedicated to St Nectan, a Welsh hermit who lived in this remote and beautiful valley during the sixth century, and this is why the church is so far from the site of the old borough. Nectan was apparently killed by robbers, and is reputed to have carried his severed head for half a mile before collapsing by the well which still bears his name. This story reminds us, among others, of St Winifride of Holywell and the legendary story of the foundation of her shrine there. Hartland was also a pilgrimage centre during the Middle Ages and many gifts, including the elaborate gilt and jewelled decorations of his staff, were made to the church here.

ABOVE: *The tall tower of Hartland Church dwarfs the huddled nave and aisles.*

RIGHT: *This magnificent waggon roof reminds us of the original splendour of Medieval church interiors.*

The setting of the church, which is probably the best in Devon, is memorable; the lofty Perpendicular Gothic tower of pinkish grey stone is set against a green valley and looks out towards the sea. Externally, the early-fourteenth-century nave windows have fine tracery, and the dressings, such as the fleurons in the moulding round the south door, are well detailed. Inside, there is a good Devonian waggon roof, but pride of place must go to the rood screen, resplendent in red, dark green and gold. Devon is justly famous for its highly decorated wooden screens, and Hartland is a very good example of the type. It is fifteenth-century work; the paired lights have cusped ogee heads and the coved top is encrusted with moulded ribs having carved bosses at the intersections. The spaces between the ribs have a unique decorative scheme consisting of flowers and shields. The cornice has five orders of busy carvings and a deep overhang – all in all a most delightful object.

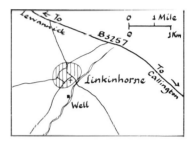

40

CORNISH HOLY WELLS, Cornwall

Cornwall, like Wales, has a varied collection of holy wells, many of which were probably revered long before the advent of Christianity. Some retained their early importance, however, and became associated with saints and miracles, often being credited with curative properties. Many wells failed to attract permanent markers or well heads, but some of the more celebrated had stone or wooden shrines built over them. The examples at Linkinhorne and Dupath are among the best surviving in Cornwall, and Linkinhorne in particular preserves an atmosphere of holiness and mystery which is entirely suited to its location in this misty Celtic land. There has always been a certain ambivalence on the part of the Church towards these shrines, and as early as the tenth century it was decreed that the worship of 'trees, stones and fountains' should cease. But it didn't, and even today suppliants still make their way to the healing waters.

Linkinhorne (the name apparently reflects an earlier dedication to a saint called Cynheorn) has a fine granite Perpendicular Gothic church with fifteenth-century wall paintings and the second tallest tower in Cornwall. But in a meadow by the church is its most unexpected treasure, the fifteenth-century holy well of St Melor, to whom the church is dedicated. This Melor or Mylor is a very obscure figure, possibly of Breton origin, and apparently a cripple who was done to death by his guardian. Yet here is his well, consisting of a small gabled granite shrine with an arched entrance surmounted by an empty niche. Inside, there is a further niche for

Map Reference Linkinhorne: SX 320734, Map 201 Dupath: SX 374693, Map 201 *Nearest Town* Liskeard Linkinhorne is 8 miles (13 km) north-east of Liskeard, signposted off the B3257 reached by minor roads to the west. In the centre of the village take the unmarked lane, past the farmyard on the left, and pull into the second gateway. Go across the field to where all the boundaries meet and in a leafy hollow is the well.

The larger well at Dupath is in Callington parish, 8 miles (13 km) east of Liskeard on the A390. The well is signposted off the Tavistock road at the junction with a B road. Follow the signs down the track and the well is located behind a farmhouse. HBMCE guardianship, open any reasonable hours.

Other holy wells can be found at: Madron: SW 446328, Map 203 Trelill: SW 676285, Map 203 Jesus Well: SW 938764, Map 200 Sancreed: SW 400289, Map 203

offerings, and the sacred spring bubbles up through a groove in the base. Beside the shrine is an oak tree and we saw a hare and lots of tiny toads when we visited. It is a timeless, ageless place, and the past seems very close in St Melor's holy valley.

The granite wellhead at Linkinhorn, so mysterious that a sprite or boggan might easily lurk in its murky interior.

41
LOSTWITHIEL, Cornwall

Map Reference Lostwithiel:
SX 105598, Map 200
St Neot: SX 185678
Goonzion: SX 170670, Map 201
Nearest Town Lostwithiel
The Stannary Court or Duchy Palace is near the River Fowey, on a street corner by Parade Square. The Convocation or Coinage Hall is now a masonic lodge and the buildings behind, which once formed the Great Hall of the Duchy Palace, have now been developed into shops. Although much altered, the buildings retain some pointed medieval window and door openings. Nearby is the 15th-century Fowey Bridge and the Parish Church of St Bartholomew, the patron saint of tinners.

The tin mines

The origins of the Cornish tin trade are lost in the mists of prehistory, but something of its early medieval development was explained in our *Norman Guide* under the entry for Lydford. During the Middle Ages tin remained an important commodity since it was a constituent of the ubiquitous bronze which was widely used for utilitarian and decorative work. The Crown, ever anxious to augment its finances, was not slow to appreciate the fiscal potential of tin production. Strict laws governed the industry and miners had to take the metal to one of four 'Stannary' (from the Latin *stannaria*, 'tin') towns in Cornwall, which were Helston, Launceston, Lostwithiel and Truro. Defaulters were despatched to the grim tower at Lydford, and suffered the notoriously harsh 'Lydford Law' which was administered there.

At Lostwithiel, we can see the shell of the huge late-thirteenth-century Court Hall of the Duchy Palace there. This building, which rivalled the scale of the Castle Hall at Winchester, was of eight bays and was finely decorated. This was but the focus of a complex of administrative buildings from which the Duchy of Cornwall was administered and the vital tin industry regulated. Here was the county court, the seat of feudal governance, and the assay office at which tin was tested and assessed for taxation. The tin arrived as ingots, from which a corner or 'coin' was removed, melted down and tested for purity. The industry burgeoned throughout the Middle Ages, and production actually doubled in the second half of the fifteenth century alone. But what evidence has this important activity left for us to see?

If we proceed to the small village of St Neot nearby, we discover something of the physical legacy of the industry. Tin occurs naturally in veins (lodes) in the parent rock, and as the rock is worn away by streams so the metal is deposited in their outwash. Deposits of this alluvial tin could on occasion reach a thickness of twenty feet, and could be easily won by removing the gravel overburden and cleaning the deposits with water. It was a logical step to begin working the tin lodes on the hillsides overlooking the valleys. This is the activity which is manifested at Goonzion above St Neot by a pattern of deep V-shaped gullies which wind irregularly down the hillside. The sides of these gullies must have been nearly vertical when they were cut, and represent a prodigious amount of hard manual work. The great scale of the workings at St Neot, which is but one of many sites in both Cornwall and Devon, attests the high value commanded by this basic raw material.

St Neot village is 8 miles (13 km) north-east of Lostwithiel on the edge of Bodmin Moor. It is signposted off the A38 and is 2 miles (3 km) north of the trunk road up minor roads. West of the church in a wall beside the petrol station, near the old smithy, the mortar stone can be seen set in a recess beside the school traffic sign.

Goonzion Down is above St Neot. The tin-working area can be seen on the slopes to the left of the road where grassy humps can be seen protruding above the bracken, gorse and heather.

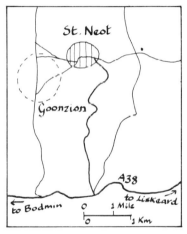

The fine fourteenth-century bridge over the River Fowey, scene of bitter fighting during the English Civil War.

Details of the preparation and smelting of the ore are in short supply as yet, but analysis of the resulting slag is becoming more common and will doubtless help to elucidate the details. In the centre of St Neot village, however, is a granite slab, now built into a wall, which bears smoothly worn rounded hollows. These indicate that it was used in a blowing or 'knacking' mill as a mortarstone upon which the tin ore was crushed by mechanical means. This stone cannot be dated with precision, but it is perfectly possible that it is medieval and that it was used in the manner later described in sixteenth-century Devon – 'three, and in some places six great logs of timber, bound at the ends with iron, and lifted up and down by a wheel driven with water'. Such a water-powered system would have been quite within the accomplishment of medieval technology, but as yet such a site has not been discovered; we must await further enlightenment from our archaeological colleagues. Finally, the splendid granite church of St Neot probably reflects the prosperity brought by tin; many churches in both Devon and Cornwall are said to have been built with the proceeds of this trade.

42
ST PIRAN'S ROUND, Cornwall

Map Reference SW 779545, Map 200
Nearest Town Newquay
Piran's Round is about 6 miles (9.5 km) south of Newquay. From Goonhavern on the A3075, take the B3285 to Perranporth. Watch out for a pink cottage on the left and a new bungalow on the right, just before the turning to Rose. Piran's Round is behind the bungalow – note the new fencing and HBMCE sign. The Cornish Gorsedd was held here in 1985. A similar theatre can be seen at St Just in Penwith (SW 370314, Map 203).

Piran's Round is a rather enigmatic site, and it is not possible to say with certainty when it was constructed. It is known that it was used at least by late medieval times as a playing place, and it was here that the Cornish Miracle Plays were performed. Piran, to whom the place was dedicated,

The Medieval playing place called St Piran's Round.

was a fifth-century Celtic monk who settled in north Cornwall and gave his name to Perranporth. His cult enjoyed great popularity in later times, and he was the patron of the Cornish tinners. Nearby is his oratory, sadly wrecked by vandals, but this interesting site has so far escaped their attentions.

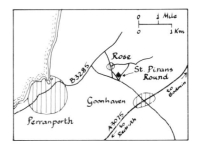

The Round is a large circular banked and ditched enclosure with two opposed entrances to the east and west, and near the centre is a hollow with a shallow ditch leading to it. It was here that the Ordinalia, the cycle of Cornish plays, was performed. This comprised the Origin of the World, the Passion of Our Lord and the Resurrection. We can perhaps imagine the spellbound audience, sitting on the grassy banks, and gazing in awe as God was manifested in his Glory, and Demons danced at the Mouth of Hell.

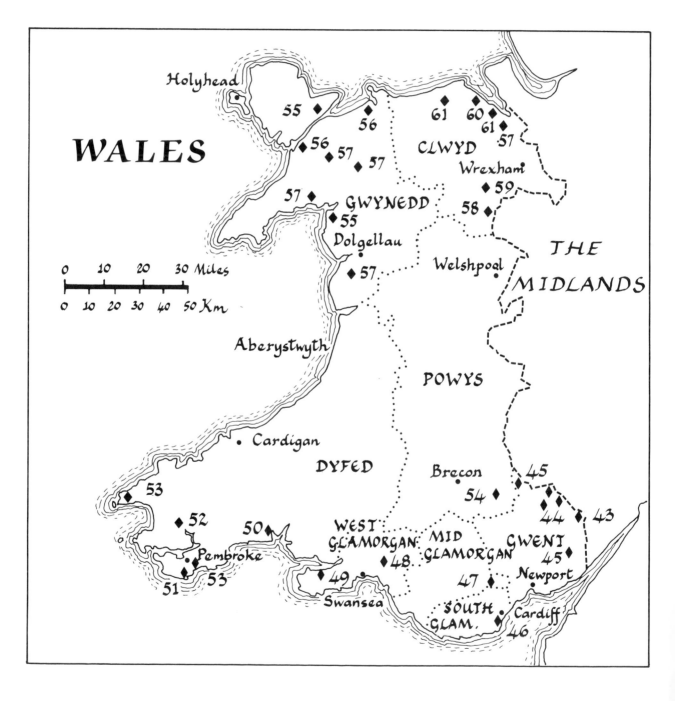

WALES

Introduction

Many of the monuments of medieval Wales are inevitably bound up with the great struggle between the princes of Gwynedd and the English. Gwynedd, with Snowdonia at its heart, was the great bastion of Welsh independence and, despite the loss of most of the rest of the country, the Princes of Gwynedd held out for a long time against their foes. Llywelyn ab Iowerth 'the Great' married King John's daughter, and took advantage of the weak English Crown to forge a Welsh alliance. He is remembered as a law giver, a statesman and a wise ruler who taught the Welsh to see the benefits of unity.

After Llywelyn's death in 1240, Welshmen still looked to the Principality of Gwynedd for leadership, and nor did it fail them. The second Llywelyn, called ap Gruffydd and known as the 'Last', took up the cause of Welsh independence. But this Llywelyn did not enjoy the advantage of a weak English ruler; he was opposed instead by Edward I, one of the most resolute kings that England ever produced. Llywelyn refused to attend Edward's coronation in 1272, and Edward promptly marched into Wales and compelled acceptance of the humiliating terms of the Treaty of Aberconwy. Llywelyn's title of 'Prince of Wales' mocked him as he was forced to go to London to give homage to Edward. When in 1282 the Welsh rebelled against the English domination, Llywelyn was not found wanting, and he distinguished himself as a brave if ill-starred leader before his death in an ambush near Builth Wells.

After Llywelyn's death the power of Gwynedd was broken, and Edward reorganized the Principality on English lines under the terms of the Statute of Rhuddlan in 1284. This really marked the end of large-scale revolt against English rule, but in 1409 Owain Glyndwr, that most charismatic of Welsh leaders, suddenly burst upon the scene and escalated a private quarrel with Lord Grey of Ruthin into a national cause. His tactics of guerilla warfare were ideally suited to the terrain, and he won strong support from the people. Glyndwr's parliaments at Machynlleth seemed to herald Welsh independence, but it was not to be. Henry IV gradually regained all the lost territory, and by 1412 Glyndwr completely disappeared, taking with him the hopes of a nation. Legend relates that he died soon afterwards in the Golden Valley, or that he lived on at his court at Sycharth, but nobody knows for sure.

What has this stirring history left to us? What is the physical legacy of medieval Wales? It is overwhelmingly a matter of castles and fortresses, remnants of the epic struggle between the two nations. Our *Norman Guide* indicated how the early castles clustered on the March, with some along the northern and southern coastal plains. Now the network was increased with, in some areas, small groups of castles working together as single units of defence. Thus Skenfrith, Grosmont and White Castle were known as the 'Three Castles' by the early thirteenth century, and they held the territory near Abergavenny.

Individual fortresses demand our attention. Tretower, for example, can show a fascinating development from shell keep to a roomy and comfortable house. Weobley Castle is likewise more a fortified house than a castle, built as it was in the quieter days after the Statute of Rhuddlan. Most remarkably of all, the great fortress of Caerphilly is the ultimate statement of the power and prestige of a great Marcher lord, who defied both the Princes of Wales and the King of England by its construction.

These castles are impressive enough, but of course the greatest treasures of medieval Wales are the mighty fortifications associated with the policy of Edward I. From the beginnings at Flint, which has a large donjon tower of a type popular in France but not afterwards used in Wales, we see a remarkable development of the concentric fortress which was the latest development of contemporary military architecture. At Rhuddlan, Harlech, Beaumaris and, most splendidly of all at Caernarfon, we see the physical effect of Edward's Welsh policy. These are some of the greatest castles built anywhere in the medieval world.

Turning away from castles and warfare, we find a good number of religious sites of various types including handsome abbeys at Neath, Llanthony and Tintern. Tintern in particular is an important and well-preserved Cistercian house, one of a number established in south Wales which waxed fat on the proceeds of sheep farming and mineral exploitation. Neath is today more famous for its tiled floors – exquisite creations, their designs still glowing with colour after centuries of burial. Llanthony lurks up a narrow valley, miles beyond the uttermost reach of civilization, a quiet and secret place; one of the bare ruined choirs of the imagination.

Dyfed, the south western part of Wales, affords a glimpse of the comfortable circumstances attendant upon the office of bishop in the Middle Ages. The two palaces at St Davids and Lamphey display every refinement of grace and design with the accent very much on comfort. Here the bishops of St Davids disported themselves and gave great feasts for their followers and guests. Doubtless much of this entertainment was of the dull and formal kind, though the splendour of the buildings, together with such distinctive flourishes as the arcaded parapets, suggest that not all was sacrificed to piety! But Christian observance of a different sort is attested by the delightful St Govan's Well, redolent of the privations of the Celtic saints, and at Holywell where the martyrdom of St Winifride was commemorated by generations of devout pilgrims.

As to the everyday life of the people, two sites come especially to mind – Cosmeston deserted village and the open fields at Laugharne. At Cosmeston, a project has been initiated which might prove to be the Welsh equivalent of the painstaking work at Wharram Percy in Yorkshire. This involves the careful elucidation of a deserted medieval village, and the preparation of its remains for display to the public. At Laugharne, by contrast, we are interested less in buildings, apart from the castle immortalized by Dylan Thomas, than in the pattern of its early fields. They remind us of the 600 years of careful husbandry which have passed since the fields here were first recorded.

43
MONMOUTH, Gwent

The fortified bridge
Monmouth was probably a Norman plantation, laid out between the rivers Monnow and Wye, in a position that was both accessible and defensible. It is famous as the birthplace of Henry V, victor of Agincourt, and the square

Map Reference SO 507125, Map 162
The bridge is at the west end of the town.

The fortified gate on the bridge at Monmouth would have provided a serious obstacle to any attacker.

twelfth-century hall keep of the castle where he was born can still be seen. Late in the thirteenth century the castle was remodelled, and it is to that period that Monmouth's chief medieval monument belongs.

This is the splendid fortified bridge over the River Monnow at the west end of the town. The bridge itself was built in about 1270, and the gateway was added about twenty years later. The gateway is flanked by twin towers and is overhung by machicolations; arrow loops cover the approaches and the whole structure retains a defiantly military aspect. The gateway is placed about a third of the way across the bridge from the town, and thus formed a sort of barbican. This gateway had to be breached before the town gate itself was reached, and must have provided a very difficult military problem, since any attacking force would have to be bunched up on a narrow front, providing an easy target for the defenders.

44

SKENFRITH, GROSMONT AND WHITE CASTLES, Gwent

Map Reference Skenfrith, SO 456203, Map 161
Nearest Town Monmouth 8 miles (12.8 km) north-west of Monmouth on the B4521, half-way between Abergavenny and Ross. The castle is owned by the National Trust and is in Welsh Office guardianship, open standard hours. The church is also worth visiting and contains some 13th-century work.

Map Reference Grosmont, SO 405244, Map 161
Nearest Town Monmouth 6 miles (9.6 km) north-west of Skenfrith on the B4347. It is in Welsh Office guardianship and open at any reasonable time. The church also contains 13th-century work.

Three Border fortresses

These three castles began to be treated as a unit of defence on the Welsh March from the twelfth century. Together they controlled a block of territory east of Abergavenny, and monitored traffic along this strategic sector of the southern March. In 1201 King John granted the 'Three Castles' (as they were by then known) to Hubert de Burgh, Earl of Kent. Hubert's career was complicated by a period of imprisonment by the French and John's churlish forfeiture of his estates, but between 1219 and 1232 he rebuilt the mainly timber castles of Skenfrith and Grosmont in stone. They were remodelled in the latest style with curtain walls having projecting semi-circular towers well provided with arrow slits.

Skenfrith presents a remarkably complete early-thirteenth-century scheme comprising a rectilinear bailey with angle towers and, at the centre, a detached round tower on a low mound. Lining the outer walls are traces of domestic and other ranges, that to the west having an undercroft, probably with a hall over. The round tower itself was raised up on a mound so as to provide effective fire over the lower outer walls, thus cheaply obtaining the advantage of a concentric plan.

Grosmont, as the name suggests, occupies a strong hilltop site and de Burgh's defences make best use of the natural resources. At the heart of the castle is a rectangular hall block with massive walls, built as the stone centrepiece of an earlier earth and timber castle in about 1210. When de Burgh returned from France he created a polygonal courtyard before this

Map Reference White Castle,
SO 380168, Map 161
Nearest Town Abergavenny
6 miles (9.6 km) east of
Abergavenny. Take the B4521
towards Ross on Wye and the castle
is signposted off to the south, about
1 mile (1.6 km) down minor roads.
It is in Welsh Office guardianship
and open standard hours.

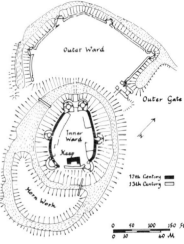

ABOVE: *Plan of White Castle showing
the Inner Ward with its twelfth century
walls, the hornwork below and the
Outer Ward, which could have
sheltered a large body of troops.*

LEFT: *The circular thirteenth-century
keep tower at Skenfrith.*

hall on the site of the earlier bailey. This had a strong outer wall, with
projecting towers providing crossfire for the defenders.

White Castle was not rebuilt by de Burgh, doubtless because it had been
provided with a square stone keep and bailey during the twelfth century. It
might be that these early walls were plastered, giving the castle its unusual
name. Late in the thirteenth century the castle was elaborately rebuilt:
massive rounded towers were added to the earlier walls, a twin-towered
gatehouse protected the entrance to the Inner Ward, and a large Outer
Ward was constructed. The Outer Ward in particular is very large, and
could have accommodated columns of troops or supplies; it was probably
designed to provide support for the Anglo-Norman conquest.

45

LLANTHONY AND TINTERN, Gwent

Map Reference Llanthony:
SO 289278, Map 161
Nearest Town Abergavenny
From Abergavenny take the A465
towards Hereford and after 6 miles
(9.6 km) take the B4423 to
Llanthony which is reached after 8
miles (12.8 km) up a beautiful and
narrow valley. The Priory is in
Welsh Office guardianship and open
standard hours.

Map Reference Tintern: SO 536000,
Map 162
Nearest Town Chepstow
Take the A466 north from
Chepstow and after 5 miles (8 km)
the Abbey and village of Tintern are
reached, delightfully situated in the
Wye Valley. Abbey is in Welsh
Office guardianship and open
standard hours.

Two splendid monasteries

Llanthony is set in a deep and wild valley carved out of the Black
Mountains; it is one of the most romantic monastic sites in Britain. The
story of its foundation is suitably delightful and concerns a knight called
William de Lacy, who took shelter in a chapel here while out hunting.
This proved to be a turning point in his life; he forsook the ways of the
world and lived here as a hermit. In 1103 he was joined by a priest named
Ersinius, who had been chaplain to Queen Matilda, and by 1108 a priory of
the Augustinian Canons had been established. The house flourished until
1135, when during a Welsh rising the priory was destroyed and the monks
had to retire to Gloucester. By the late twelfth century, they were able to
return, and most of the present buildings belong to the period 1180–1230.

The church has an aisled nave of eight bays with two western towers, the
south-western one of which is now incorporated into the Abbey Hotel.
Further east was a crossing tower between the transepts and a narrow
square-ended chancel of three bays. These remains are generally well
preserved and form an agreeably picturesque composition. The style is
Transitional, with rounded and pointed arches appearing at different
levels in the same structures. Little remains of the claustral buildings, but
the western range included three vaulted basements, one of which is now
the hotel bar. Llanthony is an excellent place to visit, and the hotel there

*The great pointed and triple-chamfered
arches of the north nave arcade at
Llanthony.*

affords the rare opportunity to both drink and sleep in the monastic buildings!

Tintern, by contrast, is a good deal more extensive and elaborate than Llanthony, though it too has a beautiful site. It was founded in 1131 by Walter fitz Richard, Lord of Chepstow, and was the first Cistercian house in Wales. During the thirteenth century the abbey was almost entirely rebuilt; work began in 1220 with the new refectory and the church was eventually finished in 1301. What remains is a mature Cistercian plan, comparing with Fountains and Rievaulx, and preserved to a remarkable degree. The church in particular is a splendid composition with a beautiful west front having twin doorways, a seven-light reticulated window and a gable light. Inside, the elevation lacks a triforium, but the triple vaulting shafts indicate that the whole church was vaulted in stone, which must have been a wonderful sight. The east window was originally of eight lights, but they have been removed, leaving only the narrow central mullion with a circular rose over. Throughout, the impression is one of surprising delicacy, although Cistercian restraint is still very much in evidence.

A decorated floor tile from Tintern.

46

COSMESTON, South Glamorgan

A deserted village

Here at Cosmeston an imaginative and long-term project is in progress — the excavation and interpretation of a deserted medieval village. The houses and other features of the village are gradually being investigated and, as they are exposed, the most durable foundations are being consolidated *in situ*. Beyond this, it is also hoped to rebuild some of the structures in order to explore the techniques used and to give visitors an impression of what a village of this sort may have looked like. This idea has much merit, and the staff of the Glamorgan–Gwent Archaeological Trust should be congratulated on their initiative.

The name of the village derives from the Norman family of Constantine, later Costyn, who followed Robert FitzHamon into south Wales late in the eleventh century. Thomas Costyn was the last of the name to own the village, and by 1317 it belonged to the de Cavershams who held it until the sixteenth century. It might be that the village was deserted some time during the fourteenth century, a period of famine, plague and economic decline in Wales just as it was in England. As with the English deserted sites of Hound Tor and Wharram Percy, these pressures bore particularly heavily on settlements in upland and marginal situations; Cosmeston was

Map Reference SS 178690, Map 171
Nearest Town Penarth
Take the B4267 coast road towards Barry, the Lavernock Road, and the medieval village site is in the Cosmeston Lakes Country Park, about 2 miles (3.2 km) from Penarth centre. The village site is open Mon–Fri 9–4, and Sun 12–5.30 April–Sept, with hourly guided tours, reconstructions of the medieval buildings, an exhibition and a shop.

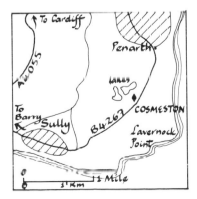

such a village. In the case of south Wales, these difficulties were exacerbated by the revolt of Owen Bren in 1316, which would have been a further spur to desertion.

So far, two tofts have been examined, one of which contained a large barn, a shed and a single-roomed house arranged round a yard. The buildings appear to have been of timber-framed construction with thatched roofs. The second plot revealed a similar house, but nearby was a large kiln or oven, possibly a communal bakehouse. All these discoveries are dated by the excavators to the early fourteenth century. Elsewhere, the foundations of a circular dovecote have been investigated, as well as further areas of farmyard. Quantities of pottery – including a jug decorated with a human face, and a curfew, used to cover the fire of an open hall at night – have been found, as well as other artefacts.

This is the first large-scale investigation of a deserted medieval village site in Wales, and it is to be hoped that it will elucidate many problems about the economy, architecture and standard of living of early Welsh villages.

47

CAERPHILLY CASTLE, Mid Glamorgan

Map Reference ST 155871, Map 171 The castle dominates the town and is in Welsh Office guardianship, open standard hours and Sunday mornings.

Citadel of the de Clares

Cast adrift in its lake, Caerphilly Castle is a fortress of overwhelming strength and majesty, citadel of the powerful de Clares, who were among the greatest magnates of their age. Caerphilly marks the high point of medieval military architecture; here were developed the techniques which Edward I was to employ at Caernarfon and Beaumaris. It is above all things a concentric castle with two effective lines of defence, not including outworks and a whole series of strongpoints which could be held independently of one another.

The de Clares, named from their caput at Clare in Suffolk, were lords of Glamorgan, when in 1268 Earl Gilbert, the 'Red' Earl of Gloucester, began to extend his territory northwards from the coastal plain. This was resisted by Llywelyn the Last, who destroyed the first castle here in 1268. Nothing daunted, Gilbert began a second castle in 1271 and, despite further opposition from Llywelyn and Henry III who sided with him, this most ambitious project was completed. De Clare continued his contumacious career until Edward I finally humbled him in 1289, but the scope of his overweening ambition is made manifest at Caerphilly.

If we look at the castle 'inside out' we find at its heart a great hall which has been restored and is still in use, together with a suite of state rooms of suitable magnificence. These are surrounded by a high inner curtain with massive towers at the angles and, in the centre of the south side, the base of the massive Kitchen Tower which covered the Water Gate. From the top of these towers and walls the defenders could command the whole site, and any foe within bowshot was imperilled. Beneath these defences was the Outer Ward which also had a curtain wall; both wards had twin-towered gateways to east and west.

Beyond the Outer Ward are the broad north and south lakes between which, like an island, lies the western hornwork which commands the approach on that side. The hornwork defences are of a rudimentary kind, and may not have been finished. On the east side, the main approach to the castle and the crucial matter of the security of its artificial water defences were accorded a high military priority as indicated by the mighty 'platforms' there. These features, unique to Caerphilly, are principally explained by the necessity of keeping the site 'wet', for without its water

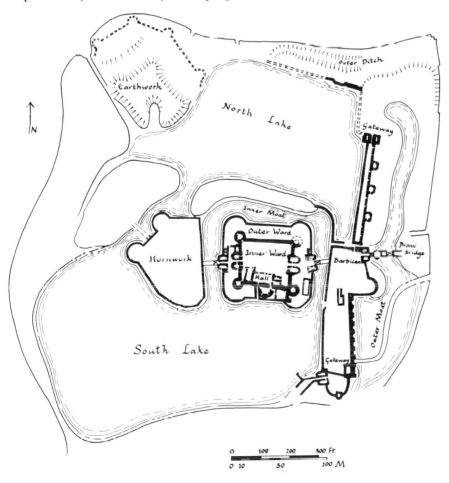

The extensive defences of Caerphilly Castle would cause even the most determined attacker a severe headache. The great lakes and cunningly designed fields of fire rendered the castle virtually impregnable.

defences the castle would still be formidable but not necessarily impregnable. So it is that we find a long defended wall north of the entrance and a broader platform to the south. They, together with the now insignificant outer ditch, would have provided an effective first line of defence against an attacker from that side.

But the broad cunning of Caerphilly's defences is augmented by the detailed strength of its towers. Each could be held as a fortalice in its own right, and a determined group of defenders could thus deny control of whole sections of the castle to an aggressor. The craggy grimness of Caerphilly's bones is still awesome, and at no other site can the stratagems of castle storming be so satisfactorily weighed in the mind's eye. It well deserves the appellation 'Giant Caerffili' bestowed by a medieval Welsh poet.

48

NEATH ABBEY, West Glamorgan

Map Reference SS 738973, Map 170 Off the Neath–Swansea road, 1 mile (1.6 km) west of Neath and 5½ miles (8.8 km) north-east of Swansea. The abbey manages to maintain an air of tranquillity despite the industrial setting. The site is in Welsh Office guardianship and is open standard hours.

Some imagination is now required to conjure the early solitude of the abbey beside the sparkling stream 'Nedd' from its industrial surroundings, but it must have seemed a promising spot for a monastery, with plenty of water, a level site and stone to be had in abundance nearby. The house was founded in 1130 and colonized by monks from Savigny, the 'Savignacs', whose Order merged with the Cistercians in 1147, and the layout is of the Cistercian type. Early quarrels with nearby Margam blighted the early history of the monastery, but the thirteenth century saw a considerable revival of its fortunes. Ample flocks of sheep paid for a new dormitory and refectory, and in 1280–1330 a fine new church was built.

The remains at Neath, called the 'fairest abbey in all Wales' by the King's Antiquary John Leland in the sixteenth century, are impressive enough, but it is to one detail of them that we would direct the visitor's attention. Earthenware floor tiles are a commonplace of many monastic sites, and the collections at Hailes and Malvern are celebrated. Among the Welsh abbeys Neath has the best assemblage, with many remaining *in situ*. During the reconstruction of the church thousands of decorated tiles were used, and they still convey an impression of lightness and colour among the ruins.

Such tiles had been in use since Saxon times in major churches, but it was during the twelfth century at sites like Byland in Yorkshire, described in our *Norman Guide*, that they once more became common. At first designs tended to be restrained, a simplicity perhaps dictated as much by Cistercian edict as by technological constraint, but by the fourteenth century, when the strict tenets of the Order were beginning to be eroded, tiles – like the architecture of the buildings which contained them – became a good deal more festive.

At Neath we find many patterns made by impressing designs into the unfired surface which were then filled with white clay. When the tiles had dried and hardened, the surface was scraped in order to enhance the contrast between the red clay of the body and the white of the design. A lead glaze was then applied before firing in a wood-fuelled kiln. The tiles so produced often featured segments of larger circular designs which were normally made up of four, nine or sixteen tiles. One area of paving at Neath shows how a sixteen-tile design could be enlarged to make a symmetrical design of sixty-four tiles, and even larger arrangements were possible. Many of the Neath tiles bear armorial and other regular patterns, but the most original depict charging horsemen, and, since one has a lance and the other a scimitar, they may show the legendary single combat between Richard Coeur de Lion and Saladin. Finally, an ode written to Llesion, last Abbot of Neath, by the local poet Lewys Morgannwg in about 1500 conveys something of the delight of these early floors, and reminds us of their ultimate derivation from marble mosaics of Classical times:

> The vast high roof in the sparkling heaven above in the sight of archangels; the floor beneath, for the people of all the men of Babel, is wrought of variegated stone.

This fourteenth-century tile probably depicts Richard I during his epic single combat with the Saracen leader Saladin.

49
WEOBLEY CASTLE, West Glamorgan

A fortified house

The death of Llywelyn the Last in 1283 and the Statute of Rhuddlan which followed it signalled a period of peace which, in south Wales at least, was to remain largely unbroken for a century. This stability encouraged landowners to think less of defence when building their homes than of comfort. Weobley is a distinctive product of this period, a small defended house set amid the beautiful landscape of the Gower Peninsula; it must have been a delightful place for its owner, David de la Bere, Steward of Swansea, to live. This early confidence was well founded, for it was not until a century later that Owain Glyndwr brought destruction upon the place.

It should not be imagined that Weobley was a 'house' in the terms that we would recognize it, however. It was still hedged about by a curtain wall, entered through a gatehouse, and the principal accommodation was

Map Reference SS 478928, Map 159
Nearest Town Swansea
On the north coast of the Gower Peninsula, between Llanrhidian and Llanmadoc. From Swansea take the A4118 and the B4271 towards the airport. From Llanrhidian take the minor road to Llanmadoc. Castle is on the north side of the road, and looks out across the River Loughor estuary. The site is in Welsh Office guardianship and is open standard hours.

The finely carved female head shows the quality of the original work.

contained in a thick-walled hall and solar block. Should dark times arrive, the lords of Weobley would be able to face with equanimity all save the most determined onslaught.

The buildings are grouped round three sides of a square. On the north side was the hall with a kitchen beneath, to the west the solar with an undercroft, and the other two sides have a strong square tower, effectively a small keep, a chapel, a range of guest chambers and storeplaces. The accommodation is comfortable enough, and the castle is chiefly memorable for its tall square towers and agreeable coastal setting.

50
LAUGHARNE OPEN FIELDS, Dyfed

Map Reference Fields: SN 290105, Map 159
Castle: SN 302107
Nearest Town Carmarthen
Take the A40 towards Haverfordwest; at St Clears (9 miles, 14.4 km) take the A4066 to Laugharne which is a further 4 miles (6.4 km). The Hugden open field system is about 1 mile (1.6 km) west of Laugharne, on a minor road from the town centre. The Whitehill Moor fields are just north of the village on the east side of the St Clears road. The Lees are near the Laugharne Marshes on the south side of the main road. The castle is in the centre of the village, overlooking the Taff estuary. It is in Welsh Office guardianship and is open standard hours. From the castle tower you get a good view of the open field systems.

The south coast plain of Wales was one of the earliest and most densely settled areas after the Anglo-Norman conquest. Feudalism took root in a region that was heavily influenced by the invaders, a process we outline in our *Norman Guide*. Open fields must, therefore, have been a common enough sight in this part of medieval Wales, but at Laugharne we can see rare traces of this historical landscape. Three open fields survive at Laugharne, the remnants of a much larger system. Their use can be traced back to a grant to the burgesses of the town by Guy de Brian in the early fourteenth century.

Of the three fields, called Whitehill Moor, the Lees and Hugden, the last is the most extensive and the most visually impressive. It lies west of the town on a rounded hillside, the strips following the contours. The individual strips are still separated by low grass-grown baulks called landscars or landskers. These are avoided by the ploughman and, on the

This view of the Hugden at Laugharne shows the separate strips on the left which are still managed by the burgesses of the town. (Photo courtesy Terry James.)

edge of the Hugdon field, small bushes and saplings growing on the baulks indicate their settled nature. As the baulks increase in height towards the bottom of the hill, they also form lynchets of the sort seen at Abbotsbury in Dorset.

In the nineteenth century the fields still had an organized system of rotation – corn for three years, followed by three years' grass – but now there are no restrictions on the cropping. The fields are still used for grazing cattle in November and December, but fencing is kept to a minimum. It is interesting in this connection to note the absence of hedges, an emotive subject elsewhere, but of course field systems like this never were hedged, except on the outer edges, and the local farmers argue that the wind dries the corn better on the open fields. Nowadays, the fields are not redistributed annually, but the layout of the strips follows the medieval arrangement. It is a remarkable piece of continuity, which stretches back over six hundred years of husbandry.

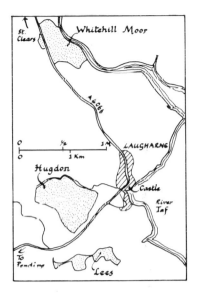

51
ST GOVAN'S CHAPEL AND WELL, BOSHERSTON, Dyfed

Map Reference SR 967929, Map 158
Nearest Town Pembroke
From Pembroke take the B4319 towards Castlemartin. After 5 miles (8 km) take the minor road to Bosherton, and carry on to the end of the road and park. The chapel is 1¼ miles (2 km) from the parish church of Bosherton. It stands in a rocky gorge on the coast. Take the path from Trevalen Downs and walk down the 52 stone steps to the chapel.

St Govan was a hermit who lived here on this lonely headland during the sixth century. He was a disciple of the Irish saint Ailbe, who was supposed, among other things, to have been suckled by a she-wolf. Legends doubtless collected about this place where Govan spent his last years, and its location beside the sea reminds us of other hermitages, such as the

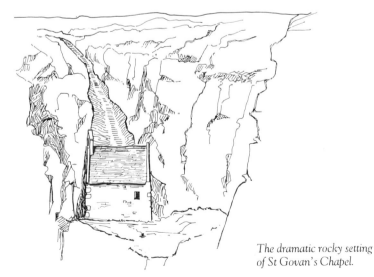

The dramatic rocky setting of St Govan's Chapel.

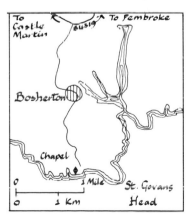

Northumbrian site at Ebb's Nook in our *Saxon Guide*. As recently as the turn of the century, cripples sought out this magical place for cures.

What remains is a small rectangular chapel with a steeply pitched roof and bellcote. The outer doorway on the north side is pointed and a second doorway gives access to a natural rock-cut chamber. At the east end is an altar, and low stone side benches provide seating. Near the entrance is a holy water stoup and beneath it a spring of clear water, which is said never to flow over the floor of the chapel. The simple detailing of the structure suggests a thirteenth-century date, and the nearby spring attests its function as a place of intercession for divine healing.

52
HAVERFORDWEST, Dyfed

Map Reference SM 952155, Map 157 Church is in the centre of the town. The nearby castle with its 13th-century remains is now a museum and information centre.

St Mary's Church
This is one of the best medieval parish churches in Wales and, although extended in around 1500, is principally of the mid thirteenth century.

Looking east in the nave of St Mary's Church. (Photo courtesy National Monuments Record for Wales.)

There had been a church here before that date, probably founded in the late twelfth century by Gilbert de Clare, who also began the castle which dominates the town. But Haverfordwest was burnt by Llywelyn the Great before his death in 1240, and the church was probably destroyed as well. It is possible that the thicker south wall of the nave belonged to Gilbert's church but, apart from that, everything else was apparently built anew in the Gothic Early English style.

The interior is graceful and carefully detailed with arcades of clustered shafts with foliate capitals and deeply moulded arches. Two of the capitals have small vignettes which reflect the scant sympathy of the inhabitants of south Pembrokeshire, 'Little England beyond Wales', for the native Welsh; one depicts an ape playing the Welsh harp, and the other a pig sawing at the crwth, the Welsh fiddle! From the fifteenth century comes a fine set of carved bench ends and a rare pilgrim's tombstone depicting him with his staff, long outer robe called a sclavine and his scrip or bag decorated with scallop shells, symbol of St James of Compostella. Later in the same century, the magnificent panelled oak roof was added, the crowning glory of a very satisfying church.

53
LAMPHEY AND ST DAVIDS, Dyfed

Two bishops' palaces

These two palaces, belonging to the Bishops of St Davids, should be much better known, since they are among the best survivals of domestic accommodation in the Middle Ages. Both grew from modest beginnings during the later thirteenth century when Thomas Bek was made bishop and found the existing arrangements inadequate. At Lamphey he added a fine solar block to the existing hall, while at St Davids itself he created a courtyard plan and built a fine hall, solar and gatehouse. After Bek, there was a lull until another wealthy bishop, Henry de Gower, was elected in 1328. He expanded the palaces, adding impressive great halls to augment the existing accommodation. These sites indicate the growing prestige of the medieval bishops, and it is clear from the scale and quality of the buildings that they lived in considerable style. This impression is further enhanced by the existence at Llawhaden nearby of a strong castle, also commissioned by Bishop Bek.

St Davids Palace lies to the west of the Cathedral across a small stream. It is arranged round a courtyard and entered through a small gatehouse opposite Bishop Gower's fourteenth-century Great Hall. On the left are Bek's hall and solar which are placed over vaulted stone undercrofts. The

Map Reference Lamphey: SN 018009, Map 158
Nearest Town Pembroke
Take the A4139 towards Tenby. Lamphey is 2 miles (3.2 km) from Pembroke. The palace is in Welsh Office guardianship and is open standard hours.

Map Reference St Davids: SM 748256, Map 157
The Bishop's Palace stands next to the Cathedral. It is in Welsh Office guardianship and open standard hours.

The west end of the Cathedral and the Bishop's Hall, with its distinctive arcaded parapet.

entrance into the later Great Hall is up a flight of steps to a handsome porch with a moulded outer doorway and canopied statue niches. This hall is of noble proportions, with large windows on the courtyard side and a rose window to the east gable. The absence of domestic apartments opening off the upper end of the hall suggests that it was intended exclusively for the entertainment of honoured guests, and we can well imagine the medieval Bishops of St Davids holding 'court' here like any lay magnate.

Lamphey is on a smaller scale, but there is similar provision of a hall and solar with undercrofts for the bishop and a Great Hall for larger gatherings. The palace stood in a deer park, and we can imagine that its owners pursued the recreations of a country gentleman. This hall, like Gower's work at St Davids, carries his distinguishing mark of an arcaded parapet and wall walk. This is a highly unusual device and argues strongly that Gower, who also remodelled the Cathedral, employed skilled workmen brought in from beyond his bishopric. Beneath the Great Hall is a stupendous undercroft, reminiscent of the arrangement at the earlier Bishop's Palace at Lincoln.

54
TRETOWER COURT AND CASTLE, Powys

Map Reference SH 186214, Map 161
Nearest Town Abergavenny
Take the A40 towards Brecon. After 10 miles (16 km) turn up the A479 to Tretower. The Court and Castle are both in Welsh Office guardianship and are open standard hours.

Tretower provides a history in miniature of domestic planning in Wales from the twelfth to the fifteenth centuries, beginning with a small Norman castle and ending with a fine courtyard house affording considerable comfort. The earliest buildings on the site were an earth and timber motte and bailey erected in about 1100. In the mid twelfth century a shell keep was built containing a hall, solar and kitchen, and in the early thirteenth century a circular Great Tower was built within the earlier keep. This tower is preserved to almost its full height, and it commanded a broad field of fire beyond the surrounding walls. The accommodation is arranged on three storeys with a basement and access at first-floor level. The two upper chambers have a pair of windows and a hooded fireplace each; the topmost room is similar but lacks a fireplace.

In the fourteenth century the lords of Tretower left the castle and instead lived next door in what became the north range of Tretower Court. This house, for such it was, is still delightful, and provides a striking contrast with the cramped conditions of the earlier keep which, although unimproved, was doubtless kept in a state of readiness. The fourteenth-century house consisted of a central ground-floor hall open to the roof with a solar and bedchamber on an upper floor at one end, and a separate first-floor chamber at the other.

In the fifteenth century Sir Roger Vaughan took the place in hand and greatly improved the accommodation. He remodelled the existing buildings and added the fine hall block with its superb cusped windbraced roof at right angles to the earlier range, forming an L-plan. Roger's son Thomas added an oriel to the hall and completed the courtyard plan by adding a curtain wall and wall walk round the remaining two sides, and provided it with a gatehouse. The provision of a mess hall points to the existence of a standing garrison, and the rich carving of the gatehouse and oriel indicates Sir Thomas's exalted position as a Knight of the Bath and grandee.

Elaborately cusped spere truss at the lower end of Sir Roger Vaughan's fifteenth-century hall.

55
HARLECH AND BEAUMARIS, Gwynedd

The iron ring

Harlech was built during Edward I's final assault on the kingdom of Gwynedd, and was the work of the celebrated military architect, Master James of St George. After the fall of the Welsh fortress of Castell-y-Bere in April 1283, the English army under Sir Otto de Grandison established a base here at Harlech. By the end of 1289 the castle was almost completed at a cost of well over £6 million at today's prices. Harlech is a concentric castle *par excellence*, sitting astride a rocky promontory, the most dramatic and spectacular fortress in a land of castles.

The groundplan is simple but effective, a box within a box, the inner walls higher than the outer and the angles strengthened with massive round towers. The inner gatehouse is essentially a keep complete with chambers, bedrooms and a chapel. The Inner Ward contains a great hall, a lesser hall, kitchen, chapel and other offices. It is a courtyard house within strong walls, an English bastion in the midst of enemy territory.

Map Reference Harlech: SH 581312, Map 124
Nearest Town Barmouth
11 miles (17.6 km) north of Barmouth on the A496. The castle is near the town centre and is in Welsh Office guardianship. Open standard hours.

Map Reference Beaumaris: SH 607763, Map 114
Nearest Town Bangor
On Conway Bay, opposite Bangor, on the Isle of Anglesey. Cross by the Menai Bridge and take the A545 for 4 miles (6.4 km). The castle is in Welsh Office guardianship and open standard hours.

Beaumaris, a small but perfect castle set on the lovely coast of north Wales. Here the concept of the concentric plan can be clearly appreciated, with the inner wall providing a further battery of fire for the defenders.

But Harlech is surely best known for its splendid song. This commemorates an event long after the castle was built but still within our period. During the Wars of the Roses it finally surrendered after enduring a long siege under its Welsh Lancastrian Constable. Harlech, which is still a Crown property, was the last stronghold held for the King during the Civil War.

Beaumaris, by contrast, set on a greenfield site in the midst of the 'beautiful marsh', belongs to a later stage of the Edwardian Settlement. It seemed that the defeat of Llywelyn in 1283 was the last act, but in 1294 there was a rising under Madog, which included an attack on the unfinished defences of Caernarfon and the temporary capture of that place. This revolt was eventually suppressed without too much difficulty, but it resulted in the construction of the largest and most refined of the concentric castles, Master James's *chef d'oeuvre*.

Work started in 1295; the familiar plan of a box within a box, both bristling with towers, was also followed here, but this time the outer walls were slightly angled to enhance the fields of fire, and the approaches were strengthened with more murder holes and other fiendish devices. Most effectively of all, the inner and outer entrances were staggered, necessitating a tight right-hand turn by an attacker, exposing him to intense flanking fire and breaking the impetus of a charge. This technique is still used in modern military road blocks, and in this simple but efficient device Master James once again demonstrated his prowess. Beaumaris was never finished; the threat evaporated, and the great Edwardian castles were left as leviathans, washed up on the shores of time, a delight for our wondering eyes.

56
CAERNARFON AND CONWY, Gwynedd

Strong castles and walled towns

Thomas Pennant, the eighteenth-century antiquarian, described Caernarfon Castle as 'the magnificent badge of our servitude', neatly reflecting the ambivalence with which the Edwardian castles are still viewed. They are, on the one hand, splendid examples of military design and planning, but they also reflect the conquest of a nation and the death of hope, represented by the defeat of Llywelyn ap Gruffydd, last of the Welsh princes. Llywelyn's treacherous death during a skirmish near Builth Wells marked the final defeat of the ancient Welsh fastness of Gwynedd, and the elegy of the Bard Gruffydd ab yr Ynad Coch eloquently expressed the nation's agony:

Map Reference Caernarfon: SH 477626, Map 115
Castle is at the west end of the town. It is in Welsh Office guardianship and is open standard hours. Remember to look at the town plan and defences.

Map Reference Conwy: SH 784774
Castle is in the eastern part of the town. It is in Welsh Office guardianship and is open standard hours.

For him the end of all things has come,
great torrents of wind and rain shake the whole land.
The oak trees crash together in a wild fury,
the sun is dark in the sky,
and the stars have fallen from their courses.

This is the background of the proud castles of Caernarfon and Conwy; they set the seal on the brilliant combined operations by land and sea which had secured the ruin of Gwynedd. Caernarfon in particular, more a palace than a castle, was conceived as the caput of north Wales, the seat of royal power. It is still owned by the Crown, and in 1969 it was used for the Investiture of the Prince of Wales. The castle consists of two wards, surrounded by high curtain walls well strengthened with angular towers. The accommodation was lavish, for this was the place from which royal dominion was to be exercised, and where Edward II, the first English Prince of Wales, was born.

To the north lies the town of Caernarfon, which was laid out in 1283 when the castle was begun. The town was primarily designed as the administrative centre of the newly won territory, and established an English presence in this stronghold of Welshness. In addition to the judicial and financial officials, there was a colony of merchants and, over it all, the great palace itself, which was both a citadel and a ready market for high quality merchandise. The town defences are exceptionally well preserved, with gates, walls and intervening towers commanding the core of the old town. Inside, the streets retain their regular angular layout, and in walking through Caernarfon we see physical evidence of the determination which lay behind the Statute of Rhuddlan.

Conwy, with its more familiar round towers, belongs more obviously to the general run of the Edwardian castles, but like Caernarfon it was favoured with impressive stone defences for the town as well as the castle. The castle, begun in 1283, was divided into two wards and has eight massive round towers with barbicans at either end. The castle is strongly sited above the confluence of the River Conwy and the Gyffin Stream, and was originally approached up a stone ramp which has since disappeared. This was a garrison town, and retains much of that atmosphere. One of the most memorable features of the place is, however, the row of garderobes which project over the wall beside Millgate. These remind us of the trials of a thirteenth-century soldier's life, but it was a situation which probably differed little in its boredom and anxiety from that of his modern counterpart.

The entrance to Conwy Castle, framed by Thomas Telford's elegant bridge.

57
WELSH CASTLES, Gwynedd and Clwyd

Map Reference Dolwyddelan, Gwynedd: SH 721523, Map 115
Nearest Town Betws-y-coed
Take the A470 towards Blaenau Ffestiniog. The castle is 6 miles (9.6 km) down this road, 1 mile (1.6 km) from the village of Dolwyddelan, just north of the road. It is in Welsh Office guardianship and open all reasonable times.

Map Reference Dolbadarn, Gwynedd: SH 586598, Map 115
Nearest Town Caernarfon
Take the A4086 to Llanberis (6 miles, 9.6 km). The castle is 1 mile (1.6 km) south-east of the village. It is in Welsh Office guardianship and open all reasonable hours.

Map Reference Castell-y-Bere, Gwynedd: SH 667086, Map 124
Nearest Town Tywyn
Take the A493 towards Barmouth and turn off after 2 miles (3.2 km) on the B4405 to Abergynolwyn. After 5 miles (8 km) take the minor road north to Llanfihangel-y-Pennant. The castle is on this minor road, in Welsh Office guardianship and open at all reasonable times.

Map Reference Criccieth, Gwynedd: SH 499376, Map 123
The castle is on the hill overlooking the town. It is in Welsh Office guardianship and open standard hours and Sunday mornings.

Map Reference Ewloe Castle, Clwyd: SJ 288675, Map 117
Nearest Town Queensferry
Ewloe is on the A55 between Chester and Holywell, 1 mile (1.6 km) north-west of Hawarden, and 2 miles (3.2 km) south of Queensferry. It is in Welsh Office guardianship and open standard hours.

Most castles in Wales were built by the Anglo-Normans during their conquest of the country but there were, of course, native Welsh castles as well; it is to these sites that we will now turn our attention. About fourteen earthwork castles are known to have been built during the twelfth century by the Welsh princes, but it was the later castles of Llywelyn Fawr, 'the Great', which are most substantial. Carefully sited on strong isolated sites, they controlled the natural routeways into Gwynedd and are chiefly distinguishable from their English counterparts by their lower curtain walls, their irregular shapes and their normal dependence on a single ward. Gatehouses tend to be weak, towers were rarely taller than two storeys and often have a distinctive D-shaped plan. These differences partly reflect the lesser wealth of the princes, but also a society which, unlike the feudal system of the enemy, did not depend on the castle as an integral part of its organization.

Llywelyn Fawr was reputedly born at Dolwyddelan, but it is thought that the castle here was his work. This was one of five major castles he established; the others were at Ewloe, Dolbadarn, Castell-y-Bere and Criccieth, all except Ewloe in his own heartland of Gwynedd. Ewloe, which is one of the best preserved, has the typical D-shaped tower as its principal element, later surrounded by a stone wall, probably added by Llywelyn ap Gruffydd in 1257. Dolbadarn is splendidly sited above the lake of Llyn Padarn, and has curtain walls of unmortared slate. It was unusual in having a hall and a great round tower, which mirror English developments at Skenfrith and elsewhere.

Castell-y-Bere, nestling at the foot of Cader Idris, is probably the most dramatic of all the native castles, and had one of the most developed plans. The Chronicle of the Princes records that Llywelyn Fawr started to build here in 1221, at the same time that he began to style himself Prince of North Wales. The castle was probably intended as much to overawe local rivals as to be a defence against the English. In plan, the castle is an elongated triangle with angle towers and a further detached tower controlling the approach from the valley. The gateway has twin towers and a barbican, and at either end are familiar D-shaped towers, that to the south acting as a keep. The northern tower was highly decorated with sculpture internally, and contained a chapel. The castle, which attests the considerable prestige of its founder, fell to Edward I in 1283 and was later besieged by Prince Madog's rebels, but after this brief fame it disappeared from the pages of history.

58
SYCHARTH, Clwyd

The Court of Owain Glyndwr

Owain Glyndwr is one of the most romantic figures in Welsh history, and it was here at Sycharth that he held his court. There is little to see beyond the great mound upon which his hall was built, but in the mind's eye we can imagine the place described by the court poet Iolo Goch, writing in 1390:

> This is its manner and appearance, in a fine
> circle of water within an embankment.
> Is not the court splendid, a bridge over the moat,
> and one gateway through which a hundred loads could pass.
> There are crucks, they are the work of joining;
> each arch joined with the other . . .

This was the wondrous dwelling of the lord Owain and his lady Mared, the best of wives. We are told that it was timbered and tiled, that it was hung with rich tapestries, and that about it was an abundance of food – a dovecote, fishpond, warren and heronry with beyond a deer park, an orchard, a vineyard and 'fair meadows of grass and hay, corn in well tended fields'. Glyndwr, born soon after the Black Death, had been educated as a gentleman and a lawyer at Westminster. He had a distinguished military career in Scotland, and by 1400 he lived here at Sycharth. But it was in that year that Owain and the other conspirators met at Glynfrdwy on the Dee, and initiated the revolt with which he is forever associated.

For this was no ordinary rebellion, no mere Border skirmish. Before they set out, his companions had declared Owain Prince of all Wales, and he led a national rising which in the space of a few years was to take him from the giddy peak of national supremacy in 1405, when he treated with the King of France and other European figures, to his obscure end as a hunted fugitive in 1417.

The site at Sycharth is essentially a motte and bailey of the familiar type, hidden in the hills west of Oswestry. Yet it appears from recent excavation not to have been of Norman origin but to have been built late in the thirteenth century. Glyndwr's house was burnt in 1403, but it seems that some occupation continued since late-fourteenth-century pottery also came from the site. Today, Sycharth appears as a large flat-topped mound, and were it not for its singular history it would join the other countless mottes in the Marches. But here is the landscape described by Iolo Goch,

Map Reference SJ 205259, Map 126
Nearest Town Oswestry
From Oswestry take the B4580 west towards Llanrhaeadr ym Mochnant. Just beyond Llansilin (7½ miles, 12 km) take the minor road south down the Cynllaith Valley. After 1 mile (1.6 km), turn down to the east side of the river and the motte and bailey castle site can be seen on the east side of the valley.

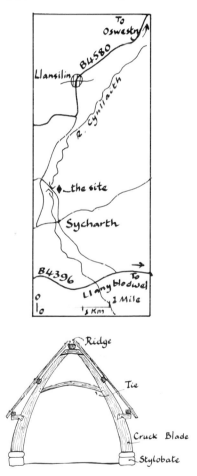

Section of a typical cruck at Sycharth, as described in Iolo Goch's poem.

and on the valley floor can be seen the choked fishponds where they cast '. . . nets where pike and fine salmon are found oftenest'. On the east side is a wooded slope still known as Parc Sycharth, and doubtless the place in which Owain was wont to hunt his deer. We have no elegy for Glyndwr; the bards could not believe him dead – some hold that he, like Arthur, sleeps beneath his hill at Sycharth, until his nation should need him again.

59
VALLE CRUCIS, Clwyd

Map Reference SJ 203443, Map 117
Nearest Town Llangollen
The abbey lies 1½ miles (2.4 km) north-north-west of Llangollen, close to the A542. It is in Welsh Office guardianship, open standard hours.

Abbey of the Princes of Powys
At first, the Welsh associated the Cistercian Order with the Norman enemy, but after the foundation of Whitland in 1140 they took them to their hearts. Valle Crucis was not founded until 1201, and the community came to the 'valley of the cross', a place of deep dynastic and religious significance for the principality of Powys. Here stood the ninth-century Pillar of Eliseg, originally bearing a cross, which commemorated the glories of the royal house. The monastery was never rich or powerful, and the church was not elaborated beyond its early aisled nave and transepted plan, but it became a focus of Welsh spirituality and burial place of the Princes of Powys, whose finely carved coffin lids can be seen in the cloister and chapter house.

The history of the abbey was largely uneventful. Marks of fire on the early-thirteenth-century masonry of the church reflect some unrecorded incident, possibly a raid, and some reconstruction was necessitated in the middle of the century. The chapter house was rebuilt later, but towards the end of the fifteenth century Abbots David and John transformed the dorter in the east cloister range into a suite of private rooms. This alteration, which marks the breakdown of the earlier plan, is startling evidence of the increased prestige and comfort attained by even Cistercian prelates late in our period. The poet Guttyn Owain praised the munificence of these two abbots, the fretted ceiling of their house and, last but not least, the resplendent decoration of the abbey choir, which he likened to Salisbury.

One of the most interesting features of Valle Crucis is its collection of over twenty sculptured slabs marking the graves of its benefactors and dignitaries. Some belong to a school of memorial sculpture which flourished in north Wales during the thirteenth and fourteenth centuries. The earliest example of this group is the slab commemorating Joan, daughter of King John and wife to Llywelyn Fawr, 'the Great', in Beaumaris Church; Llywelyn's similar slab is at Llanrwst. One of the Valle Crucis slabs, which depicts intertwined dragons with foliage, is dated 1290

A mid thirteenth-century grave slab from the Chapter House decorated with tight sprays of foliage.

and commemorates a lady called Gweirca. In the crossing is an early-fourteenth-century slab depicting an armoured half figure with shield, identified as Ievan ap Adda, Lord of Trefor. These monuments are the spirited Welsh counterparts of the slightly later West Highland monuments of Scotland.

60
HOLYWELL, Clwyd

Goal of pilgrims

St Winifride's Well, which gave Holywell its name, was an important pilgrimage place during our period. The saint lived during the seventh century, when we learn that she was the daughter of a Welsh chieftain who sheltered St Beuno, and that she was instructed by that saint in the mysteries of Christianity. She joined a convent and while there aroused the amorous instincts of Prince Caradoc. He threw his arms about her, but she avoided him and ran to the place called Dry Valley. She refused him again, and the furious prince cut off her head with his sword. Her blood permanently stained the earth, and a spring of healing water burst forth where her head first touched the ground. Fortunately, St Beuno was able to restore Winifride to life, but the hapless Prince fell victim to the saint's curse and melted away on the spot!

This dramatic tale seized the medieval imagination, and many pilgrims came to avail themselves of the healing waters. The spring is now housed in a splendid two-storeyed shrine built late in the fifteenth century by Margaret Beaufort, mother of Henry VII. The spring emerges into a star-shaped well, surrounded by a processional passage or ambulatory and covered by an elaborate vault. On the first floor is a small chapel projecting out from the hillside, and in the courtyard outside pilgrims could bathe in a long pool.

There used to be a heap of abandoned crutches by the shrine, and Holywell has a continuous history of pilgrimage stretching back into the Middle Ages. But such water shrines have a long history, and the image of the severed head was an Iron Age symbol as well; it is possible that Holywell remembers events which occurred long before the seventh century.

Pilgrimage was, of course, a major undertaking during our period, and Holywell was no exception. Early in the fifteenth century, the monks of nearby Basingwerk, who obtained custody of the well, were granted permission by the Pope to sell indulgences to pilgrims visiting the shrine. But the Cistercian monks there did not apparently derive much profit from

Map Reference SJ 185763, Map 116
St Winifride's Well is in Welsh Office guardianship and is open 11–7, Fri and Sat, April–Sept. Nearby is Basingwerk Abbey (SJ 196774), open March–Sept only.

A capital depicting a sick pilgrim being carried to St Winifride's Well.

this trade, for its buildings, parts of which still survive, are modest enough. Yet this place exercised a strong grip on the Welsh imagination:

> The drops of her blood are as the red shower
> Of the berries of the wild rose,
> The tears of Christ from the height of the Cross.

61
FLINT AND RHUDDLAN, Clwyd

Map Reference Flint: SJ 247733, Map 117
The castle is near the town centre, in Welsh Office guardianship and open at all reasonable times.

Map Reference Rhuddlan: SJ 024779, Map 116
Nearest Town Rhyl
3 miles (4.8 km) south of Rhyl on the A525. The castle is in Welsh Office guardianship and is open standard hours and Sunday mornings.

The beginning and the end

Flint, known as 'The Gateway of Wales', was the first castle of Edward I's Welsh campaign of 1277. It was the jumping-off point for his assault on the mountain fastness of Gwynedd. Construction was arranged here on the same lavish scale which distinguished all Edward's works in Wales. His army pushed along the north coast plain from Chester early in July, and the construction of the castle was quickly put in hand. By the end of the month there were 1,850 workmen here, and on 9 August 300 diggers, who had marched under armed guard from Lincolnshire, joined them. By the end of August there were nearly 2,300 diggers alone at work on the castle and fortified town, for which the regular grid of streets is the only remaining evidence.

Flint Castle, designed by the King's mason Master James of St George, prefigures many of the later Edwardian castles of Gwynedd but it was not a concentric plan. It is square in shape with angle towers, but incorporates a

Entrance to the Inner Bailey of Flint Castle.

great detached circular tower or donjon, an element not reused elsewhere. This tower, which doubled as a keep, is a stupendous construction two storeys high with a passage running round the lower storey and large central rooms on three levels.

Rhuddlan's history began rather before that of Flint, for a motte and bailey was built here in 1073 by Robert of Rhuddlan from which Norman power was extended over much of north Wales. In 1277 Edward I built the second of his castles here, and it was the first to be built on a concentric plan. The castle has a square inner ward with tall curtain walls and opposed gatehouses strengthened with twin drum towers. The outer walls are less substantial and, unusually, are provided with square towers with a broad flat-bottomed ditch beyond. There were four entrances in the outer ward and a fortified dock on the River Clwyd by which the castle could be supplied. This dock, together with the diversion and canalization of the River Clwyd, reminds us that both Flint and Rhuddlan were designed as a part of the linked land and seaborne invasion which Edward planned.

Finally, in 1284, it was at Rhuddlan Castle that Edward promulgated the Statute of that name, which is properly called the Great Statute of Wales. This settlement, which created the counties of north Wales, lasted until the Act of Union in 1536, and set the final seal on Edward I's Welsh conquests. At Flint and Rhuddlan, it can be truly said that the great adventure started and finished.

One of the mighty angle towers at Rhuddlan, the first castle to be built to a concentric plan.

Mason's marks from Flint.

NORTHERN ENGLAND

EAST-
ERN
ENGLAND

Chesterfield
DERBYSHIRE
♦ 76
♦ 75
NOTTING-
HAMSHIRE
♦ 74
♦ 77
♦ 73
Stoke
73
Derby
Nottingham

STAFFORDSHIRE
Stafford

LEICESTERSHIRE
♦ 72
Shrewsbury
Leicester
♦ 83
♦ 71
SHROPSHIRE
WEST
MIDLANDS
70 ♦
♦ 83
♦ 82
Birmingham
♦ 68
WALES
18 ♦
NORTHAMPTON-
SHIRE
♦ 69
Warwick ♦ 19
♦ 81
♦ 80
68 ♦
WARWICK-
Northampton
WORCESTER
SHIRE
Hereford
♦ 64

BUCKING-
HAMSHIRE
OXFORD-
SHIRE
Aylesbury
67 ♦ 66
♦ 65
♦ 62
Oxford
♦ 64
♦ 63

0   10   20   30 Mls
0 10 20 30 40 50 Km

THE MIDLANDS

THE MIDLANDS

Introduction

In the Midlands we find a broad range of sites reflecting our medieval
heritage, including houses, churches and landscape features. Apart from
great feudal fortresses like Warwick, the nearest approaches to true castles
here are the fortified houses at Stokesay, Acton Burnell and South
Wingfield. The first is a delectable late-thirteenth-century house spurning
the strict requirements of defence despite its location in the Marches. The
contemporary Acton Burnell, built by one of the most powerful magnates
in the land, likewise makes more of show and comfort than military
necessity. These houses, for such they were, indicate the efficacy of
Edward I's policy in Wales. Ralph, Lord Cromwell, builder of South
Wingfield, by contrast, had to fear no risks beyond the boundaries of the
kingdom. Yet he created for himself a beautiful seat in Derbyshire which
was both idyllically set and proof against all save the most determined
assault.

When we turn to lesser houses there is a fine stock, beginning with the
thirteenth-century manor house at Donington-le-Heath. This is a small
hall house with straightforward constructional details and a general aspect
of robust simplicity. Donington originally had a moat, as did the larger
house site at Aston Clinton, but here the buildings have gone, leaving
behind a set of grassy earthworks of a type familiar to medieval archaeologists. At Stanton Harcourt is the kitchen of a great house, while at
nearby Minster Lovell is one of the most beautifully situated houses in
medieval England. But we can also see lesser houses at villages like
Weobley and Pembridge which boast unrivalled collections of early
timber-framed structures. Perhaps the ultimate 'black and white' house is
Lower Brockhampton; it is a delightful moated house retaining its
contemporary gatehouse and splendid hall.

Staying in the countryside, we see a famous field system at Laxton, the
mighty trees of Sherwood, coal-mines at Catherton and huge tithe barns at
Great Coxwell and Bredon. The Midlands was above all an agricultural
region in medieval times, and the idealized concept of the three-field
system, familiar from every school textbook, only really flourished in this

part of the country. The flattish and well-favoured lands of the Midlands Plain lent themselves easily to feudalism and its organization; Laxton must stand for the hundreds of villages whose fields are now lost. Other activities there were of course, and the great forest of 'Shire Wood' occupied the lighter sandy soils of Nottinghamshire which were unsuited to arable cultivation. Whether this was the haunt of robbers must remain uncertain, but at Catherton we see the evidence of men not much above the level of outlaws eking a frugal living for themselves on the margin of society. As to tithe barns, what can we say which they cannot say for themselves? They breathe out the very air of medieval England, and are the veritable cathedrals of agriculture.

The surplus of this wealthy arable cultivation was used in no small part for the building and beautification of churches. The Chapter House at Southwell bids fair to being the most delightful medieval chamber in England, alive with subtle tendrils and nodding flowers. The Easter Sepulchres at Hawton and elsewhere are also masterpieces of the carver's art, rivalling even the royal work of the Eleanor Crosses.

Other deaths called forth their tributes, and in the mighty Yorkist church at Fotheringhay, at Stanton Harcourt, Ewelme and most emphatically in Lord Beauchamp's tomb at Warwick, we find the confident expectation of life eternal made manifest. Some of these tombs are among the most sumptuous objects ever wrought by medieval craftsmen, and they mutely remind us of the human qualities of their owners. The wonder on Lord Beauchamp's face as he looks upwards to the figure of God, the rotting cadaver beneath the Duchess of Suffolk's stately monument at Ewelme, or the simpler poignancy of the Eleanor Crosses communicate the hopes and fears of men as clearly today as they did five centuries and more ago.

There were important towns in the Midlands apart from the villages, of course, and Coventry in particular grew to national prominence as a commercial centre. The Blitz dealt heavily with the historic core of this great city, but the ruins of the cathedral, the Whitefriars and above all St Mary's Guildhall remain to demonstrate the character of its medieval past. On the west side of the city is a good collection of early town houses and in a place more famous for engineering and industry much remains to remind us of its early success. At Oxford, by contrast, the past is worn as a sort of livery, and is paraded on all occasions. Here stand some of the oldest and most revered colleges in England, reminding us that not everything in the Middle Ages was touched by the darkness of ignorance. The links of spirit and imagination transcend physical structure and demand respect and regard for an academic tradition which has been nurtured for over 700 years.

Finally, we come to that most charged of battle sites, Bosworth Field. Whatever the reader's opinion might be about Richard III's career –

whether he arranged for the princes to be murdered in the Tower and sacrificed all on the altar of his ambition – his end was a gallant one and thoroughly worthy of the royal kingship which he held in trust of God. If Richard's life was foul, then the deeds of his erstwhile friends and supporters at Bosworth were foul as well. For all that the Tudors brought change on their wings, the means of their coming opens the old debate as to whether or not the end justifies the means. But at Bosworth Field we can tread the very ground upon which this great conflict took place, and decide for ourselves the issues of the battle.

62

ASTON CLINTON, Buckinghamshire

A moated site

Medieval moated sites have exerted a strong fascination for archaeologists because they are prominent landscape features in many parts of lowland England, and yet their purpose is uncertain. We are not speaking here of castles like Bodiam and Caerphilly with broad water defences, nor yet of moated fortified houses such as Stokesay. We are concerned instead with the thousands of moated homestead sites like Donington-le-Heath and Lower Brockhampton which have no serious defensive aspirations and yet still have moats.

Many of these sites are now deserted and the moats dried up, but fieldwork has disclosed certain more or less common features. They are usually located on flat level sites, though not all are badly drained. Most have 'islands' of roughly rectangular form surrounded by a ditch, though the size of both elements varies widely. Similarly, the scale of the dwellings built on the sites shows considerable variation. Some are modest houses with few ancillary structures, whereas others are substantial and surrounded by barns, stables and other buildings. Sometimes, as at Aston Clinton, more complex sites are found with two or more contiguous moats, one containing the house and the others the outbuildings, gardens, orchards and even fishponds.

Research suggests, however, that most moats were dug to contain houses, and that they were most popular during the thirteenth and early fourteenth centuries. These were certainly difficult times, suggesting that moats may have had a defensive function, but the later times were hardly peaceful and yet the incidence of moats decreases. In any case, a moat might keep wild animals at bay and provide a ready source of water in the event of fire, but it would hardly stop a determined assault, particularly as some had permanent bridges or causeways. They could be stocked with fish or used as swanneries, and they could also help to drain their sites.

Map Reference SP 865127, Map 165
Nearest Town Tring
On the A41 between Tring and Aylesbury. Just outside Aston Clinton, in the Aylesbury direction, beyond the terraced houses in open country, look out for the track to the right by Vatches Farm. Park in the lane – the field on the corner contains the earthworks. Across the ridge and furrow you can see the bank beyond the field which contained the fishponds, and stand on the farmstead enclosure and look over to the moated homestead site. The moats still contain rushes and reeds.

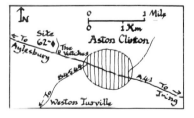

Moated site at Aston Clinton; the house stood in the main enclosure at the top, whilst the lower one contained the fish ponds as well as ancillary buildings. (Photo courtesy Cambridge University Collection of Air Photographs.)

Yet in the end it is probably wicked pride which holds the key to the phenomenon of moat-building. Practical as many of the above suggestions are, none of them really necessitated a moat because the objectives could be accomplished in other ways and normally at less cost and effort. Moated homesteads are probably best seen as an attempt by the lower feudal orders to keep up with the leaders of society. Their builders wished to emulate the castles of the wealthy and emphasize their own exclusivity by placing a physical barrier between themselves and the world at large. In this sense, the moats are symbols of the hierarchical feudal society which produced them. As you wander over the bumps and hollows of Aston Clinton, you can ponder these weighty theories, and see which you believe!

63
EWELME CHURCH, SCHOOL AND ALMSHOUSES, Oxfordshire

Map Reference SU 646914, Map 164 Nearest Town Wallingford 5 miles (8 km) north-east of Wallingford. Cross the Thames by the A423T and turn north up the A4074 in the Thame direction. In 2 miles (3.2 km) take the B4009 at Benson towards Watlington. Ewelme is reached by minor roads south of the B road. The almshouses, school and church form one of the most memorable groups of medieval buildings in England.

Ewelme is a place rich in associations with some of the major personalities of later medieval England. Kings and nobles visited after the manor came into the possession of Geoffrey Chaucer's son Thomas, who was Speaker of the House of Commons. Chaucer himself immortalized the Ewelme Spring, famed for its curative properties, in the following lines:

> In worlde is none more clere of hue,
> Its water ever fresshe and newe,
> That whelmeth up in waves bright
> The mountance of three fingers height.

In 1430 Thomas's daughter Alice married William de la Pole, Earl of Suffolk and founder of Wingfield College, Suffolk. They rebuilt the church here and founded the school and almshouses, leaving us one of the most satisfying groups of fifteenth-century buildings in England. They lived happily until de la Pole's barbarous murder in 1450; he referred to her in his will as 'His best loved wife . . . for above all the earth my singular trust is in her.'

Only the early-fourteenth-century tower predates the church rebuilt by the de la Poles in 1432. The rest, including the modish undivided nave and chancel, is an almost intact survival of an important late medieval church. At the east end, divided from the nave by contemporary wooden screens, are spacious side chapels; that to the south, containing the incomparable tomb of Alice, Duchess of Suffolk, is larger to accommodate the residents of her almshouses. The chapel interior is richly carved and painted, with flying angels on the principal roof timbers in the Suffolk style. The Duchess's tomb of 1475 is of the 'sideboard' type with an open centre containing the effigy, and an early example of a grim shrouded cadaver beneath. It is made of alabaster, exquisitely carved, and bears extensive traces of brightly coloured paint. Elsewhere there are brasses, extensive fragments of heraldic glass, and not least the font with an accomplished East Anglian style carved wooden cover.

The delights of Ewelme are not exhausted by its wondrous church, however. Beside it lie the de la Pole Almshouses, founded in 1437 and, perhaps in deference to nearby Oxford, the first in England to be arranged round a quadrangle. They were established to house thirteen poor men and two chaplains, one of whom was also to teach at the school.

A flying angel roof boss in the Suffolk style.

The almshouse cloister at Ewelme, a place of quiet peace for its fortunate inhabitants.

The accommodation now comprises nine comfortable dwellings; the Bedesmen are allowed to live with thier wives and are no longer required to attend daily services. The Almshouses are of timber-framed construction with brick infilling and stone dressings on the outer walls. The use of brick recalls the origins of the de la Pole fortunes in the brickyards of Hull with their Flemish connections, as does the distinctive 'crowstep' gable over the north door.

Finally we come to the school, founded at the same time as the almshouses and also built of brick. Over the porch is the 'Grammar Master's Room' still used by the Headmaster after over 500 years; this is thought to be the oldest school building used as a state primary school in England. Upstairs is a handsome fifteenth-century arch-braced timber roof, and the original west door of the church is reused in the porch. This ancient school, which still offers the village children their education 'freely without exaccion of any Schole hire' as the Suffolks' charter stipulated, reminded us once more of Geoffrey Chaucer:

O yonge fresshe folkes, he or she.

64
GREAT COXWELL AND BREDON,
Oxfordshire, Hereford and Worcester

Map Reference Great Coxwell, Oxfordshire: SU 269940, Map 163
Nearest Town Faringdon
2 miles (3.2 km) south-west of Faringdon between the B4019 and the A420. The barn is owned by the National Trust and is open every day at reasonable times.

Map Reference Bredon, Hereford and Worcester: SO 919369, Map 150
Nearest Town Tewkesbury
3 miles (4.8 km) north-west of Tewkesbury on the B4080. The barn is west of the church and belongs to the National Trust, open Wed, Thur 2–6, and Sat, Sun 10–6. It is near a sharp bend in the road, past an obelisk milestone.

Two tithe barns

Tithes were introduced into England before the Norman Conquest, and were the tenth part of a parishioner's income donated in kind to the Church. This was a weighty tax, and the tithes of a wealthy parish could be extremely valuable. During the twelfth and thirteenth centuries, therefore, lay founders of monasteries often chose to endow a new house with church livings or 'benefices' rather than land *per se*. This involved the monastery becoming the corporate rector of a parish, and it would thus receive the tithes. A vicar was then appointed, so called from the Latin *vicarius*, 'substitute', and he would receive the 'lesser tithes'. These normally consisted of perishable foodstuffs like milk and eggs, or immature stock like calves and piglets. But the 'greater' tithes, which included corn, hay or wood, would be the prerogative of the monastery itself.

The barn at Great Coxwell was built by the Cistercian Abbey of Beaulieu (Hampshire) soon after it received the manor from King John in 1204. Barns like this were so important to monastic building funds that they were often built before, or at least at the same time as, the monastic church itself. It is a huge structure with roughly coursed limestone walls

Great Coxwell Tithe Barn, one of the 'cathedrals' of Medieval agriculture.

and fine ashlar dressings. The stone side walls and aisles of slender oak posts have supported the colossal weight of the Cotswold stone roof for over 700 years, and the structure is still perfectly sound. The aisle posts rest on square stone pillars and their tops are joined by horizontal tie beams which have paired diagonal bracing struts. The roof is supported on the principal posts which alternate with base crucks of the sort seen at Bradford-on-Avon.

Bredon, which also has a fine parish church, has a rather later barn, with different origins. There had been a monastery here in Saxon times, but after its destruction by the Danes its endowments were settled on the Bishopric of Worcester, and it remained a possession of the Bishops of Worcester until the sixteenth century. Thus the Bishopric stood in place of the monastery here, and it was responsible for appointing the Vicar of Bredon. The barn was probably built in the fourteenth century; it has two porched entrances, one containing an upper room with a fireplace and privy reached by an external flight of steps. This was the office of the official called a granger (from the Latin *granum*, 'grain'), who was responsible for keeping account of the produce stored here. The barn has recently been reconstructed after a fire, but its walls and principal timbers are all intact.

These barns are but two survivors of the hundreds – or, more probably, thousands – which once existed, and are priceless examples of medieval craftsmanship. William Morris lived near the Great Coxwell barn, and he hailed it as 'the finest piece of architecture in England'; we know just what he meant!

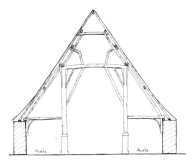

A section of the Great Coxwell tithe barn showing a pair of aisle posts and details of the roof construction.

65
OXFORD, Oxfordshire

Map Reference SP 530050, Map 164
As a general rule most colleges are
open to visitors in the afternoons.

A medieval university

The origins of the City of Oxford as a centre of learning reach back into the twelfth century at least, and from the middle of that century the number of scholars in the city increased rapidly. At first they lived where they could, at inns and lodgings, but gradually they banded together to hire houses – which was probably where the 'halls' originated. During the thirteenth century the arrival of the Friars gave the nascent university further impetus. It was then that the first colleges were founded which, as their name suggests, embodied the same principle of communal living in separate quarters but with a common hall and chapel as is found in religious foundations like Archbishop Chichele's college at Higham Ferrers.

We might well ask why students came to the University, and what they studied. The answer to the first question is simple enough: the University was the principal path to professional and social advancement open to the sons of middle-class families. If they wished to obtain high office in Church or State they went to University, and afterwards became, initially at least, a clerk or secretary in some great household, preferably the king's. As to the second question, they studied seven years for the degree of Master of Arts, composed of two sections: one of three years, the 'Trivium', and one of four, the 'Quadrivium'. The first covered Grammar, Rhetoric and

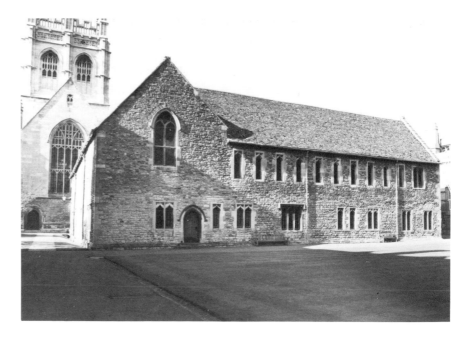

The late-fourteenth-century library with its delicate cusped ogee traceried windows.

Logic, and the second Arithmetic, Geometry, Music (meaning the science of harmonies) and Astronomy. Afterwards, most students went on to study for the Doctorate of Theology, a process which took ten years, reminding us of the dominance of the Church throughout the University.

There is much argument about which of the Oxford colleges was founded first, but certainty is precluded by a scarcity of evidence. Merton, founded by William de Merton, sometime Chancellor of England, claims to predate the foundation of University College in 1249 and Balliol in 1263. Three more colleges were established during the fourteenth century before William of Wykeham, Bishop of Winchester, established his innovatory double foundation of a school next to his cathedral linked to a college, called New College, in the University of Oxford. By the end of the Middle Ages there were ten colleges, four others attached to monastic houses, and a staggering seventy 'halls' in which scholars also lived.

Merton College has the earliest major buildings. Its chapel, built in the years after 1290, has superb geometric tracery, and work on the western parts began soon afterwards. Incredibly, this building was to have been but the choir of a huge church which was never completed. But chapels can be seen elsewhere; the peculiar interest of Merton attaches to the early collegiate buildings comprising the Hall and the Mob Quad. The Hall is essentially of the late thirteenth century, but was rebuilt later incorporating parts of the original structure. It is now entered through a later porch, but the door, with its finely flowing ironwork is original. The Mob Quad was not laid out as such, but evolved this plan as buildings were added during the fourteenth century. The style is restrained, the doorways all being simply chamfered with plain hood moulds, the exception being the late-fourteenth-century library entrance on the south side.

Whereas Merton Quad was the result of a gradual process of accretion, the concept of the quadrangle, which approximated to the 'courts' of houses of the period and monastic cloisters, proved popular. At New College, founded in 1379 to specialize in the study of law, the principal buildings were arranged from the first round the 'Great Quad'. The gatehouse, Perpendicular chapel and other elements of the early plan survive, but much has been remodelled later. New College established the pattern for later foundations. At Magdalen and All Souls good fifteenth-century buildings can be seen, with the hammerbeam roof and reredos of All Souls Chapel being particularly memorable.

Perhaps the most agreeable aspect of a visit to Oxford and its colleges is the great continuity which it represents, of buildings still used for their original purpose. While it is true that as early as 1517 the foundation charter of Corpus Christi College dismissed the earlier foundations as 'monkish', they lit a flame of scholarship that has never been extinguished.

66
MINSTER LOVELL HALL, Oxfordshire

Map Reference SP 324114, Map 164
Nearest Town Witney
3 miles (4.8 km) west of Witney off
the B4070. An HBMCE
guardianship site open standard
hours, a 200-yard walk from the car
park. The ruined house is in a
beautiful setting beside the River
Windrush.

Minster Lovell, which occupies a delightful site in the Windrush Valley, records its two principal associations in its name. A minster or 'mother church' was established here in Saxon times to serve a wide area before parishes were formed. The 'Lovell' element recalls the time at which the manor came into the ownership of that family late in the thirteenth century. When William, the 7th Lord Lovell, returned from the French wars in 1431 he decided to rebuild the house here, and in 1440 obtained a royal licence for a deer park, which would have added the final flourish to this delectable mansion.

Although ruined, the original form of the house is quite clear on the ground; it was arranged round a courtyard open to the river on the south side which was always its focus. The vaulted entrance porch is approached down a pretty patterned cobbled path, which appears to be medieval. The porch is aligned on the screens passage of the hall, at the upper end of which is a projecting stair tower leading to an upper solar. Beyond, on the north and west sides of the courtyard, are suites of high-status accommodation. The east range meanwhile was given over to the kitchen and other domestic offices with, unusually, a stable at the lower end. The buildings are finely detailed throughout, and the site affords a rare opportunity to examine at close quarters the domestic arrangements of a great medieval magnate.

Even magnates had to live, however, and here at Minster Lovell there is a further survival which sheds some light on this aspect of medieval life. Dovecotes were a common sight in medieval England, and good examples can be seen here and at Sibthorpe (Nottinghamshire). We are really talking here less of 'doves' than of pigeons, for the purpose of this great circular building with its splendid conical roof was strictly functional, as its location in the manorial farmyard indicates. It was a medieval 'battery house', albeit one from which its inmates could sally forth in order to supplement their rations. The pigeons nested in the hundreds of square boxes along the walls, and they could exit through a hole in the roof, which was originally regulated by a louvre. Here eggs were gathered and young birds, called 'squabs', were reared before providing the Lords Lovell with many a tasty meal.

It might well be asked why Minster Lovell has survived in such an unaltered condition. It is because Sir William's grandson John espoused the Yorkist cause. After the Battle of Bosworth he was accused of treason and his lands, including Minster Lovell, were confiscated. Lovell's end is a mystery, however. Some claim he died on Stoke Field in 1487, but another report says that he escaped and died in a 'cave or vault'. During the eighteenth century it was said that a vault containing a skeleton had been found here at Minster Lovell, his family home . . .

The ruined house beside the Thames at Minster Lovell with the handsome cruciform church beyond.

67
STANTON HARCOURT, Oxfordshire

A great kitchen and a memorable church

The great medieval house of the Harcourt family was unfortunately demolished during the eighteenth century, but two of the original buildings remain: Pope's Tower, which contains a late-fifteenth-century chapel on the ground floor, and the Great Kitchen. The kitchen is late-fourteenth-century and one of the best in the country, the others being at Raby Castle and Glastonbury. It is square on plan and has an octagonal pyramidal roof, which, like the small two-light windows, is fifteenth-century work. This later roof has no louvre on the crest in the manner of Glastonbury, which would have reduced its effectiveness in clearing the smoke and heat produced by cooking over the three large open fireplaces. Instead, shutters were fitted below the roof which could be adjusted to suit the prevailing wind. The roof is vast, an assemblage of eight ribs supported on stone corbels, linked together by two tiers of collars with windbraces.

The loss of the medieval house is compensated for in some measure by the splendid church of St Michael. This contains some twelfth-century fabric, but the major interest attaches to the chancel, remodelled in the mid thirteenth century and in a remarkably complete condition. The

Map Reference SP 416057, Map 164
Nearest Town Witney
5 miles (8 km) south-east of Witney. Stanton Harcourt is signposted off the roundabout on the A40 ring road east of Witney. The house is open once a week from April to the end of September. Write for information since opening times vary each year.

The existing house at Stanton Harcourt is dominated by the Medieval kitchen to the left, which gives some impression of the scale of the original structure.

The thirteenth-century wooden screen at Stanton Harcourt is a rare survival.

chancel walls were provided with graduated triplets of lancets, one set in the east wall, and originally two each down the sides. The southern windows were destroyed by the erection of the Harcourt Chapel, but this proved a lucky blow since the remaining jambs on that side are superbly preserved and retain their original painted decoration. A further important survival is the contemporary wooden chancel screen, which matches the lancet shafts of the windows and has trefoil headed openings.

As if all this were not enough, the church also contains a prodigious collection of medieval and later monuments to members of the Harcourt family difficult to parallel elsewhere. The Harcourt Chapel, built in about 1470, is possibly the work of the Oxford mason William Orchard, who designed the delectable vault of the Divinity School there. This, by contrast, is restrained work with panel traceried windows retaining some contemporary glass, and containing the fine alabaster effigies of Sir Robert Harcourt and his wife. This splendid church, with its costly fittings and furnishings, illustrates the range and skill of the craftsmen which a great medieval household could call upon; what must the house have been like?

68
THE ELEANOR CROSSES, Northamptonshire

Map Reference Geddington: SP 896830, Map 141
Nearest Town Kettering 4 miles (6.4 km) north-east of Kettering on the A43 in the Corby direction. The cross is in the centre of the village and is in HBMCE guardianship.

Northamptonshire is fortunate indeed to possess two of the famous Eleanor Crosses. Edward I's Queen, Eleanor of Castile, died at Harby in Lincolnshire in November 1290. The grief-stricken King had her body embalmed, and decreed a sombre funeral procession to her burial place at Westminster Abbey. The 'crosses', actually polygonal pillars carrying crosses, were erected at each place that the cortège rested. The stopping places, all having royal castles or major monasteries, were Lincoln, Grantham, Stamford, Geddington, Hardingstone, Stony Stratford, Dunstable, Cheapside and, most famous of all, Charing Cross. The crosses were erected between 1291 and 1294; John of Battle was commissioned to build them and William of Ireland carved the statues of the Queen.

The Hardingstone Cross is the most elaborate, with an octagonal base of three stages; the top of the shaft, which presumably supported the cross, is now missing. The base has panelled buttresses between which are lights beneath flat ogee arches, apparently the earliest appearance of such an arch in England. On every second side is carved an open book, doubtless originally painted with a suitable text. Above are cusped gables, a frieze of flowers and a pierced parapet. The second stage has four deeply recessed canopied niches containing statues of the queen. The third stage is square and canopied, and from it rises the broken cross shaft. The Geddington Cross has a triangular base, and is much more restrained; it is an object of great delicacy, still commanding the centre of the village after 700 years.

We know that the idea of erecting crosses to mark the stopping places of

Map Reference Hardingstone:
SP 754582, Map 152
Nearest Town Northampton
The cross is on the outskirts of Northampton on the Hardingstone road, just before the outer ring road, near the main roundabout and Police HQ.

Even in its reduced form, the Eleanor Cross at Hardingstone, Northampton is a moving monument to Edward I's love for his queen.

Gentle Geddington, with at its heart the Eleanor Cross, symbol of Edward I's great love for his devoted queen.

a funeral procession was not new, for it had been done for the cortège of Louis IX of France in 1271. But the Eleanor Crosses almost certainly represented something more profound than Edward merely wishing to vie with his enemies. For this was the queen who had, among other things, borne him his heir and saved his life when she sucked poison from a dagger wound he sustained in the Holy Land. The Eleanor Crosses remain one of the most poignant symbols of their age, and display an unlooked-for sentimentalism on the part of the 'Hammer of the Scots'.

69

HIGHAM FERRERS, Northamptonshire

Map Reference SP 960687, Map 153 Nearest Town Rushden
Just north of Rushden, on the A6. The Chichele College is in HBMCE guardianship and open (exterior only) at any reasonable time. The church, school and bede house are located together. In the field to the north of the church are fishponds and rabbit warren earthworks. In the market-place is a medieval cross.

Birthplace of Henry Chichele

Henry Chichele, Archbishop of Canterbury, was born at Higham Ferrers, a prosperous market town, in about 1362. He was the son of a merchant and may have owed his early education to John of Gaunt, who was lord of the manor. The town had been granted a charter in 1251 and had a market and an annual fair. This early prosperity explains the substantial thirteenth-century work in the church and its stylish fourteenth-century additions. But as well as the fine church we can also see at Higham the school, college and bede house which the Archbishop established in his home town.

The church has a spectacular collection of late-thirteenth-century sculpture on the tympanum over the western doors. It is carved in low relief with roundels depicting the Life of Christ, evidently inspired by glass or manuscript originals. The work is of the highest quality and bears comparison with contemporary carvings at Westminster. Inside is a memorable collection of brasses including those of Chichele's family, but the finest commemorates Laurence St Maur, Rector of the parish, at the time of the second building campaign some time after 1327. The church was almost doubled in width, the chancel remodelled and a Lady Chapel built, but the crowning glory was the recessed crocketed spire, one of the best in a county famous for its steeples.

Archbishop Chichele did not forget his birthplace, and in 1422 he founded a college here for seven chaplains, four clerks and six choristers with at its head a Warden who was also vicar of the parish church. The collegiate stalls and misericords can still be seen in the church, one bearing Chichele's portrait and another his arms. In College Street the ruins of the collegiate buildings, consisting of a chapel, hall and lodging arranged round a courtyard and entered by a gatehouse, can be visited. Over the gateway are three empty niches which contained statues of St Mary the

Virgin, St Thomas, and St Edward the Confessor to whom the college was dedicated.

One of the priests was also deputed to teach at the Grammar School which Chichele refounded in 1422. The three-bay school hall stands in the churchyard, with three-light windows down the sides and larger windows at the ends. The final link with the bountiful Archbishop is the Bede House, founded in 1428 for twelve old men and a woman attendant. This is a splendid structure of banded ironstone and limestone consisting of living quarters divided into cubicles with a chapel at one end. The college, school and bede house form a most interesting group of monuments to the generosity of a man who sprang from lowly origins and who is chiefly remembered today as a patron of learning and as the founder of All Souls College, Oxford.

The fine perpendicular window in the west end of Higham Ferrers church.

70

FOTHERINGHAY, Northamptonshire

Map Reference TL 059931, Map 142
Nearest Town Oundle
Beside the River Nene, 3 miles
(4.8 km) north-east of Oundle, on a
minor road north off the A605.
Near the church in the main village
street is the medieval Old Inn.

Shrine of the House of York

The church at Fotheringhay is one of the most remarkable sights of medieval England, stately and magnificent, a Perpendicular masterpiece set against green Northamptonshire meadows. This splendid church was already over 150 years old before the execution of Mary Queen of Scots at Fotheringhay Castle. For while the village is now chiefly known for that event, it was famous long before. Richard III was born here in 1452, and this was the collegiate church of the mighty House of York.

We have encountered many collegiate churches elsewhere, but few were as grandly conceived or built with such art as this. The college had a complicated history, however, chiefly due to the untimely demise of its first two Yorkist patrons. Edmund Plantagenet, Duke of York, began the project as early as 1370, but the college was not actually founded by his son until 1411. The present building is largely the result of a contract dated 1434 between Richard, Duke of York, and the freemason William Horwood. Only the western parts of the church remain, the chancel and

ABOVE: This brightly painted pulpit was donated to the church at Fotheringhay by Edward IV, though the tester is an addition.

RIGHT: Fotheringhay across the riverside meadow, the noble shrine of the House of York.

cloisters having been demolished after the Reformation, but even in its reduced condition it is a superb monument to a powerful dynasty.

The tower is of three storeys with a great west window and an elegant octagonal belfry with tall triple lights. Externally, the nave is dominated by huge windows separated by slender buttresses and pinnacles supporting the narrowest of flying buttresses. Inside, the Perpendicular structure is forced to its uttermost, and the broad nave is filled with light. This would be even more pronounced but for the blank walls across the chancel and the entrance to the vanished cloister on the south side. The nave roof has curved principals, a technique achieving strength without mass which is also used in the external flying buttresses.

The finest feature of the interior is the pulpit, donated by Edward IV and recently restored to its original livery of green, red and gold. Most of the glass has gone but fragments remain to show its quality, and we know that in the cloister alone there were eighty-eight stained-glass windows. Memories of the Plantagenets are not far to seek. When Queen Elizabeth I visited the church she found the tombs of Richard III's parents mouldering in the ruined choir. She caused two new tombs to be built in the nave and they stand there still, massive and solemn, the falcon and fetterlock badge of York prominently displayed. Finally, lest we forget, the Chapel of All Souls was dedicated as recently as 1982 in memory of the noble House of York.

71
BOSWORTH FIELD, Leicestershire

Few battles in English history can have generated so much discussion about their course and significance than the Battle of Bosworth in 1485. Henry Tudor landed at Milford Haven on 7 August with about 2,000 French mercenaries and a few Lancastrian knights and nobles. He received no check to his advance through Wales, and gathered reinforcements as he went. He entered England and marched east by way of Shrewsbury, Stafford and Atherstone. Richard III was at the royal castle of Nottingham, and he marched to Leicester on 19 August; by the 21st the two armies were close to each other a few miles south of Market Bosworth in Leicestershire. Richard had strength of numbers, fielding some 8,000 men to Henry's 5,000. The Stanley brothers, with a further host of 4,000, were also expected to support Richard.

Richard chose a high place called Ambion Hill for his position, a site which was later criticized as offering too little manoeuvring space for his army. He missed his chance at an early stage by failing to attack the rebel

Map Reference SK 401001, Map 140 *Nearest Town* Hinckley From Hinckley take the A447 north towards Market Bosworth. After 6 miles (9.6 km) turn west to Sutton Cheney. The Battlefield Centre is about 1 mile (1.6 km) west of the village. It is run by Leicestershire County Council and has a Visitor Centre and outdoor interpretation of the battle. The trail is open all year during daylight hours. The centre is open 3 April–27 Oct, Mon–Sat 2–5.30, Sun 1–6. Tel Market Bosworth 290429. Sutton Cheney Church is small and simple, open daily, and housing a memorial to Richard III, for it was here that he heard his last mass on 2 August 1485, the eve of the battle.

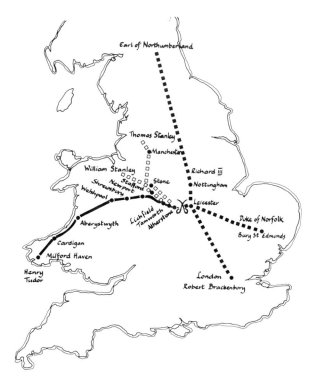

The routes of the forces to Bosworth Field in August 1485; Richard's narrow numerical superiority was vitiated by the uncertain loyalties of his troops.

army while it was forming up. The royal position was attacked and the Duke of Norfolk, Richard's chief supporter, was killed. For an hour the fight was evenly matched, but when the Stanleys defected with their troops the whole course of the battle changed. This treachery was compounded by the Earl of Northumberland's failure to engage the enemy with his rearguard, but it is possible that he was unable to deploy his troops on the restricted site. Richard led a desperate counter attack, but was hacked down; it is said that he died with a cry of 'Treachery!' on his lips. Whatever might be said of Richard's career, his death was a noble one – scorning flight, he became the only English king to be killed on the battlefield since the Norman Conquest.

The significance of this battle has been hotly disputed, and few would now suggest that it uniquely marked the end of the Middle Ages. It was not even the end of the Wars of the Roses, because the Battle of Stoke in 1487 marked the last bloody twitching of that conflict. It did, however, usher in the Tudor dynasty which raised the nation to a level of prosperity and international influence undreamed of in the period covered by this book. Yet when we tread the muddy clay of Bosworth Field, we can still sense Richard's shade crying, 'Treachery!'

72
DONINGTON-LE-HEATH MANOR HOUSE, Leicestershire

Donington-le-Heath is a rare survival of a small thirteenth-century manor house in a relatively unaltered condition. Houses of this general pattern, set within a moat, the accommodation arranged on a U-plan and the Great Hall on the first floor in the Norman style, must have been a common enough sight in medieval England, but most were remodelled in late times. Donington lost its status during the seventeenth century and slumbered on as a farmhouse, its owners having neither the finance nor inclination to alter its comfortable but basic accommodation. As a result the Great Hall, raised over an undercroft, retains its early roof; many of the door and window openings of both stone and wood are original and, thanks to sensitive repair, the house preserves much of its medieval character.

The manor was built in about 1280 of coursed rubble stone with thin ashlar buttresses at the angles. The early openings are pointed and chamfered, and a doorway in the front wall indicates an original first-floor entrance, making it look more like Boothby Pagnell in our *Norman Guide*. This doorway led into a passage or service room divided from the hall by a timber-framed screen, the mortices for which can be seen in the underside of the roof truss at that end. Having thus established the 'geography' of the house, we know that the left-hand wing contained the services, and that the solar and chamber were on the right. The hall has a later fireplace, presumably replacing an earlier one, and a fine open trussed roof with

Map Reference SP 421136, Map 129
Nearest Town Coalville
1 mile (1.6 km) south-west of Coalville. The house is signposted off the A50 Leicester to Ashby de la Zouch road. It is run by Leicestershire Museums, Art Galleries and Record Service and open 3 April–30 Sept, Wed–Sun, 2–6, admission free. Refreshments in the barn. Tel Coalville 31259. It is pleasantly set with a herb garden.

The first-floor hall was originally entered via a staircase to the upper pointed doorway.

collars and chamfered ties. One of the chambers has been imaginatively restored with painted walls, tapestry hangings, rugs and furniture, demonstrating an entirely believable standard of comfort in this modest and agreeable house.

73

HAWTON AND SIBTHORPE, Nottinghamshire

Map Reference Hawton: SK 788511, Map 120
Nearest Town Newark
1½ miles (2.4 km) south-west of Newark on a minor road off Leicester Road.

Map Reference Sibthorpe: SK 763455, Map 129
Nearest Town Newark
Lies in the flat lands of the Trent plain between the Fosse Way and the Great North Road. From the A46, 6 miles (9.6 km) south-west of Newark, take the east turn to Flintham and Sibthorpe. Just outside the village, on the east side, is a fine medieval dovecote which is also worth seeing.

The Easter Sepulchres

The medieval church developed an elaborate ritual for the celebration of Easter which reached the peak of its complexity early in the fourteenth century. An important part of the commemoration consisted of placing a consecrated wafer, the Body of Christ, in a symbolic 'tomb' between Maundy Thursday and its 'resurrection' on Easter Sunday. This sort of dramatized liturgy must have had a strong appeal in the Middle Ages and echoes the contemporary Mystery Plays. In earlier times the receptacle used was just a wooden box placed in some convenient cupboard or corner, but later a permanent sculpted sepulchre was provided, and the example here at Hawton is reckoned the best in England.

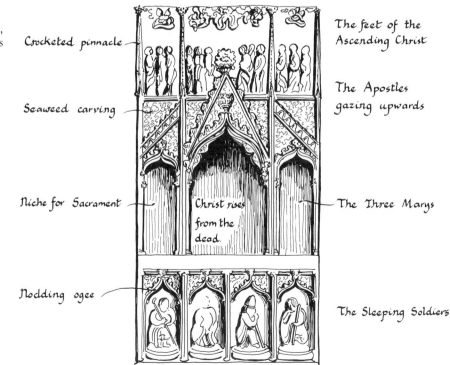

Hawton Sepulchre is one of the finest fourteenth-century sculptures in England, alive with movement and detail.

The sepulchre is in the usual position on the north side of the chancel, and next to it is the tomb of its builder, Sir Robert de Compton, who died in 1330. Beyond is the contemporary door into his chantry, and this juxtaposition reminds us of the clear link between this architectural rendering of the resurrection story and the donor's hopes of eternal life. The doorway and tomb recess have richly moulded ogee arches with pinnacles, and the basic tripartite form of the sepulchre itself is almost overwhelmed by the mass of representational and freestyle carving.

At the base are shown the images of the Sleeping Soldiers before the tomb, each under an appropriately 'nodding' ogee arch. Above, in the rear panels of the sideboard-shaped recess, Christ rises from the dead, clad in his grave clothes, with the Three Marys to the right and the niche for the Blessed Sacrament to the left. Above the crocketed gables, with 'seaweed' carving in the spandrels, is a long panel showing the Apostles gazing up at the feet only of the Ascending Christ. This is a rare and delightful composition, and includes some excellent carving.

These same masons made the similar sepulchre at Sibthorpe nearby, and also probably the Lincolnshire examples at Navenby, Irnham and, most splendid of all, at Heckington, where the whole chancel, sediliae and all, was rebuilt in sumptuous style by Richard de Potesgrave, Chaplain to Edward III.

74
SOUTHWELL CHAPTER HOUSE, Nottinghamshire

Southwell Minster has appeared in both our earlier guides, and we cannot travel medieval England without seeing its incomparable Chapter House, dated to around 1290, for it contains the first medieval collection of carved foliage in England. The Chapter House is reached by a passage leading from the north side of the church and terminating in a vestibule. Both passage and vestibule are elaborately arcaded, and the passage was originally open to the east, like a cloister. The two doorways into the Chapter House have delicate pierced cusped heads and are separated by a trumeau supporting a hollow quatrefoil.

Inside, the octagonal chamber has thirty-six seats round its walls, and the roof consists of an unsupported star vault with a leafy boss at the centre. Five ribs spring from each side of the octagon and meet to form an elaborately patterned ceiling. This admirably complements the gabled stalls, the rich geometrical tracery of the windows and their shafted reveals. It is a masterpiece of movement and light shaped into a grand upward sweeping design which is a jewel of the Gothic style.

Map Reference SK 702538, Map 120
Southwell Minster is open daily.

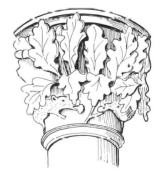

A capital from the Chapter House at Southwell showing two piggies greedily guzzling acorns under the oak leaves.

The detailed carvings of the Chapter House are even more famous than its overall design. They are chiefly found in the gables over the stalls, and depict leaves and flowers with breathtaking realism. The carvings, made of the hard-grained Magnesian limestone from nearby Mansfield, are both free-flowing and controlled; the leaves cluster and wave as if in the open air, but are also 'arranged'. The effect is therefore almost overly naturalistic, and it can be suggested that this work passes the peak of art because it strives only for reality. But what a reality it is: the undercutting, the balance and the finish of the work are all beyond praise; buttercup, hawthorn, hop, vine and ivy can all be identified with ease, for these leaves are still 'green' after six centuries.

75

LAXTON OPEN FIELDS, Nottinghamshire

Map Reference SK 722670, Map 120
Nearest Town Ollerton
From Ollerton take the A6075 towards Tuxford. Laxton is 5 miles (8 km) east of Ollerton on a minor road south-east of the A road. Newark District Council has published a trail of Laxton which is available in the village. The 3 main open fields are West Field, South Field and Mill Field (also on the south side). The fishponds are near Mill Field and can be seen from the clearly marked public footpath.

Laxton is the most famous of our surviving open field systems, and it is well worth visiting. Originally there were four fields here; the East or Town Field has disappeared, but the South, Mill and West fields remain. As at Braunton, some consolidation of strips has inevitably occurred and what we see today is not really the early layout of individual strips but of the larger groups or 'furlongs'. This is because a decision was taken earlier this century to amalgamate the original scattered strips into larger blocks for ease of cultivation. It is, of course, precisely this process which has led to the total disappearance of such field systems elsewhere, but the changes at Laxton seem to have been halted for the present.

There are 483 acres of open fields remaining at Laxton today, and the system is administered in a manner which enshrines many aspects of medieval practice. The 'Field Court' is responsible to the 'Court Leet', which meets in the village pub and controls the system. All the occupiers of properties in Laxton are on the Suit Roll of the Manor, and are supposed to attend meetings of the Court upon payment of a fine or 'essoign' of two pence. Villagers are appointed by the Court as Pinder, who detains stray cattle in the Pinfold, and a twelve-man jury under a Foreman who inspect the crops, make sure the ditches are kept in good repair and check the landmarks of the fields. The costs of the court are met by the sale of hay grown on the commons and sykes of the village, which were unploughed areas left either because of the lie of the land, or because they afforded access to the fields. The Court no longer supervises the apportionment of strips, but it does enforce the strict three-course rotation of the fields.

The Laxton fields preserve their open appearance to a considerable degree, and hedges are confined to the larger enclosures or to the original

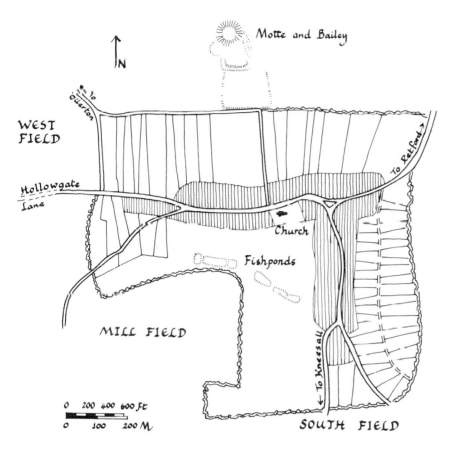

WEST FIELD

MILL FIELD

SOUTH FIELD

Motte and Bailey

Church

Fishponds

Hollowgate Lane

To Ollerton

To Retford

To Kneesall

N

0   200 400 600 ft
0   100   200 M

Plan of Laxton village showing the remaining strips round the village.

great field boundaries. The curving reversed-S shapes of the furlongs are clearly visible on the ground, and the baulks between the different furlongs are minimal. Apart from the fields themselves, there are other features of the medieval village layout to be seen. To the north are the grassy earthworks of the small motte and bailey castle built by the de Caux family soon after the Conquest. East of the village is Hollowgate Lane, which, as the name suggests, has been worn into its distinctive 'hollow' profile by many years of traffic, providing a good example of such an early trackway. In the valley south of the village is a fine set of at least five linked rectangular fishponds, so arranged to facilitate breeding and catching the fish. Finally, at the centre of the village is the parish church of St Michael, which is mercifully undistinguished, providing a perfect foil for this place which is so exceptional now, but which once must have resembled hundreds of other villages of the Midland Plain.

76

SHERWOOD FOREST, Nottinghamshire

Map Reference SE 621682, Map 120
Nearest Town Ollerton
At Edwinstowe on the west side of
Ollerton is the Sherwood Forest
Visitors' Centre, run by
Nottinghamshire County Council.
This is well signposted on the
B6034, north of Edwinstowe. There
are displays of the history of the
forest. There are also trails within
the forest, many of which include
the Major Oak.

The great 'Shire Wood' of Nottingham enjoys a high place in the popular
imagination of medieval England by virtue of its supposed connection with
Robin Hood, the swashbuckling outlaw. Robin is first heard of in Langland's *Vision of Piers the Plowman*, composed about 1377, when the
character of Sloth owns to knowing the 'rhymes of Robin Hood'. The
earliest text is of the mid fifteenth century and called 'Robin Hood and the
Monk', but the most informative is the 'Gest of Robyn Hode'. They tell of
an outlaw living in the Greenwood, in the area of West Yorkshire called
Barnsdale, near a place where robberies are known to have taken place on
the Great North Road. The most likely candidate is a certain Yorkshire-
man called Robin Hood who was described as a 'fugitive' in 1230. The
Sherwood connection seems to have come about through repeated mention of the unpopular Sheriff of Nottingham in the ballads, but it has
stuck.

If we go to Sherwood today, we find individual trees like the 'Major Oak'
which are unlikely to be more than 500 years old; but elsewhere in the
forest, and notably at the place called Birkland ('birch land'), we can see
what is essentially a medieval forest landscape like the one at Hatfield in
Essex. Here are several hundred magnificent oak trees, their great bran-
ches sticking stiffly outwards from vast trunks, the tops quite dead,
apparently from some ancient ecological disaster. They too are about 500
years old and form a living link with the Middle Ages. The ground is
choked with bracken, and there are many birches too, probably descendants of the original trees growing when the place was named before the
Norman Conquest. Whatever the facts might be, it provides excellent
cover for robbers!

*King John a-hunting, from a thirteenth-
century manuscript. Notice how the
coneys start from their burrows and the
regal stag flies before the couples of
hounds.*

77
SOUTH WINGFIELD MANOR HOUSE, Derbyshire

Ralph, Lord Cromwell, served in the English army in France and fought at Agincourt in 1415; this early exposure to foreign influences must have affected him deeply, and he was certainly very ambitious. He became Constable of Nottingham Castle, Warden of Sherwood Forest and, in 1433, Chancellor of England. It was at that time he began building residences here at South Wingfield and at Tattershall (Lincolnshire) commensurate with his new status. The two are very different, but it is perhaps unwise to stress the domestic nature of Wingfield too much; it is on a strong natural site, and its walls could readily be defended.

Map Reference SK 375547, Map 119
Nearest Town Alfreton
The village is on the B5035, 2 miles (3.2 km) west of Alfreton. The ruined manor house stands apart from the village on a lofty hill affording magnificent views of the surrounding countryside. The manor is being consolidated by the Historic Buildings and Monuments Commission prior to being taken into guardianship. It is currently open daily, admission free. Go through the village to the west side and take the marked footpath to the site, a walk of about ½ mile (0.8 km). Another medieval house can be seen locally at Haddon Hall near Bakewell (SK 2365), owned by the Duke of Rutland, open April–end Sept, Tues–Sat, 11–6.

View of the Great Hall from the tower showing the embattled entrance porch and the oriel window beyond the gap to the right.

Cromwell began Wingfield in 1441: it is a truly beautiful place, with two ample courtyards and suites of state rooms. Over the inner entrance he had carved his arms and the double money bags which symbolized his office of Chancellor. The Outer Court is strongly walled and provided with a barn and a long range down the east side which could have been accommodation for soldiers or retainers. The wall between the two courts is substantial and has square buttresses. At the west end is a tall rectangular keep which would have provided a secure retiring place in time of trouble.

The gateway to the Inner Court lines up with the screens passage of the Great Hall forming a grand axis. The hall itself is ruined, but the square porch and canted oriel at the dais end with their elaborate panelled battlements survive to show its quality. At the lower end are the customary three service doorways, and in the gables are large three-light windows; the windows to the north were altered later. Beneath the hall is one of the finest features of the site, a great undercroft, the vaulted roof of which has massive moulded ribs supported on stubby pillars, the ribs meeting in large flat circular bosses with shallow trefoiled decorations. West of the hall are the domestic offices and kitchen on the ground floor with the great chamber, office and private apartments above. Chickens scratch where Lord Cromwell once held sway, and vegetables are grown in the Outer Court, but this combination of domesticity and finery is probably a pretty accurate reflection of the original atmosphere, and certainly makes South Wingfield a delightful place to visit.

78
THE CITY OF COVENTRY, West Midlands

Map Reference SP 335790, Map 140 The Cathedral is in the centre of the city and well signposted. The ruins are open at all times, the new Cathedral from 9.30–7.30 in summer and from 9.30–5.30, Oct to Easter. To the south in Bayley Lane is St Mary's Guildhall, open subject to Civic requirements. Whitefriars is off Whitefriars Lane, south of the Herbert Art Gallery and Museum, and now close by the elevated inner ring road. It is open daily from 10–5, except Sunday. Spon Street is on the west side of the inner city area, an extension of Fleet Street.

Coventry was one of the most prominent woollen cloth centres of medieval England, and during the fourteenth century, when it was the fourth town in the land, its success was recognized by the grant of royal charters. By 1449 there were many master drapers, weavers, fullers, dyers and tailors in the town, and 'Coventry blue' dye was famous. The basic elements of the plan had been established in the twelfth century, with a castle and town defences as the principal components. At the heart of the town is the great medieval parish church of St Michael, later the Cathedral, but reduced to a scorched ruin by the Blitz of 1940. It remains as a stark reminder of the horrors of war, and the shattered walls with their delicate medieval carvings are almost unbearably poignant.

Beside the Cathedral is St Mary's Guildhall, begun in 1340 and enlarged in 1400; its splendid hall has a vaulted undercroft and retains its large four-light windows and panelled roof. At the service end are three pointed service doors, while at the upper end is the exuberant guild chair. The lavish gilded carving looks altogether too medieval to be true, more like something out of Pugin's version of the House of Commons, but it is only when we see such a fabulous seat that we understand fully whence the nineteenth-century Gothicists derived their inspiration. It dates to the mid fifteenth century, richly carved with blank tracery and, atop one of the styles, an elephant and castle.

Before leaving the Coventry Guilds, we must mention the haunting Coventry Carol, sung at the Pageant of the Shearmen and Tailors during the fifteenth century, and performed before three kings, including both Richard III and Henry VII. These lines were sung as Herod's soldiers came in to slay the children:

Herod the king, in his raging
Charged he hath this day
His men of might, in his own sight
All young children to slay,

A further rare survival of medieval Coventry is the magnificent dormitory of the Carmelite Friary, built soon after the foundation of the house in
1343. The presence of friaries in a medieval town was an infallible sign of
its importance, but few escaped later destruction. The friars came to
England in the first half of the thirteenth century, at a time when popular
enthusiasm for the established monastic Orders was waning. Their com-
mitment to a life of preaching and example, signalled by their houses being
located in towns rather than the countryside, made them more acceptable
than the cloistered Orders. Brothers of the Dominican, Franciscan and
Carmelite Orders, popularly called the black, grey and white friars from
the colours of their habits, became familiar and respected figures.

Excavations of the Coventry friary have revealed a huge church with a
broad nine-bay 'preaching' nave like St Andrew's Hall at Norwich. The
cloister was laid out to the south, but all save the eastern range has
disappeared. The vaulted cloister walk survives on this side and is lit by
triple pointed windows. Half-way along is the vestibule of the vaulted
chapter house, and to either side are the warming room and parlour. It is
on the first floor that the greatest surprise awaits us, since we suddenly
emerge from the top of the stairs into the dormitory. It is a huge room,

The dormitory roof at Coventry
Whitefriars.

eleven bays long, and has a magnificent sixteenth-century roof with massive timbers.

Finally, in Spon Street on the west side of the town, a remarkable group of late-fourteenth-century timber-framed terraced houses can be seen. One block of six was apparently built as a speculation, rather like the Abbey Cottages in Tewkesbury. They are of the 'Wealden' type, an unusual choice for urban housing, and consist of a ground-floor hall to the left, open to the roof, with a jettied first-floor solar to the right, partly over the screens passage and partly projecting into the hall. These houses, and others like them in this part of the town, demonstrate Coventry's considerable prosperity during the later Middle Ages, when it acted as a huge market-place set at the very heart of England.

79

WARWICK, Warwickshire

Map Reference SP 282650, Map 151 The Church is in the centre of the town in Church Street. It is open daily. The Castle is off West Street and stands beside the River Avon. It is open daily; 1 Mar–31 Oct, 10–5.30, 1 Nov–28 Feb, 10–4.30.

The Beauchamp Chapel

The Church of St Mary dominates the town of Warwick, rather than its mighty castle, yet their histories are similar. Both started in Norman times and, as the castle developed under the Beauchamps during the fourteenth century, so the church grew as well. A fire in the church in 1697 necessitated extensive rebuilding and, while still impressive, it is no longer of medieval inspiration. The castle was not visited by a single act of destruction, but successive modernizations have cumulatively rendered the medieval structure difficult to appreciate. The east front above the river is unforgettable, but it is largely a show. Inside, the feeling is as much Victorian as Gothic. Yet Warwick retains one glorious link with its medieval past: the incomparable tomb of Richard Beauchamp, Earl of Warwick.

A famous knight and warrior, Knight of the Bath and the Garter, he visited the Holy Sepulchre at Jerusalem to pay his vows in 1408, was Lord High Steward at the Coronation of Henry V, and held important commands in France. He died at Rouen in 1439, having earlier decreed in his will:

> I will, that when it liketh God, that my Soule depart out of this World, my Body be interred within the Church Collegiate of our Lady in Warwick, where I will, that in such place as I have devised (which is Known well) there be made a Chappell of our Lady, well, faire, and goodly built, within the middle of which Chappell I will, that my Tombe be made . . .

Chantries were common in medieval England and the best of them, as here, could be very elaborate. But the existence of such special chapels in churches should not make us forget that many lesser people simply wished a priest to pray for them after death. For a chantry was a private mass said at a side altar for the founder and other named persons and it was thought to be the most effective way of engaging the mercy of God on the soul of the deceased. Chantries became very popular later in the Middle Ages, and the very wealthy, like Richard Beauchamp, built special chantry chapels and endowed priests in perpetuity to say masses for their souls. Lord Beauchamp actually arranged for three priests to sing soul masses thrice daily for ever.

The incomparable tomb of Richard Beauchamp, Earl of Warwick.

Richard Beauchamp gazes in wonder at the image of God in the east window of the chapel.

When we enter the Beauchamp Chapel we notice how the founder's tomb, set directly before the altar, still dominates the scene. It took over a decade to complete the arrangements before Lord Beauchamp could be laid to rest here. The Purbeck marble tomb base was made by John Bourde of Corfe, the brass effigy was cast by William Austen of London, the fine carving was done by John Massingham, and the whole was polished and gilded by Bartholmew Lambespring, a Dutch goldsmith. There were other contracts too, some of which survive, and these were in addition to the building of the chapel itself. The resulting work is of great beauty, and the finely featured face is clearly modelled from life; but whose face is it? It has been suggested that because the contract with Austen mentions only 'an image of a man armed', it was not intended as a portrait. Yet in that same contract also appears Roger Webb, Warden of the Barber Surgeon's Company. If there was a death mask from which the face on the effigy was made, Webb would surely be the sort of man to have made it.

Whatever the details, the monument is remarkable. The representation of the probably Milanese full plate armour of the effigy is faithful in every detail, and was probably made in Milan. His head rests on a helm and crest, and at his feet are a muzzled bear and a griffin. Over the effigy is a gilded metal hearse with enamelled stops to carry a rich pall on special occasions. Round the sides of the tomb are copper gilt figures of the 'weepers', as the members of the family were called in the original contract, with angels between. One of the weepers, the easternmost of the south side, is identifiable as Warwick 'the Kingmaker' from his arms beneath.

Finally, the Earl holds his hands slightly apart, as if in wonder, and gazes fixedly upwards. He is enraptured by the sight of the gilded image of God over the east window, surrounded in paint and glowing glass by the Whole Company of Heaven.

80
LOWER BROCKHAMPTON, Hereford and Worcester

A timber-framed house

The early-fifteenth-century moated house at Lower Brockhampton is one of the most picturesque sites in this book. It is set in a remote wooded valley and now has only a farmyard for company; there was originally a small village, as the ruined Norman chapel indicates. The house is a good example of the sort of small and lightly defended moated site discussed in the entry for Aston Clinton. The contemporary gatehouse is a rare survival and, like the house itself, is timber-framed. The angle posts have moulded capitals from which braces support the jettied upper floor.

As originally built, the house had an H-plan, with the surviving hall block linking two gabled cross wings at either end, the right-hand one of which is preserved. The house is entered through the original studded door to the screens passage at the lower end of the hall and retains its spere truss. Inside, the two-bay hall is still open to the roof in the medieval style, and its side walls are made of large square panels with closely set vertical posts. The roof truss has a cambered collar with curved arched braces and the studs have quatrefoils, though the scalloped windbraces are probably nineteenth-century. This is a remarkably well-preserved example of a small-scale open ground-floor hall, and must stand as a reminder of many a vanished house elsewhere.

Map Reference SO 688560, Map 149
Nearest Town Bromyard
From Bromyard take the A44 Worcester road. After 2 miles (1.2 km) take the narrow turning north beside a gate lodge, signed to Lower Brockhampton. After a delightful 1½ miles through woods and farmland, the house can be seen at the bottom of the valley complete with moat and gatehouse. Owned by the National Trust, the Hall is open Easter Sat–end Oct, Wed–Sat 10–1 and 2–6, and Sun 10–1. (*Note.* Do not confuse with the other Brockhampton in this county, which is 4 miles south-east of Hereford.)

Quintessential England; the fifteenth-century manor and gatehouse at Lower Brockhampton.

81

WEOBLEY AND PEMBRIDGE, Hereford and Worcester

Map Reference Weobley SO 402516,
Map 149
Nearest Town Leominster
Weobley is 9 miles (5.4 km)
south-west of Leominster, on the
south side of the A4112 towards
Brecon.

Map Reference Pembridge SO
390580, Map 149
Nearest Town Leominster
Pembridge is 8 miles (4.8 km) west
of Leominster on the A44 in the
direction of Rhayader.

Wood was the commonest building material of medieval England, and the Welsh border counties had copious quantities of it. Oaks grew here in profusion, and so it comes as no surprise to discover that timber-framing and cruck construction were used for all save the most important buildings. At Weobley, we see a small town which retains a considerable number of early houses and a general medieval scale. Pembridge, on the other hand, shows us an important individual building, the impressive timber-framed bell tower, which reminds us that even high-status buildings like churches could be partly or wholly built of wood.

There was a Saxon settlement at Weobley, and after the Conquest the de Lacys of Ludlow built a castle at the south end of the village and laid out a borough with an irregular street plan. The original castle was of earth and timber construction, but stone defences were probably added during the thirteenth century. The church has some Norman work, notably the reset south doorway, but the principal building period appears to have been the late thirteenth and early fourteenth centuries. The timbered houses, by contrast, belong to the later fourteenth and fifteenth centuries, when the town appears to have prospered, probably on account of its sheepwalks.

Broad Street has a whole series of timber-framed houses, and at the north end, near the church, is the Red Lion Hotel, originally a fourteenth-

A view of Weobly showing a cruck-built structure on the right with a jettied fourteenth-century house beyond, which is now the Red Lion Hotel.

century house with a jettied upper floor, large square framed panels, and two early windows with trefoiled ogee headed lights and cusped spandrels in the front wall. Behind the inn, an outbuilding preserves two cruck trusses and large square panels in the side walls. On the opposite corner is another fourteenth-century house, now a gallery and teashop, which has a hall block that was divided into two storeys during the seventeenth century; here can be seen arch braces to the principal members and square framed panels. Further down Broad Street on the opposite side can be seen a house with a central hall block and cross wings at either end, and on the corner of High Street is a rectangular block of the fifteenth century. Round the village, many further examples of early houses can be seen in a more or less intact condition; steep roofs, originally made for thatch, and irregular walls containing frames are a common sight, and we are fortunate indeed that Weobley has survived so well.

Pembridge is another timber-framed village and good examples of early houses, notably in East and West Streets, can be seen here. It is the fourteenth-century bell tower which interested us, however, since it is a fine example of a major timber structure which has retained its original function. Before looking at it in more detail, it is worth pointing out that the church beside which it stands is contemporary, and has excellent

The fourteenth-century timber-framed bell tower at Pembridge with the contemporary stone-built chancel on the right.

stonework with good reticulated tracery and fine carved details. Why should the bell tower have been made of wood when plenty of money was apparently available for a stone church?

The fourteenth-century timber-framed belfry is octagonal on plan and has three diminishing stages with hipped and pyramidal roofs covered with stone slates and wooden shingles. The ground stage is of stone, and the entrance is in the south-west angle. The massive pegged inner framing is supported on four major angle posts linked by cross framing which appears not to be original, since there is evidence for diagonal braces which have since been removed. There is a walkway round the inside of the belfry, which still contains the bells and clock.

82
CATHERTON COMMON COAL-MINES, Shropshire

*Map Reference SO 620780, Map 138
Nearest Town Cleobury Mortimer*
Catherton Common is 3 miles (1.8 km) north-east of Cleobury Mortimer, south of the village of Farlow. From Cleobury take the A4117 west towards Ludlow. Beyond Hopton Wafers take the northern turning towards Farlow. The mining site can be seen either side of the road in about 1 mile (0.6 km).

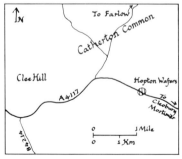

Coal was a recognized source of energy in medieval times, but problems of bulk transportation must always have made it an expensive commodity. It

The physical evidence of life on the margins of Medieval England; between the 'islands' of fields are the rounded tips of spoil resulting from ad hoc coalmining. (Photo courtesy Cambridge University Collection of Air Photographs.)

was largely the prerogative of higher-status sites like the Edwardian castles of north Wales which are known to have received coal supplies by sea. Excavation of industrial sites has produced evidence of coal-burning at pottery and tile kilns, as well as at the iron-working sites of the Weald. Coal has been found on some inland village sites, so it was obviously traded quite widely, although it was perhaps used only for specialized purposes. Coal production was an important industry by the fourteenth century in the Tyne Valley, and sea coal was gleaned from early times, but elsewhere the winning of coal appears to have been a more haphazard process.

Here at Catherton Common, we see the physical evidence of just such *ad hoc* activity. It is important in this context that Catherton is a common, for it meant that it lay on the fringes of settlement beyond the ambit of strict feudal regulation. The people who lived here were squatters, finding a living as best they could by clearing small irregular fields from the furze-grown common and grazing their stock on the thin upland pastures. But between these 'islands' of clearance they quarried the shallow coal seams with small pits, leaving behind rounded heaps of upcast having small depressions at the centre, marking the tops of the shafts. When we visit Catherton Common we see evidence of the dwellers on the 'bottom rung' of medieval society, eking out their living as best they could.

83
STOKESAY CASTLE AND ACTON BURNELL, Shropshire

Two fortified houses
These two sites, which are almost exactly contemporary, belong to the last twenty years of the thirteenth century. They were built during the reign of Edward I, and we must imagine that it was his Welsh conquests which permitted two such lightly defended great houses to be built here in the Marches. Stokesay is a fortified manor and Acton Burnell a tower house, the differences in their planning and architecture being largely explained by the very different ranks of their owners. Bishop Burnell, who also built the splendid Great Hall at the Bishop's Palace at Wells, was Chancellor of the Realm, whereas the builder of Stokesay was but a provincial merchant, with a household to match.

Stokesay is one of the most delightful sites in this book, and affords a fascinating glimpse of late-thirteenth-century life in England. The manor was bought in about 1280 by Lawrence of Ludlow, a great wool merchant. He demolished most of the existing buildings, leaving only the lower two storeys of the north tower, and built the present Great Hall and solar block. In 1291, he obtained a licence to crenellate the house and added

Map Reference Stokesay SO 437816, Map 137
Nearest Town Ludlow
7 miles (4.2 km) north of Ludlow on the west side of the A49. Recently acquired by HBMCE, it is now in guardianship and open daily (except Tues), 4 Mar–31 Oct 10–6 (10–5 Mar and Oct).

Map Reference Acton Burnell SJ 534019, Map 126
Nearest Town Shrewsbury
On minor road 8 miles (4.8 km) south of Shrewsbury. Take the A458 towards Bridgnorth. After 5 miles (3 km) turn south towards Pitchford and then Acton Burnell. The castle is in HBMCE guardianship and open at any reasonable time.

the irregular polygonal tower in the south-west corner. The house therefore comprised a Great Hall and solar of the normal pattern, with a kitchen and services at the lower end in the base of the earlier tower, augmented by a tower of refuge to the south, a curtain wall and a moat.

The principal element of the site is, of course, the Great Hall, and it is here that the triumph of comfort over defence is immediately apparent in the large windows on the external wall. There are three of them, having two lights with transoms, cusped heads and circles over. Interestingly it appears that the hall, which is now open, may originally have been aisled.

Stokesay Castle: the Great Hall is at the centre and the tower of refuge to the right.

At the south end, twin arch braced vertical posts may fossilize the lines of the earlier arcades, but this was apparently superseded in the fifteenth century when the principal timbers of the present roof were built. The solar and southern tower were remodelled in the seventeenth century, but preserve a feeling of homeliness absent at many sites.

Acton Burnell, by contrast, has little of the 'home' about it, nor was it ever likely to have had. It was the mansion of a great magnate and provided accommodation for himself, his immediate family, and probably his Constable, who may have lived on the ground floor. The main block is rectangular, of two storeys, with towers at the corners. It would have been the central element in an enclosure containing barns, retainers' lodgings and other offices. We again encounter large windows, and there are even some on the ground floor here; we would be most accurate in thinking of this place as a country house. On the first floor was the Great Hall, open to

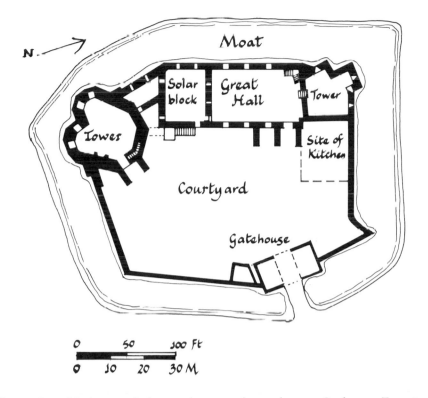

N.

Moat

Solar block

Great Hall

Tower

Tower

Site of Kitchen

Courtyard

Gatehouse

0   50   100 Ft

0   10   20   30 M

Stokesay has a compact plan within its encircling moat, but it was always more of a fortified manor house than a castle.

the roof, and lit by two-light windows similar to those at Stokesay. Even in its ruined state, the hall block is highly impressive, its square plan and battlements ironically making it look just like a castle in a child's picture book!

EASTERN
ENGLAND

100
Louth

Lincoln
♦ 101
LINCOLNSHIRE
♦ 99
98 ♦

♦ 102

♦ 96

King's Lynn ♦ ~ 95

THE   Spalding

Norwich

MIDLANDS   ♦ 103   NORFOLK   94 ♦

CAMBRIDGE-
SHIRE
· Huntingdon   93 ♦

92
90 ♦
♦   91

SUFFOLK   ♦ 89

Bedford   Cambridge
BEDFORD-   88 ♦   Ipswich
SHIRE
♦ 86
87 ♦ ♦   84 ♦
♦ 104
♦ 85
Chelmsford
HERTFORD-
SHIRE
ESSEX   0   10   20   30 Miles

0   10 20 30 40 50 Km

EASTERN ENGLAND

Introduction

To visit the east of England in search of medieval monuments is to understand more fully the impact of the New World on our island's history. Before the Voyages of Discovery, trade was directed towards the Continent, the Baltic and more remotely to the Mediterranean. The east coast was ideally placed for this trade, and it waxed fat on the proceeds of its Continental contacts. Within a century or so the pattern had begun to change and counties like Essex and Lincolnshire, which had been vastly wealthy in the early Middle Ages, fell into an obscurity from which EEC membership and greater European trade have only recently begun to rescue them.

That early prominence has left a dazzling series of monuments, however, beginning with the two seaports of Boston and King's Lynn which between them dominated early medieval trade. At Boston is the great church called the 'Stump', the outward and visible sign of the town's early importance; at Lynn two churches and a fine guildhall tell the same tale. Further south, along the Suffolk coast, we encounter a moving legacy of failed ambition. At Walberswick, Dunwich, Blythburgh and many lesser settlements, outsize churches and bumps in the ground indicates that these places prospered before their late medieval decline.

The landscape of the east has for long been distinguished by its broad corn-growing acres, rich pasture and fenny coastline. This was broadly correct for the Middle Ages, but then as now the landscape was put to a wide variety of uses. In Lincolnshire, for example, salt was won from the estuarine mud at places like the aptly named Saltfleet, where the resulting mounds of spoil can still be seen. Near the Norfolk coast, the winning of peat by dint of almost unimaginable labours resulted in the creation of the Broads. On the thin sandy soils of the Breckland near Thetford, rabbits were bred in numbers which necessitated their protection by a warrener who lived in a defended house which yet stands. Essex has always been celebrated for its woodlands, and it is there at Hatfield Forest that we can understand something of the character of a medieval wood. When we walk its rides and see trees still managed according to medieval practice, we gain a precious insight into an important and renewable resource of medieval England.

Secular buildings are well represented in the region, with some individual structures standing out as being especially important. The splendid timber-framed tithe barn at Widdington was built under the aegis of William Wykeham, Bishop of Winchester, as part of his foundation of New College, Oxford. It is a strange history indeed which links this honest barn with the sophistication of an Oxford college, but then even scholars have to eat! Two domestic towers claim our attention. Ralph, Lord Cromwell, built the extraordinary brick edifice at Tattershall, probably in imitation of Lowlandish rather than French tastes, while at Longthorpe we see an earlier tower containing a stunning collection of contemporary wall paintings. These pictures provide a rapid refresher course on the sources of medieval synthesis and logic, for here are biblical elements, images from the Bestiary and other works of fantasy, moralizing themes and straightforward representational works which were probably intended to do no more than amuse the owner!

The towns and villages of the east are often a source of great delight. Saffron Walden with its lavish parish church and the incomparable Sun Inn, a monument to fifteenth-century domesticity, and nearby Thaxted with its enigmatic Guildhall come immediately to mind. Both towns are stuffed with early timber-framed buildings, a characteristic shared by Clare and Long Melford in Suffolk as well as lesser places like Wingfield. Of the stone towns, Lincoln must surely hold the palm; the great city sprawls down its hill crowned by the majestic Cathedral, the greatest wonder of medieval England and the imperishable memorial of Lincoln's own St Hugh. Grantham is less well known, but the soaring spire of its parish church and the dignified façade of the Angel Hotel mark it out as a seat of the medieval muse.

It will be for the wealth and diversity of its churches that the east of England will for ever stay in the memory of the visitor. They range from such miniature masterpieces as Gipping Chapel with its huge and tranquil windows to the greater marvels of Blythburgh and the fenland magnificence of Norfolk and Lincolnshire. A lifetime would be too short to understand this great Christian heritage of stone, wood, plaster and glass. Trunch and Salle in Norfolk stand out as much for their overall conception as for their details, but there are others too, the 'best' of which we have listed. Little Maplestead has been restored almost to a point at which the innate mystery of its associations with the Knights Hospitaller has been lost, yet something waits there still. Here as elsewhere in the eastern counties we are in the presence of a great and memorable past of which the monuments we catalogue here are but the shattered remnants.

84
LITTLE MAPLESTEAD, Essex

A round church

The Order of the Knights of the Hospital of St John of Jerusalem, otherwise known as the Knights Hospitaller, was founded after the capture of the Holy City by the Crusaders in 1099. The Knights took monastic vows which were generally strictly observed, and wore black habits blazoned with a white cross. Like the Templars they proved very popular, and attracted many endowments of land. In England the order had about fifty estates called 'commanderies' which were ruled by the headquarters at St John's Priory, Clerkenwell, London. The revenues produced went to finance the fight with the infidel, and to provide hospitality for pilgrims visiting the holy places. Here at Maplestead, we see one of the distinctive round churches which the Order built in conscious imitation of the Church of the Holy Sepulchre at Jerusalem.

This church would have been but one element of a group of buildings on the site, most of which would have been geared to the administration of the estate. The estate was run by brothers or 'confratres' and had a staff of chaplains, squires, chamberlains, foresters and servants in addition to farm labourers. Each house had to provide hospitality for the poor and, in this as in their vows of poverty, chastity and obedience, the Knights remained true to their high ideals. The commanderies supplied fish and flesh as well as the three types of bread and two classes of beer which were commonly produced. Cereals were therefore important, but sheep provided the main economic basis here as elsewhere.

Map Reference TL 822339, Map 168
Nearest Town Halstead
From Halstead take the A131 north towards Sudbury and after 1 mile (1.6 km) take the turning north-west to Little Maplestead. The church is well set with a large oak tree in the churchyard on the western edge of the village.

The nave of the Hospitaller church at Little Maplestead.

While it must be admitted that Maplestead church was somewhat savagely restored during the nineteenth century, it retains many features of interest. The fourteenth-century circular nave has a complete set of trefoil piers supporting simply moulded arches, and gives a good impression of the original space; the deep fillets to the piers lend a decidedly foreign appearance. The chancel was apparently reserved for use by the Knights during the Middle Ages, and hence the nave alone remained in parochial use after the Reformation. There was originally a screen between them against which the Knights sat, and the effect must have been rather like the pulpitum of a monastic church. The west doorway is, like the nave piers, rather unusual and while the details might have been recut during the restoration, enough remains to show that this church looked well beyond England for its inspiration.

85
HATFIELD FOREST, Essex

Map Reference TL 534200, Map 167
Nearest Town Bishop's Stortford
Take the A120 (the Stane Street Roman road) east in the direction of Braintree. The forest is signposted south down a minor road some 3½ miles (5.6 km) east of Bishop's Stortford. The National Trust owns and manages 1,000 acres of Hatfield Forest. There is an admission fee for cars and an exhibition at Shell House by the lake. Note the large log store on the corner with the A road selling off the coppiced wood.

A medieval greenwood

Something of the origins of royal forests was explained in our *Norman Guide*, and Hatfield Forest was until 1446 part of the Royal Forest of Essex, an area subject to the Forest Laws. The legal designation of an area as a 'forest' did not necessarily imply that it was covered with trees. As with our national parks, the name refers to an area in which certain legal restrictions pertain rather than to its land use. Similarly, forests were not exclusively devoted to hunting deer and sport; they were economic entities which provided revenue in the form of fines, meat from deer, rabbits and other creatures, grazing for cattle, as well as a variety of wood and timber which could be used for many purposes depending upon its age and quality. Hatfield, however, was both a legal and a physical forest and it is of peculiar importance today as the best surviving example of a medieval forest in Britain.

Hatfield demonstrates the complexity of medieval forest management, in which all the competing requirements for food and raw materials were held in balance. It still supports deer, for example, which were originally managed and culled as carefully as any domestic herd. Cattle graze its rides and plains at certain times of the year in keeping with the natural cycle of regeneration and growth. Rabbits are no longer kept in its warren, and the ancient customs of the forest, such as the annual right of the local blacksmith to the second best oak, recorded in 1328, have lapsed. But the physical appearance of the place is very much as it would have been during the Middle Ages.

One of the pollarded trees at Hatfield; this was done to prevent animals eating the tender young shoots after the poles had been harvested.

When we visit the forest today, we do not see a tangled mass of trees but a generally dispersed pattern with some larger individual trees called 'maidens' and denser stands with distinctive patterns of growth. Two basic techniques of tree management were used, coppicing and pollarding. They produced the large quantities of poles and small wood which were needed for fencing, hurdles, charcoal-burning, lightweight constructions and, of course, for fuel. Coppicing involved the cutting of a tree at a level just above the roots and the stump thus left was allowed to grow a crop of poles. The poles grew rapidly and were carefully harvested at intervals of between five and ten years, depending upon the scantling of the timber required. The stump or 'stool' then produced another growth of poles, and so the process went on, often for centuries, and it is thought that one ash stool in Suffolk may be a thousand years old.

This technique worked well enough in 'compartments' of the forest which were fenced against deer and other grazing animals, but in the pastures and plains at Hatfield pollarding had to be used to prevent the animals eating the tender young shoots. Instead of cutting the tree at ground level it was cut between eight and twelve feet above the ground. The tree again produced a crop of poles, but they were above the height at which an animal could eat them. Both techniques appear at Hatfield, and it is easy to distinguish between the ground-level 'hands' of the coppice and the 'hands and arms' of the pollarded trees. At Hatfield, coppicing has always been carried on, and recently some of the old pollards have been cut as well.

To walk in Hatfield Broadoak Forest is to step back into the landscape of medieval England. Yet it is not a 'wild' landscape, it is kept and managed by the hand of man according to uses which were already ancient by the Middle Ages. It is thought that the earliest evidence for coppicing is found in the Neolithic period, 5,000 years ago, when thousands of poles were used for the recently excavated trackways across the Somerset Levels. It is only in later times that man has been so prodigal of natural resources as to finally clear large areas of woodland which had previously kept entire communities in firewood, constructional timber and a bewildering variety of other uses from rakes to barrels.

86
THAXTED AND SAFFRON WALDEN, Essex

Map Reference Thaxted: TL 610310, Map 167
Nearest Town Saffron Walden
From Saffron Walden take the B184 in a south-easterly direction for 7½ miles (12 km).

Map Reference Saffron Walden: TL 537386, Map 167
The Sun Inn is owned by the National Trust and is privately run as an antique and book shop. It stands on the corner of Market Hill and Church Street. Other good late medieval timber-framed buildings can be seen in Bridge End Street.

Essex is exceptionally rich in medieval timber-framed buildings, and has some delightful small towns which retain much of their early scale. Thaxted and Saffron Waldon achieved prominence late in the Middle Ages basically because of their association with the cloth trade, but in the case of Thaxted, cutlery was also an important early industry. Apart from its splendid church, Thaxted retains another important physical legacy of its medieval past, the Guildhall. This elegant timber-framed building stands at one end of the market-place, and has given rise to much speculation. Opinions as to its date and function are widely divided, with some maintaining that it was built in about 1400 as a guildhall while others argue that it is in fact a sixteenth-century market hall. It is sobering to realize that in the present state of the study of timber-framed buildings a century can separate expert opinions, and at present there is no certain way of distinguishing between them. It is to be hoped that the development of tree-ring dating will assist these deliberations in the future!

At the Old Sun Inn in Saffron Walden, we are on somewhat surer ground, since it retains a decorated doorway and a pierced traceried light to the service wing which can be dated with some confidence to the mid fourteenth century. This is an impressive timber-framed building, now a bookshop, which was built to an H-plan with a central hall flanked by jettied cross wings. The hall was entered via a screens passage at the lower end through the finely carved doorway near the centre of the building. It has finely carved kingpost roof trusses in all three units, and great curved braces support the tie beams. The exterior is now covered by decorative plasterwork partly dated to 1676, although the priest's house at Clare reminds us that similar decoration was also used in the fifteenth century.

As might be expected from their busy late medieval histories, both these towns have fine Perpendicular churches. St Mary's at Saffron Walden is one of the largest in Essex and one of the most lavish, having tall nave arcades enriched with cusped quatrefoils in the spandrels. Above are continuous clerestorey lights of the most generous proportion and the roof with its angel supporters is original. The feeling of light and space is continued at Thaxted, largely due to the loss of its original glass. The iconoclasts dealt severely with the interior of this church, and apart from the font and its elaborate cover it is very much as it must have appeared after the excesses of the seventeenth century.

The Old Sun Inn, Saffron Walden. The basic structure is of the fourteenth century, but most of the external plasterwork was done later.

87
WIDDINGTON, Essex

Map Reference TL 538319, Map 167
Nearest Town Saffron Walden
Take the B1383 south to Newport.
Widdington lies 2 miles (3.2 km)
south-east of Newport on minor
roads. The barn is well signposted
and stands in a farmyard beside a
length of former moat. It is in
HBMCE guardianship, open
summer season only, standard
hours.

Prior's Hall Barn

The farm now called Prior's Hall is west of the church, and was granted in
the twelfth century to the priory of St Valery in Picardy. Inside the
farmhouse is thirteenth-century stonework which probably belonged to a
grange farm on the site. During the French Wars of Edward III's reign the
position of the 'alien' priories, which were French houses having lands in
England, became invidious. Many looked to prominent laymen and
ecclesiastics for protection from national xenophobia. In the nature of
things, the protectors often saw an opportunity to buy up the monastic
estates which they guaranteed, and this is what happened at Widdington.
In 1379 William of Wykeham established his colleges at Winchester and
Oxford and Widdington formed part of the original endowment of New
College, Oxford.

As is discussed under the entry for the tithe barn at Great Coxwell, it
was important for new foundations to make provision for the efficient
raising of revenue from estates in order to finance their building programmes. Barns, with their capacity to collect and store the produce from
estates, were an important part of that process, and so it is thought likely
that the fine timber-framed barn at Widdington was built soon after 1379.
The building is thus an important late-fourteenth-century example of
English carpentry, and in the quality of its design and execution it well
illustrates this aspect of the medieval structural achievement.

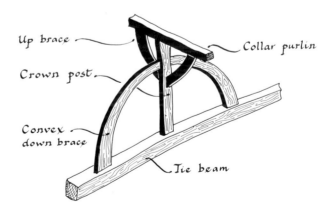

*Crown-post roof truss of the type used
in the Widdington barn.*

The barn is now weatherboarded, as it would always have been, and the
flint plinths to the ground walls and plain tiled roof probably also follow
the original pattern. There are gabled entry bays at either end, and the
barn itself is ten bays long. The roof is of crown post construction and is

supported on free-standing aisle posts which have jowled tops and curved braces. The details of the construction are ingenious and repay careful examination. The use of 'knees' to strengthen the ties of the aisle roofs is an early example of the technique, and the whole structure bespeaks the highest standards of craftsmanship, as we might expect from such a distinguished patron as the Bishop of Winchester.

88
CLARE AND LONG MELFORD, Suffolk

Clare is still dominated by the strong motte and bailey castle built at the southern end of the town by Richard de Clare, friend of the Conqueror and founder of the great dynasty of that name. The top of the motte affords an excellent prospect of the little town and beside it are the remains of the friary founded in 1248 by Gilbert de Clare and which again supports a community of the Augustinian Friars. In the opposite direction is the market-place with the parish church standing at the north end. The castle controlled the bridge over the River Stour, a town grew up beside it, and the patronage of the de Clares attracted monasteries to the new town – first a Benedictine house which moved to nearby Stoke-by-Clare, and then the friars. Later still, in the fourteenth and fifteenth centuries, the cloth trade brought further prosperity to Clare as it did to nearby Long Melford.

Apart from the castle, the priory retains early-fourteenth-century work including the former infirmary range which is now the church, and parts of the Prior's lodging which were converted into a house after the Reformation. The parish church is largely a product of late-fifteenth-century remodelling, but the Decorated nave piers indicate the quality of the earlier building. In the churchyard is the 'Ancient House', a rare survival of a priest's house and obligingly dated 1473. The walls are encrusted with decorative plaster pargetting and it serves to remind us of the delights of Suffolk's rich heritage of timber-framed medieval houses.

Long Melford, by contrast with Clare, came to prominence only in late medieval times, and it was then a haunt of cloth merchants rather than ancient titles. But the relatively sudden prominence of the place has left a rich legacy of timber-framed domestic buildings of the late fifteenth and early sixteenth centuries. Pride of place here must go to the church, an immense and exuberant essay in the Perpendicular style with many refinements brought about by the wealth and piety of its mercantile benefactors. The entire fabric was rebuilt between 1460 and 1495 and, although the west tower is actually a twentieth-century addition, it is a most felicitous work.

Map Reference Clare: TL 769455, Map 155
Nearest Town Haverhill
Take the A1092 east for 8 miles (12.8 km). The castle is a country park and is accessible, affording good views of the town. The priory has been used by the Austin friars since 1953, and is open to visitors. The Priest's House can be seen by the churchyard.

Map Reference Long Melford: TL 865467, Map 155
Nearest Town Sudbury
3 miles (4.8 km) north of Sudbury on the A134. The church stands slightly above the town in a magnificent setting against a wide green. The small town has fine late and post-medieval timber-framed houses along the main street.

Inside the church there is a banquet of fine arches, roofs, stained glass, screens, brasses and paintings sufficient for the most ardent gourmand. It is, however, with the Clopton family that the church will be forever associated, and their resplendent chantry chapel can still be seen. It was John Clopton who financed the construction of the unique Lady Chapel late in the fifteenth century. This remarkable structure is a separate church in itself, complete with ambulatory, and was perhaps used for guild services.

Detail of one of the plaster panels on the priest's house, which is dated 1473.

Inside John Clopton's Lady Chapel at Long Melford. Notice the rich blank arcading and the canopied niches, which would originally have contained statues.

89
GIPPING, Suffolk

A private chapel

The chapel was built in 1474–80 as an adjunct to Sir James Tyrell's mansion which stood to the east. It is a fine example of Suffolk flint flushwork and is embellished with motifs, initials and emblems relating to the family. The late Perpendicular windows make the chapel interior very light, but rather strange is the relationship of the windows above the side doors, which might be an afterthought. Similarly, the reveals of a blocked western opening suggest some replanning during or shortly after construction. The north chapel is a small square room open to the roof and unusually provided with a fireplace. It is improbable as either a chapel or a priest's dwelling, the first because it has no eastward projection and the second because it is so comfortless. Perhaps it was simply the family pew.

The original tie beam nave roof survives with cable moulded wall plates and principal beams. At the west end is a collection of contemporary bench ends, one with a poppyhead and another bearing the ubiquitous Tyrell knot. The east end of the chancel is a spectacle in itself with fifteenth-century glass depicting the donor and his wife, all in ogee canopies and now bizarrely flanked by painted eighteenth-century *trompe-l'oeil* columns. This chapel is a splendid example of the sort of private establishment common in medieval England. It never received rights of burial which were lucrative and retained by the parish church, but served solely to fulfil the daily spiritual requirements of a great lord and his household. Gipping is more than this, however; it is a small jewel of a building upon which Sir James Tyrell lavished much love and perfection.

Map Reference TM 072636, Map 155
Nearest Town Stowmarket
From Stowmarket take the B1113 north towards Diss. Gipping is signposted off to the east after 2 miles (3.2 km). The church is set at the end of a small lane, signposted 'Gipping Church ¼ mile' (0.4 km). It stands in a tree-lined churchyard overlooking fields with opposite a fine vernacular farmhouse.

The Tyrell knot on one of the bench ends.

Doorway into the North Chapel at Gipping inscribed, 'Pray for Sir Jamys Tirell· Dame Anne his wyf'.

90
THORNHAM PARVA RETABLE, Suffolk

Map Reference TM 109727,
Map 155
Nearest Town Diss
From Diss take the Ipswich road for
8 miles (12.8 km). Thornham Parva
is on the west side of the A140 and
the church stands on its own in the
small village with sparsely set
vernacular houses. Because of the
fine retable the church is normally
locked; enquire at the village shop
for the key.

The little church of St Mary at Thornham is a delight in itself. It is
thatched, contains some good Norman work and its walls are enlivened by
thirteenth-century wall paintings depicting the life of St Edmund, King
and Martyr. This is a feast enough, but the church is also possessed of a
stunning object which, although out of place here, calls eloquently to
mind the vanished glories of our medieval church interiors. Behind the
altar is the celebrated 'retable', still performing its original function of
closing the rear of the sanctuary. The panel glows with gold and rich
colours, a masterwork of medieval art, kept here in this tiny church to the
glory of God and to the delight of congregation and visitor alike.

*The sumptuous retable with St Peter
with his sword and Edmund, King and
Martyr, with his arrow to the right of
the Crucifixus.*

This is a painting of the highest quality, and bears comparison with
contemporary royal work at Westminster Abbey. The design is based on a
central Crucifixus flanked by St Mary and St John with, to either side, four
saints contained in niches. The saints to the left are Dominic, Catherine,
John the Baptist and Paul, while on the right are Peter, Edmund, Margaret
and Peter the Martyr. The cusped niches containing the figures stand on
round columns and in the spandrels between are roses and oak leaves in
low relief. The fields behind the figures are similarly textured and divided
into chequers bearing fleur-de-lis, lions rampant, paired birds and other
motifs.

The origins of this panel are not certainly known. It was discovered in
the house of a local Roman Catholic family as recently as 1927 and

donated to the church. The appearance of St Edmund suggests an East Anglian origin, and the presence of two Dominican saints, Dominic himself and St Peter the Martyr, who died in 1252, suggests that it might have been commissioned by a church belonging to that Order. The friary at Thetford has been suggested as the probable church, and this may be true; we will almost certainly never know. We can only be thankful that this transcendant object was preserved from the terrible destruction which overcame so many others.

91
BLYTHBURGH AND THE COAST, Suffolk

This part of the Suffolk coast saw many changes during the Middle Ages, and perhaps its most famous monument is the deserted town of Dunwich. Dunwich had flourished mightily during the early Middle Ages, but in the fourteenth century the River Blyth cut a new channel to the sea and the harbour began to silt up. The town's trade was diverted to Walberswick, Blythburgh and other lesser ports like Covehithe which thus enjoyed considerable prosperity during the fifteenth century. What is left now is a landscape of failed and deserted settlements, often possessed of great late medieval churches which, either intact or in ruins, witness this strange tale.

Covehithe has a spectacular ruined church, but nothing can compare with the ruined majesty of St Andrew's, Walberswick. This building was a product of the town's substantial seaborne trade in fish, salt, coal, corn and timber. In 1451 there were thirty-two fishing boats belonging to the port, and thirteen ships traded to Iceland and the Baltic. The ruined church was dedicated in 1493, just twenty years after an earlier church near the marshes had been demolished. During the sixteenth century the town's decline began and this great building with its flushwork decoration, finely traceried windows and above all its great size fell into decay. Walberswick and its church joined the ranks of failed settlements along the unforgiving Suffolk coastlands.

A similar tale can be told of the decayed town of Blythburgh, for here too the fifteenth-century boom was unsustained. Time has dealt more kindly with the mighty church of the Holy Trinity, however, and it is both an architectural masterpiece and, on its commanding site above the marshes, one of the most moving sights of late medieval England. Outside there is flint flushwork in profusion, including the delightful and recently restored dedicatory inscription on the east wall. Beneath the scintillating clerestorey is a pierced parapet crowned with regal beasts, and below are

Map Reference Blythburgh: TM 450753, Map 156
Nearest Town Southwold
On the A12 (T) Lowestoft to Ipswich road, 5 miles (8 km) west of Southwold. The church is on a prominent mound looking across the marshes and to the coast beyond.

Map Reference Walberswick: TM 490747, Map 156
Nearest Town Southwold
On the south side of the Blyth estuary from Southwold. Take the B1387 east off the A12 for 4 miles (6.4 km). The church stands some way from the older part of the village which has a large green close by the river with fishing boats along wharves.

Map Reference Covehithe: TM 523819, Map 156
Nearest Town Southwold
5 miles (8 km) north of Southwold, east off the B1127

Map Reference Dunwich: TM475706, Map 156
Nearest Town Southwold
From Blythburgh take the B1125 south; Dunwich is reached by minor roads to the east.

The mighty church of Blythburgh from the south showing the large windows, pierced aisle parapets and massed clerestorey windows.

'*Sloth*', *depicted as one of the Seven Deadly Sins on the Blythburgh bench ends.*

the great aisle windows. Inside, all is Perpendicular light and warmth and, although lacking much of its medieval splendour, it is enlivened by the silver grey of the carved oak bench ends and the beautiful tie beam roofs which escaped the depredations of the Puritans. It is a vast and satisfying structure; a dawn visit in summer prompted us to these well-intentioned lines:

Early Morning at Blythburgh

Quietly standing by the river
When the bird sung morning
  comes
Feel the reed beds gently quiver
As the sun soft sea breeze runs.

High above the mist bound marshes
The mighty church of Blythburgh
  stands
Where its finely finished arches
Gaze across rich Suffolk lands.

Watcher of a thousand dawnings,
Come ye thankful people come,
Easily blessing countless mornings;
Symbol of the great work done.

92
WINGFIELD CHURCH, CASTLE AND COLLEGE, Suffolk

Wingfield is an obscure enough place today, set in the heartland of rural Suffolk, but it was the principal seat of the later medieval Earls and Dukes of Suffolk. In 1360 Katherine, daughter of Sir John de Wingfield, President of the Black Prince's Council, married Michael de la Pole, a wealthy merchant of Hull. Sir John died in 1361, and his executors gave effect to his wish to form a college of chantry priests here at Wingfield. The de la Poles were afterwards elevated to become Earls of Suffolk, and Michael, the 2nd Earl, built the fine castle here after 1384. The fortunes of Wingfield were thus founded on a liaison between an obscure local family with a dynasty of merchant princes, something of whose history is outlined in the entry for Ewelme (Oxfordshire).

The church is Wingfield's premier monument to its medieval prominence. The present building was begun in 1362 when the parish church became collegiate, following the terms of Sir John de Wingfield's bequest. The chancel and chapels were built first, the nave and west tower following soon after. On the north side of the chancel is the handsome founder's tomb bearing Sir John's armoured effigy beneath an ogee arch. But this earlier work was eclipsed by that of the de la Poles. Michael, the 2nd Earl, added the south chapel, built in a most sumptuous style, and his tomb, set under an arch bearing shields and wings for 'Wingfield', features beautiful wooden effigies of himself and his wife. In 1430 William de la Pole, 1st Duke of Suffolk, rebuilt the chancel and provided the fine collegiate stalls and other fittings.

Map Reference College and Church: TM 230769, Map 156
Castle: TM 222772
Nearest Town Diss
7 miles (11.2 km) east of Diss off the B1118. Wingfield College is open from Easter Saturday to 29 Sept on Sat, Sun, and Bank Holidays 2–6. Write for information about the Arts and Music season at the College; a concert in the Great Hall is a memorable experience. Wingfield Castle is currently not open to the public.

The Medieval college at Wingfield still lurks behind Squire Buck's late-eighteenth-century front on the right, whilst the parish church is visible on the left.

Apart from the church, Wingfield can boast a fine castle and, a structure of the greatest rarity, a timber-framed medieval college. The first is obvious enough, with a handsome show front having a central three-storey gatehouse, flint flushwork decoration and brick battlements. The use of brick both here and in the church reminds us of the de la Poles' early interests in the brickyards of medieval Hull. Inside, however, much is changed, and the existing house is of the sixteenth century. The college, by contrast, is much less obvious from the outside, but survives in a remarkably intact condition.

Beside the church stands the handsome Palladian house called 'College Farm'. The front is entirely a confection of the eighteenth century, and its somewhat unusual proportions conceal a major survival of the medieval college buildings. It appears that much of this structure was actually built before the college was founded in 1362, and so was technically built as a house rather than a collegiate building *per se*. But the timber-framed Great Hall remains, and a corridor beside it probably represents one range of a projected cloister. It is pleasing to relate that the college is now retained in sympathetic use after a lapse of nearly 400 years. Concerts take place in the hall where the chantry priests met for the meals which punctuated the perpetual round of masses celebrated at the founder's tomb.

93
THETFORD WARRENER'S LODGE, Norfolk

Map Reference TL 839841, Map 144
Nearest Town Thetford
2 miles west of Thetford on the B1107 to Brandon. The site is not signposted. Go past the golf course and take the first narrow turning left into the Brecklands District Council car-park. Take the track towards the south. The site is located in the open woodland. It is in HBMCE guardianship and open at any reasonable time.

Thetford lies in that part of Norfolk called the 'Breckland', an area of thin sandy soil which, although cultivated at various periods of the past, proved unable to sustain intensive agriculture. This low soil fertility today finds its recognition in Forestry Commission plantations and military training grounds, the classical attributes of 'marginal' lands. In the Middle Ages the priors of Thetford developed similar low-intensity uses for the Breckland, the principal one of which appears to have been the breeding of rabbits. Rabbits, like pigeons, were a useful source of winter protein in medieval times, and their fur could also be used for garments and trimmings. Rabbit bones have been found on monastic sites like Kirkstall near Leeds, as well as at secular sites, and it is clear that rabbit meat was well favoured after the introduction of the species in Norman times.

Artificial rabbit warrens, in the form of low earth mounds sometimes containing stone 'nesting boxes', are known from many parts of England, and examples can be seen as far afield as Dartmoor and Northamptonshire. The Breckland did not, apparently, require such facilities, even if they could have been constructed in its shifting sands, and instead the whole

The Warrener's Lodge at Thetford retains a strong sense of isolation in the midst of the sandy Breckland.

semi-arid landscape became a huge rabbit reserve. Since rabbits were valued as a source of meat the concomitant risk of poaching had to be averted, and to that end small but strongly built tower houses were built in the area. One of these survives near Thetford, and it bears more than a passing similarity to the contemporary fifteenth-century tower houses built in the Borders, although there they defended cattle rather than rabbits.

In this lodge, the Warrener could sleep safe at night and keep watch from the roof, for while the Thetford Lodge is now rather hemmed-in by plantations, it would originally have controlled a broad sweep of country. The lodge represents a step in the bloody progress of the 'poaching wars', which were carried on with the utmost ruthlessness by both sides, and which remained a besmirching feature of English rural life right up to the nineteenth century.

94

THE NORFOLK BROADS AND ST OLAVE'S PRIORY, Norfolk

It is a staggering realization that the 2,500 or so acres of the Norfolk Broads are the result of medieval man's endeavours. They were apparently formed by the large-scale exploitation of peat which was won from shallow diggings, and which kept the chills at bay in many a medieval household. The Romans probably began the removal of the peat, and doubtless some small-scale activity continued during the Saxon period, but it was only with the rise of monastic enterprise during the twelfth century that the trade was effectively organized. Hundreds of thousands of blocks, generally called 'turves', were burnt at the cathedral priory of Norwich alone, and

Map Reference TM 459996, Map 134
Nearest Town Great Yarmouth 5.5 miles (8.8 km) south-west of Great Yarmouth on the A143, the priory, which is in HBMCE guardianship, is open summer season, standard hours. Great Yarmouth preserves a medieval town plan. The town was largely rebuilt after World War II, but its city walls survive. The Broads are the shallow lakes within the triangle of Norwich, Lowestoft and Sea Palling, fed by the Rivers Yare, Bure and Waveney.

A typical Broadland view; it is still difficult to believe that these great sheets of water were created by the hand of Man.

that great and burgeoning city must have consumed much of the output from the Broads workings.

The secret of the industry and the presence of the Broads lies in a difference in sea level between early medieval and modern times. Before the climatic deterioration late in the thirteenth and fourteenth centuries, the sea level was about thirteen feet lower than it is today. This meant that the peat diggers kept their feet dry, and monasteries like the Augustinian house of St Olave and St Mary were able to control this lucrative trade. At a time when woodland resources were already coming under pressure in eastern England, this source of fuel must have been a great boon. Early in the fourteenth century the diggings at South Walsham alone were yielding over 200,000 turves a year and this impressive output was only finally halted by flooding. As early as 1315 water began to collect in the South Walsham cuttings, and by the close of the century inundation was almost complete.

We are therefore left with a maze of flooded cuttings, originally sharply defined, but now cloaked with reeds and mud. The waterways thus formed are a favoured haunt of holidaymakers, and provided that pollution, coypus and other threats can be controlled, they will remain so for many years to come. Yet how many of the carefree boat people reflect on the origins of these waterways? As a tribute to the hard work and organization of medieval man they are as impressive in their way as many a castle and cathedral elsewhere.

95

TRUNCH AND SALLE, Norfolk

Notable churches

Choice between the churches of Norfolk is invidious, but we draw the reader's attention to these two corkers. Trunch is a fine church with octagonal nave piers, a memorable hammerbeam roof and a handsome screen. But its most celebrated feature is the wooden font canopy, a confection from the very end of our period which strangely prefigures eighteenth-century 'Gothick'. The font itself, enriched as it is with flushwork flint panels to the base, is dwarfed beneath this extraordinary free-standing erection which culminates in a corona of niches and a crocketed cupola. The available surfaces are alive with vegetation notable for its luxuriance and vivacity. This is the climax of a great sequence of English font covers which had begun with the strict practicality of measures against witchcraft as early as the thirteenth century. We must be grateful indeed that the attentions of witches were so feared!

The church of St Peter and St Paul at Salle (the name comes from the 'sallow' or willow wood) is a *tour de force* of the Perpendicular style. It is, of course, large and light, and externally the great west tower, dated by the occurrence of the arms of Henry V on the west doorway to 1405–20, is the most dominant feature. The porches both have the finest flint flushwork, a speciality of the place, and East Anglian angels are much in evidence on the west tower and, more familiarly, on the intersections of the nave

Map Reference Trunch: TG 288349, Map 133
Nearest Town North Walsham
From North Walsham take the B1145 north and after 1.5 miles (2.4 km) take the minor roads north to Trunch. The church stands pleasantly in the centre of the village.

Map Reference Salle: TG 110249, Map 133
Nearest Town Aylsham
Salle is on the B1145, 6.5 miles (10.4 km) south-west of Aylsham. The village is just off the road on the north side. It is signposted from the centre of Reepham.

ABOVE: *Some of the luxuriant carving on the font at Trunch.*

LEFT: *The Church of St Peter and St Paul at Salle, a* tour de force *of the Perpendicular style.*

roof. This roof is a triumph of the carpenter's art, with massive moulded purlins and principal rafters, all springing from the lightest stone corbels imaginable.

The details of the structure should not be overtaken by the mass. The chancel roof bosses have delicate Scenes from the Life of Christ, and the splendid Seven Sacraments Font with its pinnacled canopy is among the best in a county famed for these sumptuous creations. In the south transept are six stained-glass figures of the Norwich School and brasses of the fifteenth-century benefactors abound. One monument to John Brigge dated 1454 has an early example of *memento mori* comprising a cadaver in a shroud. The choir stalls continue the high standards of workmanship in their spirited misericords, and are complemented by a fine set of poppy-head benches. Even the pulpit has painted fifteenth-century panels, although the upper parts are later. The whole building is a celebration of God and of the tremendous creative power which worship unlocked in the heart of medieval man.

96

THE SHRINE OF OUR LADY OF WALSINGHAM, Norfolk

Map Reference TF 935363, Map 132
Nearest Town Fakenham
5 miles (8 km) north of Fakenham on the B1105. Walsingham Abbey grounds are open 2–5 on Weds in April, on Weds, Sat and Sun in May–July and Sept, and in Aug they are open on Mons as well. Each weekend from Easter till the end of October pilgrimages are held at the new Shrine. On Spring bank holiday the National Annual Pilgrimage is held, when thousands of pilgrims come from all over Britain.

Early in the twelfth century a lady called Richelde de Faverches, who was devoted to the Cult of the Virgin, had a vision here at Walsingham. The Blessed Virgin Mary appeared to her and showed her the small wooden house in Nazareth in which the Angel Gabriel had foretold the Birth of Christ. Richelde had a further vision, in which she was besought to remember the precise dimensions and appearance of the 'Holy House', and she was instructed to build a replica of it at Walsingham. The village carpenter made the house–shrine, and they attempted to place it on a site near two holy wells. But angels came at night and moved it to a second site, 'two hundred fote and more in dystaunce'. News of these extraordinary events set England ablaze, and Little Walsingham, a hitherto obscure village on the north Norfolk coast, became a major pilgrimage place.

Many offerings were made at the shrine, including a phial of the 'Virgin's Milk' brought back by Crusaders returning from the Holy Land. The early arrangements were inadequate, and an Augustinian Priory, remains of which can still be seen, was established here. Later still, in 1327–8, a Franciscan Friary was founded under the patronage of Elizabeth de Clare, and its ruins, although in private ownership, can be glimpsed from the gateway to the site on the Fakenham Road. Walsingham prospered from its newfound celebrity; a market was granted and inns and lodgings for pilgrims proliferated. What remains is a small market town, with a fine group of historic buildings and, to the south, the much reduced priory. The east wall of the church still stands with a large window and elaborately decorated buttresses. The conventual buildings are represented by the refectory, which has good thirteenth-century work and retains the staircase which led to the reading pulpit.

But pilgrims still come to Walsingham today, and it is not to the old Priory that they make their way, but to the Anglican shrine nearby. This structure, built in the years after 1931, makes few concessions to artistic merit and rather lacks a devotional atmosphere. But here and at the Roman Catholic Slipper Chapel at Houghton St Giles, some link is maintained with the thousands of medieval pilgrims who flocked to see the Holy House of Walsingham.

The east wall of the great pilgrimage church at Walsingham.

97
KING'S LYNN, Norfolk

Map Reference TF 625200, Map 132
Walk around the centre of King's
Lynn and explore the fine churches
and market-places. The Hall of the
Trinity Guild, now the Town Hall,
is open to visitors and still houses
amongst its civic regalia the
fourteenth-century cup of silver gilt
known as King John's cup. Notice
the deep sites of the houses, with
rear wings and warehouses on the
river frontages.

A medieval port

The town was called 'Bishop's Lynn' throughout the Middle Ages, a name
which reflected its origins as a 'new town' of the Bishops of Norwich and its
site by a lake or 'len'; the old name was changed by Henry VIII. The origins
of Lynn go back to the time of Herbert de Losinga, Bishop of Norwich. In
1101 he granted the site of the town, which consisted of the church of St
Margaret, an area of land and a Saturday market, to the monks of his
cathedral. This early initiative was reinforced later in the twelfth century
when Bishop William Turbe granted 'Newlands' to the north to the
monks, together with a second – Tuesday – market and a chapel. The
nascent town was granted a charter by King John in 1204, and during the
thirteenth and fourteenth centuries it rose to giddy heights of commercial
success, rivalling Boston, London and Southampton.

The legacy of this urban growth is to be seen in the plan of the town with
its large Tuesday Market square and the site of the Saturday Market which
is marked by the Holy Trinity Guildhall built in 1421. This is a handsome
building with a front of chequered flint and ashlar, a steeply pitched gable
and a broad traceried window. The early town had walls of earth, made
from the old sea banks, and wooden gateways which were intended less for
defence than to control commercial traffic and the dues which it generated. Lynn's principal trade lay in the export of food and raw materials,
notably grain, salt and the inevitable wool. In return, timber, iron and fish
came from the Baltic and fine cloth, wine and furs from the Low Countries.

The churches of Lynn are of great interest, with St Margaret's in
particular retaining not only important Norman and medieval fabric, but
also two of the biggest and most famous civilian brasses in England – to
Adam de Walsokne who died in 1349 and Robert Braunche dated 1364.
They are of superb quality with massed niches and canopies, floral patterns
in the fields and, on the earlier brass, an unusual representation of a
windmill. St Nicholas Church began as the chapel of ease founded late in
the twelfth century by Bishop Turbe. The present building is almost
entirely a product of one building campaign early in the fifteenth century,
however. It is eleven bays long with an undivided nave and chancel, a fine
essay in the Perpendicular style with a notable south porch with serried
niches, elaborately decorated blank panels, and a well-moulded outer
doorway. The Greyfriars was founded in 1230–5, and its fine octagonal
tower, an important seamark, still stands. Finally, in the Red Mount
Chapel, licensed in 1485, we see an intriguing example of a wayside chapel
on the pilgrimage road to Walsingham.

The growth of Lynn began early in the
twelfth century in the area of the
Saturday Market and St Margaret's
Church; later in the same century there
was a northerly extension which
included the Tuesday Market-place.

98
BOSTON, Lincolnshire

A medieval seaport

Boston, like its sister Wash port of King's Lynn, enjoyed considerable prosperity early in the Middle Ages, and during the thirteenth century in particular Boston was shipping more sacks of wool than London and Southampton. This early success was partly a reflection of the town's siting on the Marsh with its attendant flocks of sheep, but also because it acted as an outport for Lincoln where goods could be transhipped prior to their journey up the Witham. The early trade was far-flung in its contacts and impressive in its scale. Furs, falcons, cloth and wine came from northern Europe, and spices, glass, silk and wax came from the Mediterranean.

The visitor to Boston will see two principal features of the town, the Market-Place and the parish church, which immediately demonstrate its early significance. The Market-Place is huge, a great triangular space laid out in a bend of the Witham, the site of the Great Fair held on 17 June, the Feast of St Botolph, to which merchants came from all over Europe. At the south end of the Market-Place is a restored late medieval timber-framed building called Shodfriars Hall, and beyond again is the fifteenth-century St Mary's Guildhall, a handsome brick building with stone dressings and a kingpost roof.

Map Reference TF 327441, Map 131
The Guildhall is open to the public daily as a museum. Other remnants of the medieval period can be seen behind the façades in the Market-Place and down the narrow alley ways. The church is open daily.

The glorious Church of St Botolph symbolizes the triumph of the spirit over the woes of the fourteenth century.

The second great legacy is the parish church with its famous 'Stump'. This colossal west tower is a triumph of the hand of man over the broad Fenlands which surround it, and it is sobering that it was probably originally intended to support a spire. The church was begun in 1309 and largely completed apart from the Stump, a century later. It is one of the most remarkable medieval parish churches in England; its site, scale and quality all demand unqualified admiration. The mighty west tower is above all things a mark for both land and sea, being visible for a distance of some forty miles. The church is a major work of the Decorated Gothic style, very large and fully matching the grandeur of the west tower. The nave has slender seven-bay quatrefoil arcades, wave moulded arches and large windows decorated with flowing tracery which matches the superb contemporary south door.

99

TATTERSHALL CASTLE AND COLLEGIATE CHURCH, Lincolnshire

Map Reference TF 209575, Map 122 *Nearest Town* Woodhall Spa 3.5 miles (5.6 km) south-east of Woodhall Spa on the A153 Sleaford to Skegness road. The Castle is owned by the National Trust and open all year Mon–Sat 11–6.30, and Sun 1–6.30. The red tower of the Castle can be seen for many miles across the flat fen landscape.

Tattershall belongs to the same group of 'Frenchified' late medieval tower houses as Nunney and Wardour, built by gentlemen returning from the late wars with France during the early fifteenth century. Here Ralph, Lord Cromwell, High Treasurer of the Realm, dwelt in considerable state and great security. Cromwell died childless and so, instead of founding a dynasty, put his money into a magnificent chantry church here at Tattershall in which prayers could be said for his soul. These two buildings together, the fortress built of brick and the church in the more traditional stone, comprise an important example of late medieval preoccupations with secular and spiritual security.

The tower is built of warm red brick with darker coloured diapers and stone dressings. The prominent machicolations are a borrowing from the French, as are the height and scale of the building. The interior contained a suite of domestic accommodation arranged on four major floors with a basement beneath. Unlike Nunney, however, Tattershall did not apparently contain a kitchen and other domestic offices, suggesting that it was but the principal element of a more extensive range of buildings, rather than a self-sufficient unit. The principal rooms were panelled, and the surviving fireplaces indicate the quality of the original interior. On the first floor was a hall, on the second an audience chamber with a fine brick vaulted anteroom, and on the third floor was a bedchamber. The fireplace in the audience chamber featured the Treasurer's purse, proudly displayed over the inner gateway at Lord Cromwell's other house at South Wingfield.

Construction of the nearby collegiate church was completed under the supervision of Lord Cromwell's chief executor, Bishop Waynflete, after his death in 1456. The church is cruciform in plan and it is brilliantly lit by huge Perpendicular Gothic windows which were, until the eighteenth century, filled with stained glass. The style and scale of the building are strongly reminiscent of the great Lancastrian collegiate church at Fotheringhay and, like it, detailed decoration is subsumed in the flowing lines of the structure. Inside are the original screens and pulpit, all with fine traceried decoration, and these, together with the glass which is now mostly in Stamford, would have lent a sumptuous appearance.

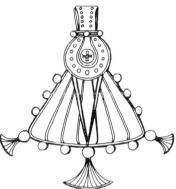

The Treasurer's purse was prominently displayed by its proud owner.

Ralph, Lord Cromwell's great keep at Tattershall.

100

MARSHCHAPEL AND THE SALT SITES, Lincolnshire

Map Reference TF 360988, Map 113
Nearest Town Cleethorpes
Marshchapel is on the A1031
Cleethorpes to Mablethorpe Road,
9 miles (14.4 km) south-east of
Cleethorpes. The church is on a
minor road south of the main road.
The salt mounds can be seen by
following any of the minor roads out
to the coast. Other fine churches
can be seen at Tetney (TA
317009), Grainthorpe (TF 387966)
and Theddlethorpe All Saints (TF
464881).

The churches of east Lincolnshire are celebrated for their great size and exquisite craftsmanship. The sources of the prosperity which built them are not far to seek. Overwhelmingly, it was the wool clip of the great marsh flocks which underpinned the local economy, but from early times salt-making had been a significant local industry. Salt was an important commodity in medieval England, affording as it did an efficient means of preserving fish and meat against the long winter months. By means of either dry salting (in which the meat was placed in a bed of salt) or else brine curing (particularly used for fish), a supply of protein was assured, as was a ready supply of fish for fast days and Friday observance. The salt was either extracted as 'rock salt' from mines in Cheshire and Worcestershire, or else from estuarine mud and seawater on the coasts of East Anglia.

This mud was collected after high tides brought salt water up the coastal creeks and channels, the mud being stored in shelters to keep the rain off.

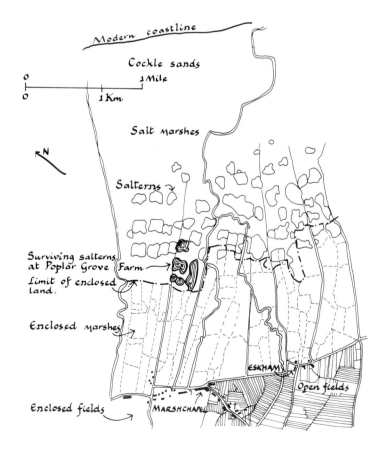

This map is based on one drawn by William Haiwarde in 1569, and shows the high density of saltern sites between the village and the coast.

The mud was separated from the brine by filtering or settling in shallow clay-lined pits called 'floors'. Once the concentrated brine solution was procured it was placed in wide pans of lead or latten, and slowly warmed over fires of charcoal and turves. The water was evaporated off, and the salt residue scraped out of the pans; as with other medieval industries the risks of lead poisoning were not apparently appreciated.

The industry was obviously very intensive along certain stretches of the Lincolnshire coast. Round Marshchapel, for example, can be seen many of the low rounded mounds called 'red hills' or 'hot beds' which were formed from the great accumulations of exhausted saline mud which built up on the saltern sites. As the industry developed, so the salters moved further eastwards towards the coast, and the earlier hills formed useful areas of dry ground for grazing and eventually occupation. The hills often contain fragments of reddish fired clay, from which their name is derived, as well as charcoal fragments and occasional sherds of pottery. It must have been a damp and difficult life along the North Sea coast, with the constant possibility of marine inundation and difficulties of transport inland. But the market was seemingly inexhaustible, and the low salt mounds and the splendid churches remain as evidence of this early exploitation of the marshland.

101
LINCOLN CATHEDRAL AND CITY, Lincolnshire

Our two previous *Guides* introduced the earlier history of this great city, and at the opening of our period Lincoln still enjoyed considerable prosperity. It was a clothmaking centre and in 1326 it became one of the Staple towns through which trade in wool, skins, hides, timber and tin were channelled. The city was also granted regular markets for these products, and new officials and courts were established. These measures extended Lincoln's existing functions as a market and administrative centre and brought additional prosperity. One sign of this was the arrival of the 'Grey' or Franciscan Friars in 1231; their chapel and undercroft now house the City and County Museum.

But Lincoln was always dominated by the royal castle and above all by its incomparable Cathedral. The Diocese of Lincoln was the largest in England, and reached from the Humber to the Thames. The wealth of this great tract of middle England was channelled into the construction of one of the greatest Gothic churches in the land. The key to this story lies with one man, St Hugh of Avalon, who was a competent and respected bishop during his episcopacy in 1186–1200 and, after his death, a popular saint.

Map Reference SK 981717, Map 121 The Bishop's Palace is in HBMCE guardianship and open in the summer season, standard hours. It stands on the south side of the Cathedral, in the grounds of the diocesan office, Edward King House. The Castle is administered by the Council and open daily.

One of the angels from the spandrels of the great choir built to house the body of St Hugh of Lincoln.

This wooden vaulting boss in the cloister is thought to depict toothache, which was doubtless a common medieval problem!

Map Reference SK 915357, Map 130 The Angel Inn, in the High Street, is still a hotel and can be visited for a pleasant drink or meal. The church and chained library are normally open 9.00–6.00, Mon, Thurs and Fri, and on Sat 9.00–1.00.

Hugh was an unusual choice as bishop, since he was a Carthusian monk, the same contemplative Order that built the monastery at Mount Grace in Yorkshire. He reorganized the diocese, and strongly asserted the independence of the Church in the face of encroachments by the Crown. He was able by dint of his humour and intellect to encourage kings towards greater spirituality, and to inspire the reverence of the people. He also began the rebuilding of the Cathedral, which is unusual in being essentially a product of one major thirteenth-century building programme. Hugh's choir with its famous 'crazy vault', an early experiment in the Gothic style, still stands. Hugh was canonized in 1220, and Lincoln became a popular pilgrimage centre. Work started on the Angel Choir, a magnificent extension of the earlier fabric comprising both presbytery and retro choir, and the saint's body was moved there in 1280. This great Cathedral is thus a monument both to Hugh's reforming zeal and to his popularity, for it was largely financed by contributions made at his shrine.

A lesser-known product of Hugh's building achievement lies immediately south of the Cathedral. The Bishop's Palace is an important example of domestic planning, and despite considerable destruction during the Civil War it retains much medieval work. The site had been granted to the diocese in 1135–8 by King Stephen, and the earliest hall there belongs to Bishop Chesney's original layout. Its remarkable structure consists of superimposed upper and lower halls, with lancet windows lighting the side walls. The principal chambers were at the south end of the hall, and the north end was remodelled during the fifteenth century.

Hugh added a large aisled hall to the west with three service doorways in the south end, which is one of the earliest English examples of such an arrangement. The flanking doorways led to the buttery and pantry, and the central door gave access to a passage leading to the kitchen. This was a magnificent construction, raised over a vaulted undercroft and containing five broad fireplaces, the tiled back walls of which survive. These buildings reflect the requirements of the great diocese which the Cathedral served; Hugh himself maintained his ascetic vegetarian lifestyle and provided a model for the responsible exercise of power.

102
GRANTHAM, Lincolnshire

A fine inn and an important church

Grantham, until it was bypassed a few years ago, was a well-known stopping place on the Great North Road, and many of the town's facilities were geared to this traffic. The medieval town was prosperous enough, as the magnificent Church of St Wulfram demonstrates, but we are fortunate here in being able to see a fine medieval hostelry which has provided shelter for many travellers. The fifteenth-century Angel Hotel was built in a most prosperous style, with a grand ashlar front having a central vehicle arch and a delightful oriel window supported by a carved corbel.

It is an example of the 'gatehouse' type of inn in which the principal apartments were arranged in the main block to the street. It will be noticed that the right-hand canted bay is rather wider than that to the left, and it is probable that the hall lay on that side. This is borne out by the large fireplace in that room. The parlour therefore probably lay to the left of the central passage, with the kitchens and other offices on the site of the later rear ranges. The upper floor of the front range is now open, but may originally have been subdivided to form chambers open to the roof. The interiors of the bays retain finely carved ribs and bosses, and the detailing is of the best quality. A handsome building indeed, and one which admirably combines conviviality with conservation.

As to Grantham's great church, a minster before the Conquest, the visitor will immediately be struck by the lofty steeple, not the tallest but certainly among the earliest and finest of these structures in England. It was an addition to a church which had its structural origins late in the twelfth century, as the three middle bays of the nave indicate. Early in the thirteenth century the aisles were extended westwards and the exterior was later remodelled in a rich Geometric style which owed much to Lincoln. The building campaign culminated in the upper stages of the great west tower and spire, which are enriched with copious quantities of ballflowers and crockets, the leitmotifs of the early fourteenth century. The interior of the church reflects later changes in its fittings and furnishings, but there is a crypt beneath the Lady Chapel, and a chained library which, although of sixteenth-century origin, reminds us of medieval practice.

Angel bearing a crown on the underside of the oriel window of the Angel Hotel at Grantham.

103
LONGTHORPE TOWER AND WALL-PAINTINGS,
Cambridgeshire

Map Reference TL 163983, Map 142
Nearest Town Peterborough
The tower is on the outskirts of
Peterborough new town, signposted
off the A47 ring road on the west
side of the city. It is in HBMCE
guardianship and open standard
hours, although closed for lunch
and on Monday and Tuesday
mornings. It is now rather hemmed
in by modern houses, but the
adjacent house, in private
ownership, is the earlier building to
which the tower was added.

*The Wheel of the Five Senses, with a
monkey, a vulture, a spider's web, a
boar and a cock, which represent taste,
smell, touch, hearing and sight
respectively.*

*The figure on the left might be a
representation of the Church-Ecclesia –
since she points to the word 'Ecclesiam'
on the scroll she is holding.*

The village of Longthorpe has been absorbed into the sprawl of outer
Peterborough, but at its centre the remains of a large medieval house
remind us of its earlier history. The celebrated Tower was actually an
early-fourteenth-century addition to an existing house built by William de
Thorpe; the 'long' part of the name came later. His son Robert, Steward of
the Abbey of Peterborough after 1310, probably built the Tower, and his
son, another Robert, probably commissioned the wall-paintings. Longthorpe is thus an example of a hall house to which a tower of refuge was
added, a sequence paralleled at Stokesay and elsewhere. This is interesting
enough, but here at Longthorpe is preserved an early and elaborate
sequence of wall-paintings, which constitutes one of the best surviving
domestic interiors of medieval England.

The paintings are in the principal chamber of the Tower, and depict
religious as well as secular themes, mostly based on allusions to morality
and good living. Apart from directly biblical elements like the nativity,
pairs of apostles, the symbols of the evangelists and King David with his
harp, there are moralizing themes like the 'Three Living and the Three
Dead' which point out the emptiness of earthly attainments. The Wheel of
the Five Senses is here illustrated by various animals representing the
faculties, such as a spider's web for Touch, a boar for Hearing and a cock for

Sight or Watchfulness. Here are also the Labours of the Months, a theme familiar from the fonts in our *Norman Guide*, and a charming portrait of a teacher lecturing a pupil. These bright pictures, interspersed with heraldry, bizarre creatures from the Bestiary, and some abstract decoration, are a splendid evocation of medieval England, as stimulating and thought-provoking today as when they were first painted.

104
LEIGHTON BUZZARD, Bedfordshire

A small town and its craft

This small market town has two medieval features of particular interest. The first is the handsome fifteenth-century market cross which is one of the best of its type in England, and which still commands the centre of the town. The cross has an unusual pentagonal plan, and an open vaulted ground stage surmounted by a corona of niches and a tall central crocketed pinnacle. The carvings are robust and the details of the four centred arches and the cusped canopies to the upper stage are well handled. It is a most satisfying construction, redolent of the late medieval civic pride which built it, for Leighton's market was already 400 years old when the cross was built – and the builders' confidence in the future has proved to be well founded.

The other aspect of the town which demands our attention is the splendid ironwork on the west door of the church, and its probable link with a famous medieval craftsman of the town. One Thomas de Leghtone was commissioned in 1294 to make the iron grille for Queen Eleanor's tomb at Westminster Abbey, and this doubtless explains the presence of other good ironwork in the area. On the west door of Leighton church, at Eaton Bray and at Turvey, can be seen excellent thirteenth-century ironwork. These are delightful examples of the busily springing arabesques which were such a speciality of metalwork at the time. Eaton Bray is probably the best, and on the south door can be seen tight scrolls with leafy terminals, the scrolls curving evenly from the solid hinge pieces, all formed out of the solid bar metal.

Map Reference SP 925250, Map 165
If you are able to sort out the one-way system that operates here, you will find the market cross in the centre of the market-place, and the church to one side of it.

The handsome fifteenth-century market cross at Leighton Buzzard.

THE BORDERS

Durham

DURHAM

NORTHERN ENGLAND

♦ 117

CLEVELAND

Northallerton

♦ 115   ♦ 116

♦ 114   ♦ 112

NORTH YORKSHIRE

♦ 114

113 ♦

♦ 111

York ♦ 110

HUMBERSIDE

♦ 118

Lancaster

LANCASHIRE

Leeds

WEST YORKSHIRE

♦ 107

Hull

♦ 106

♦ 119

♦ 109

♦ 105

♦ 119

♦ 120

GREATER

SOUTH YORKSHIRE

Liverpool

♦ 120

Sheffield 108 ♦

MANCHESTER

EASTERN

♦ 121

♦ 120

ENGLAND

CHESHIRE 123 ♦

♦ 123

♦ 122

♦ 124

THE MIDLANDS

Chester

120 ♦

0   10   20   30 Miles

0   10 20 30 40 50 Km

NORTHERN ENGLAND

Introduction

The north of England during the Middle Ages was a region of considerable prosperity and, until the later fourteenth and fifteenth centuries at least, one of rising population and income. The early reverses attendant upon the 'Harrying of the North' by the Conqueror and the uncertainty engendered by the wars with Scotland had some effect, of course, but in general there is little evidence of serious political instability. Instead we find a wide range of medieval sites, most of which are concerned with domestic life and the Church.

Castle Bolton is a good example of the type of grandiose fortification which a magnate built for himself during the later fourteenth century. Its siting is also instructive; certainly its builder, Lord Scrope, had the Bolton lands as his barony, but the siting of the castle in this remote place probably had more to do with the contemporary Peasants' Revolt. Other castles were at York and Tickhill, while both York and Hartlepool had town defences. But it is noteworthy that the defences of these northern castles were generally, like those at Pickering, left pretty much in their late Norman condition, with only the minimum being spent on their care and maintenance.

When we turn to the towns and villages, we find an interesting picture of changing fortunes. York itself burgeoned throughout the Middle Ages, but even that great city experienced some check during the general malaise of the later years. But what a city it was, with the great Minster at its heart, merchants from all over the known world visiting its fairs and markets, and a collection of houses, guildhalls and other buildings to delight the eye. On a smaller scale, Beverley shared in the success of the east coast. Here again we find defences but built of brick, as well as two churches demonstrative of the early prosperity of this handsome town.

In the matter of villages, Wharram Percy must hold the crown not merely for the north but for the whole of England. Yet it is not now a village at all; it is the site of a failed settlement, a green valley filled with memories, like many another on the marginal lands of England. Such villages were casualties of the changing times at the end of the Middle

Ages. Climatic deterioration, labour shortage after the Black Death, the increase of pasture over arable and shrinkage of the national economy resulted in many less favoured settlements like Wharram becoming depopulated. Yet here the story of the village is being retold through the efforts of archaeologists and specialists from many other disciplines. The site is a sort of total research project in which the very bones of medieval life and society are being laid bare.

A distinctive legacy of the north-west of England are the late medieval timber-framed halls at places like Samlesbury, Rufford, Smithills and Bramhall. These buildings continued ancient traditions of carpentry and provide a startling insight into domestic conditions during the fourteenth and fifteenth centuries. With their elaborate decorative framing, generous halls and snug living accommodation, they clearly indicate that medieval England was by no means the chill and dreary place which many commentators suggest. At Markenfield in Yorkshire, by contrast, is a fine stone house, a structure paralleled by the ruins of the rectory at Warton in Lancashire. The moral here is that people built with whatever materials were available to them; if stone, then stone, but if you lived in the margins of the huge forests of the north-west, wood was the obvious material, and the survival of timber houses and churches indicates its longevity.

The monastic Orders made a great contribution in the north. The Cistercians were introduced in our *Norman Guide*, and under the entry for the 'Yorkshire Abbeys' in this book we trace the later development. These monasteries were more than powerhouses of prayer, they were great centres of agricultural and industrial expansion which had a profound effect both directly and by spawning lay imitations. But there were other Orders as well. Mount Grace is the best preserved Carthusian house in Britain and its great cloister surrounded by the small individual cells retains an air of quietness and peace. At Norton Priory we see something of the detail of a medieval monastery as excavation and interpretation continue there, while at Thornton Abbey the gatehouse attests the prestige enjoyed by the monks there during the late fourteenth century.

Parish churches are varied, but with some superb individual examples and features. Tickhill is a good Yorkshire church in creamy Tadcaster stone, while in Cheshire are the unusual timber-framed churches at Lower Peover and Marton. These two structures must stand to remind us of the hundreds if not thousands of wooden churches which existed in medieval England, and the sight of them is quite extraordinary. At Hartlepool is a grand Early English church dominating the site of the Saxon monastery, while at Patrington in South Yorkshire is a Decorated Gothic church which lurks in the memory as much for its dramatic setting as for its architecture.

Finally, there are two other Yorkshire shrines which stand out: one is the delicate bridge chapel at Wakefield, and the other is the parish church at Pickering with its marvellous wall-paintings. The Wakefield chapel stands in the midst of nineteenth- and twentieth-century sprawl and industry, a reminder of the ancient days of the wool trade which ultimately brought the city such prosperity. But at Pickering we can actually step back into the fifteenth century, surrounding ourselves with the colour and beauty and gravity of medieval worship. The boldness and clarity of these pictures, together with their high artistic merit, mark them out as masterpieces of representation; a stupendous legacy which should be studied with care and great joy.

105
THORNTON ABBEY GATEHOUSE, Humberside

The abbey was founded as an Augustinian house by William le Gros, Count of Aumale, in 1139. Most of the buildings belong to the thirteenth and fourteenth centuries, however, and the chief interest of the site resides

Map Reference TA 115190, Map 113
Nearest Town Scunthorpe
10 miles (16 km) north-east of Scunthorpe on minor road north of A160, signposted. In HBMCE guardianship, open standard hours. When visiting the Abbey note also the fine 13th-century plate tracery in the Chapter House.

The great fourteenth-century brick gatehouse with the sixteenth-century barbican before it. Notice the use of stone for the cladding of the ornamental buttresses, the parapets and niches

in its spectacular gatehouse. It was apparently built late in the fourteenth century, and the depredations of the Peasants' Revolt in 1382 have been cited as a possible cause. This is the most impressive monastic gatehouse of its date to survive, as well as being an important early example of the use of brick.

After the departure of the Romans, no bricks are known to have been made on a large scale in Britain before the fourteenth century. At that time the area around the port of Hull, which traded with the Low Countries and the Baltic, began to show some familiarity with the use of brick. This is scarcely surprising since it was in those very countries that the use of brick was most common. Hull had no stone but was quickly found to have plenty of brick clay, and so the industry began. The powerful de la Pole family, closely associated with Wingfield in Suffolk, controlled the nascent concern. Brick became a common, if still aristocratic, building material in the later Middle Ages, as the other local sites of Tattershall Castle, Gainsborough Old Hall and The Chancery at Lincoln indicate.

But here at Thornton, brick was still only used as the common walling material; stone was employed for the dressings and sculptures above the archway, and the lower parts are faced in ashlar. The original composition has been rather marred by the addition of the sixteenth-century barbican, but the sculpture of Our Lady flanked by St John the Baptist and possibly St Augustine the Doctor dressed as a bishop attest the quality of the work. Curiously, there is some disagreement about the function of the building. At first-floor level is a fine hall, and it has been suggested that the Abbot would have lived here. But there is no kitchen, and food would have to have been brought up a narrow staircase from outside, a most inconvenient arrangement. Perhaps the gatehouse was merely intended as a statement of the importance of the house – a *folie de grandeur*, and tribute to the late medieval 'bending' of the austere rules of monasticism.

106
PATRINGTON CHURCH, Humberside

Map Reference TA 315226, Map 113 *Nearest Town* Kingston upon Hull The spire of the church can be seen for miles around. It is in the centre of the village on the south side of the main road. Patrington is on the A1033 10 miles (16 km) south-east of Hull. The church is normally open and has a good bookstall.

'The Queen of Holderness'
The fourteenth century saw many spectacular church building projects, but few are displayed to such advantage as Patrington Church. Sir John Betjeman likened it to a stone galleon, sailing 'over the wide, flat expanse of Holderness'. Elements of the present building, notably the central tower, fossilize the earlier plan of the church, but it is essentially an essay in the Decorated Gothic style and is the northern counterpart of Hawton and Heckington.

Patrington Church displays the fourteenth-century Decorated Gothic style to perfection.

Externally, the graceful spire claims the attention. It is supported on an open octagonal corona which deftly handles the transition from the tall square tower to the tapering spire. The prominent stepped external buttresses are all crowned with chunky crocketed pinnacles, and they provide an excellent foil to the delicate flowing tracery of the windows.

Inside, the dominant impression is created by the clustered shafts of the nave arcades and crossing piers. They terminate in rich leafy capitals, which in a curious way seem to 'grow' out of the shafts. The moulding of the arches and responds and the carving of the capitals are everywhere of the best quality, but the contemporary Easter Sepulchre overtops them. The function of these sepulchres is discussed in the Hawton (Nottingham-

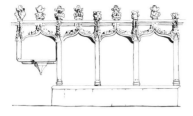

The elaborate piscina and sedilia.

shire) entry, and the example here is clearly of the same pattern. The sleeping soldiers repose beneath ogee arches encrusted with crockets and foliage. Above the central recess a shrouded Christ rises rather awkwardly from the grave, flanked by two censing angels.

Finally, it might well be asked why such a jewel of a church is situated in the midst of this rather unpromising country. We are looking at an area which saw its halcyon days at about the time the church was rebuilt, the first half of the fourteenth century. At nearby Beverley we see something of the prosperity which the wool trade could generate, and Holderness had its share.

There were two weekly markets here and three annual fairs. The nearby town of Hedon was actually founded as a port, and under the sea to the south lie the remains of other lost ports, Ravenserodd and Ravenser. These towns, like the more famous Dunwich in Suffolk, were inundated and lost. Patrington, belonging as it did to the Archbishops of York, would have fitted well into such a successful area. It is a reminder of the golden days before the Black Death, climatic deterioration and political troubles closed remorselessly in.

107
BEVERLEY, Humberside

Map Reference TA 037392, Map 107
North Bar is on the north side of the town and St Mary's Church is in the same street. The Minster lies on the south side of the town, and is usually open daily except on Saturdays.

Two splendid churches

This town on the River Hull deserves to be better known and appreciated. It boasts a fine collection of buildings of later periods, and from the Middle Ages come two incomparable churches which amply display its mercantile success. For although far inland, the medieval merchants of Beverley dealt in the plenteous Yorkshire wool clip and travelled widely over northern Europe. One result of these foreign contacts was the use of brick which here, as at Thornton Abbey, was used as a prestige material, in this case for the town gates. The remaining North Bar, built in 1409 at a cost of £96 0s. 11½d, is a handsome edifice with moulded string courses, stepped battlements and shield-shaped plaques; it would not be out of place in the Low Countries.

The first charter was granted in 1129 by Archbishop Thurstan of York, and by the fourteenth century Beverley had become one of the leading English towns. The tenurial history is complex, but in essence the Archbishops of York controlled the northern end of the borough, and the Provost and Canons of the Minster the south. This ecclesiastical background brings us to the twin highlights of the place: the Minster of St John and the parish church of St Mary. Both are of outstanding quality, with the

Minster being memorable for its scale and St Mary's for its rare beauty.

The Minster was founded in about 690 as a college of secular canons. It was later destroyed by the Danes and, although rebuilt, the present building is all of c. 1220 and afterwards. It is of cathedral size, and has an elaborate plan incorporating twin transepts. The eastern parts were built first, and are executed in an exceptionally pure Early English style with many echoes of Lincoln. Purbeck marble shafts, dogtooth arches and moulded vaults provide a bewilderingly rich interior. The nave was begun in about 1310, and complements the richness of the sanctuary by the use of trefoiled arches in the triforium and in the massing of its numerous columns, which lend a rather Continental impression.

St Mary's Church has many remarkable attributes, not the least of which is its excellent collection of mid-fifteenth-century misericords. Externally, the most commanding feature is the central tower, which has the large belfry lights and delicate pinnacles characteristic of the East Riding Group, including Hull and Hedon. This is actually a replacement of the original which fell down during a service in 1520, killing several members of the congregation! Inside, the nave is also of the sixteenth century, but the north chapel, which has a ribbed vault studded with carved bosses and windows with exquisite curvilinear tracery, is a delight.

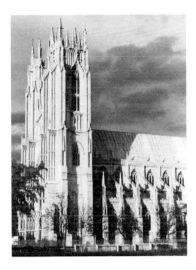

The magnificent twin Perpendicular towers were added to the west end of Beverley Minster c. 1400. Sir John Betjeman described it as 'one of the finest Gothic churches in Europe'.

108
TICKHILL CHURCH, South Yorkshire

A Yorkshire gem

Tickhill was an important early lordship and its castle controlled the route eastwards from the Pennines into the Vale of York. It was evidently a busy place, having an Austin friary and, in Northgate, the Hospital of St Leonard, the timber-framed façade of which dated 1470 can still be seen. Little remains of the castle, but the parish church of St Mary is one of the grandest in Yorkshire, and attests the early importance of the town.

Built of creamy white Magnesian limestone, the west tower in particular is a feast for the eyes. The lower parts were built in the thirteenth century, as the display of dogtoothing on the side arches reveals. In the later fourteenth century the Fitzwilliam family, whose arms appear on the structure, paid for the middle stage which is distinguishable from the earlier work by its angle buttresses. But as late as 1429 a 'cart with hoss' was bequeathed towards the cost of completing the tower. It is to this later period that the splendid pierced parapet belongs. This distinctive feature, unusual in Yorkshire, is here further enriched by the addition of ogee arches above the embrasures.

Map Reference SK 591931, Map 111
Nearest Town Doncaster
7 miles (11 km) south of Doncaster on the A60, near the Nottinghamshire border. The church is in Church Lane and St Leonard's Hospice is on the east side of the Doncaster Road.

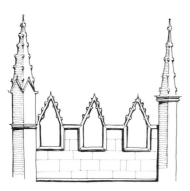

Detail of the parapet.

Although large, the plan originated in the thirteenth century – as the work in the tower and the chancel indicates. The fourteenth-century four-bay nave arcades have piers of complex section and foliate capitals, all of a piece with the reticulated windows, handsome north chapel and its ogee headed tomb recess. This puts us in mind of the contemporary work in Lincolnshire at places like Ewerby and Heckington where north chapels were *de rigueur*.

A further unusual feature of the church is the occurrence of an east window above the chancel arch, a distinctive fourteenth-century addition more at home in Gloucestershire. This window, together with the fretted tower parapet, suggests an unusual degree of experimentation, and should presumably be attributed to the wider connections of its builders, the Fitzwilliams.

The base of Tickhill tower is thirteenth-century, but the great west window is late fourteenth, and the tower was not finally completed until the 1430s, to which period the handsome pierced parapet belongs.

109

WAKEFIELD BRIDGE CHAPEL, West Yorkshire

Wakefield was a prosperous cloth town before the rise of Leeds and Bradford, and its splendid parish church, since 1888 a cathedral, retains important medieval fabric, particularly of the fifteenth century which saw the apogee of the wool trade. But the most distinctive product of the town's medieval prosperity is the bridge chapel of St Mary. A moment's reflection will show the appropriateness of this monument: wool had to be carried round the country on packhorses, so tracks, trails and roads were essential for the success of this trade. The Wakefield chapel was built partly as a shrine, but also as a means of collecting money for the upkeep of the bridge itself.

The chapel is at the centre of a bridge of nine pointed arches which was built over the River Calder in 1342. In 1356 Edward III granted a licence vesting offerings to the chantry in two priests, and the bridge chapel, which is generally accepted as the finest in England, was probably built then. Despite a thoroughgoing restoration by Sir George Gilbert Scott in 1847, and further work in 1939, the original scheme is clear enough. It is a small jewel of the Decorated Gothic style with an elaborate façade of five bays and three doorways. There is much flowing tracery, crockets and reliefs of scenes from the Life of Christ as well as the Virgin, to whom the chapel is dedicated, and St Christopher, patron saint of travellers. The side walls each have three traceried windows of three lights.

Inside is a low pitched tie beam roof, and to the right of the altar is a canopied niche where a statue of the Virgin stood, before which a light would have burnt. The present statue was removed from the exterior

Map Reference SE 338202, Map 104
On the south-east side of the city. From the centre take the A638 Doncaster road. Just after a railway bridge turn left and the old bridge can be seen running parallel to a new road bridge over the River Calder. The chapel is open by appointment only and by contacting the Vicar, 31 Peterson Road, Wakefield, tel 375600. A service is held there every Sunday at 3 pm. A similar but more restored chapel can be seen at Rotherham and also at St Ives in Cambridgeshire.

St Mary's Chapel on Wakefield Bridge. The young Earl of Rutland was slain near this place during the Battle of Wakefield on 30 December 1460.

during the 1847 restoration. Beneath the chapel is a small crypt, and a single bell hangs in the north-east turret. Many merchants must have paused in this place to give thanks for a good day's trading at Wakefield Market.

110
YORK, North Yorkshire

Map Reference SE 603521, Map 105 Clifford's Tower, Castle Street, in the south-east part of the city is in HBMCE guardianship and open standard hours and Sunday mornings in summer. Merchant Adventurers' Hall is in Fossgate and is open 1 April–31 Oct, 9.30–1, and most afternoons until 4; 1 Nov–31 March, 9.30–1 except Sundays. Merchant Taylors' Hall stands by the city wall at the east end of St Andrew Gate, open most days. The walls are always available and a walk around them affords admirable views of the city and its fine medieval gates.

The second city of medieval England

York reached the height of its wealth and influence between 1200 and 1450 and was often, especially during the Scottish wars, the seat of national government. The most obvious physical sign of the city's prestige are its splendid walls, which began to be rebuilt in stone from about 1250. All told, their circuit is about three miles and, apart from Chester, they are the most complete set in England. The royal castle was also rebuilt at this time, and the quadrilobal Clifford's Tower added. By the mid fourteenth century the city was well developed, and good examples of fifteenth-century houses can be seen in Goodramgate, North Street and the Shambles. There are many great medieval buildings, such as St William's College near the Minster which was enlarged in 1455–67 to form a house for chantry priests, and the King's Manor, rebuilt in brick after 1483, for which the original contract with Richard Cheryholme, bricklayer, survives.

During the twelfth century, various trades began to organize themselves as guilds, which became very important. At their height there were about eighty guilds, existing to regulate trades and to secure the living standards of their members. The guilds also had welfare and religious functions, and all shared in the great annual Corpus Christi procession which, by the fourteenth century, included the performance of what came to be known as the York Cycle of Mystery Plays. These plays are still performed, and they offer a rare experience of the fertile creative imagination of our period.

A further legacy of the guilds merchant are two halls. The Merchant Taylors' Hall has a later brick exterior, but inside is the timber-framed hall with its tie beam roof of *c.* 1400. The more famous hall is that of the Merchant Adventurers. This title, vibrant with the optimism of the reign of the first Elizabeth, was not introduced until 1581, however. When the hall was first built in the mid fourteenth century it was called the Guild of Mercers and Merchants. The hall today, though restored, is essentially as built in 1357–61 with a brick and stone undercroft and a timber-framed first-floor hall divided by a row of wooden pillars. The York merchants exported wool and cloth to the Low Countries, France, Spain and

Bootham Bar: the fourteenth-century gateway with its bartizan angle towers is supported on a Norman arch.

Germany, and brought back wine, fish, iron, dyestuffs, timber and many other commodities.

York was, of course, more than a military and commercial centre. At its heart is the great Minster, and the present writer was privileged to take part in the archaeological work there during its restoration. The recent fire in the south transept, a disaster with many echoes in our period, imperilled the magnificent tomb of the founder of the present building, Archbishop Walter de Grey. Perhaps the finest feature is the stained glass; it has the largest collection in England. Apart from the Minster itself, there were thirty-nine parish churches in medieval York of which nineteen are left, as well as monasteries and charitable institutions such as hospitals. The most famous was St Mary's Abbey, the ruins of which can be seen in the Museum Gardens. In second place was the Priory of the Holy Trinity, Micklegate, and parts of the original building survive in the church of that name. Early in the thirteenth century the mendicant friars came to York and all had houses here, but no traces remain above ground.

'. . . and his kingdom was full of darkness; and they gnawed their tongues for pain' (Rev. 16:10). A panel from the great east window (1405–8) by John Thornton, depicting the Apocalypse.

111

WHARRAM PERCY, North Yorkshire

Map Reference SE 859645, Map 100
Nearest Town Malton
6 miles (9.5 km) south-east of
Malton. Take the B1248 and,
½ mile (0.8 km) south of Wharram
le Street, follow signposts to site
right down a minor road. Park at
Bella Farm and walk to the site (¼
mile, 0.4 km) down a steep track.
Not suitable for the infirm, and
boots advised in bad weather. Site is
in HBMCE guardianship and open
at any reasonable time. Some
explanatory boards are permanently
fixed at the site. Other nearby
deserted medieval villages are at
Argam (TA 112710), Cottam (SE
993648), Cowlam (SE 965655),
Little Givendale (SE 823530),
Riplingham (SE 960320),
Towthorpe in Londesborough
(SE 867439).

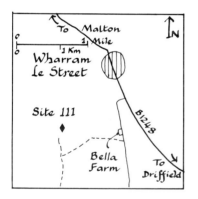

A deserted village

The name of this village, which probably ceased to exist as a community by
about 1500, has become famous in the annals of British archaeology. It is
here that the devoted labours of Professor Maurice Beresford and Mr John
Hurst on behalf of the Medieval Village Research Group have fleshed out
our skeletal picture of medieval village life. For over thirty years the
complicated task of excavating the church, manor and peasant houses has
been in progress, and the result is an interpretation of the history and
development of this place unrivalled in Europe. But what was Wharram
Percy, and why was it deserted?

The area about Wharram (the name derives from the Old English *hwer
hamm*, meaning 'an enclosure in a kettle or pot-shaped valley') has
evidence of prehistoric and Roman settlement, but a village does not seem
to have been established here until Saxon times. In 1177 the village was
held by William de Perci, from which the second element of the name was
derived.

With the arrival of the Percy family, a stone manor house was built, and
the same masons' marks have been found during excavation of the apse of
the parish church, suggesting that it was extended at this time. The village
was clearly prospering, and a regular pattern of peasant garden plots called
'tofts' and houses called 'crofts' was laid out as a northern extension to the
earlier village.

The thirteenth century began well enough, but later there began a
gradual deterioration in the climate with wetter and cooler conditions
prevailing. This made upland villages like Wharram and Hound Tor on
Dartmoor less rewarding to farm, with consequent pressure on the population. Matters got worse, and by the early fourteenth century cattle
murrains and crop failures increased as a result of the still worsening
climate. Then in 1348 the Great Pestilence, which we know as the Black
Death, arrived in England and decimated the population.

It is against this background that we must view the fate of Wharram
Percy. When first established, the village was doubtless well able to
support its inhabitants with a surplus remaining for trade and taxes. This
quiet plenty continued into the twelfth century when a rapidly increasing
national population would have stimulated the production of food by
arable farming even in this relatively unfavoured place. The years about
1200 probably marked the apogee of Wharram's fortunes.

But the poor climate, plague and inflation which occurred after the
Black Death as wage rates rose among the surviving peasants resulted in

The ruined church of St Martin at Wharram Percy. The two surviving cottages can be seen beyond and most of the Medieval village houses were located above the slope to the left.

the progressive depopulation of villages like Wharram. The Great Pestilence certainly finished off numbers of villages on less favoured sites but many, like Wharram, managed to survive a little longer. The *coup de grâce* may have been administered by the Hilton family, who probably deliberately depopulated the village in around 1500 and turned its site and the old arable fields around it into a sheepwalk. This process was going on all over England, and was the basis of the tremendous prosperity of the late medieval wool trade.

What has this curious, and in some ways very sad, history left for us to see? The major monument, as one might expect, is the parish church of St Martin. This building reflects the fortunes of the village both in its standing structure and in the buried evidence beneath it. During the eighth century a small timber church was built here, the postholes of which were found by excavation. Later in that century, a stone church was built which was itself replaced in late Saxon times. These changes indicate the gradual enlargement of the Saxon village on the lower terrace of the valley. In the twelfth century, with the arrival of the Percys, an apse and south aisle were added, reflecting the expansion of the village. During the thirteenth century a north aisle was built, and later a north chapel was added.

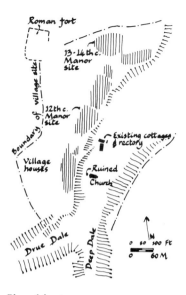

Plan of the site.

The late thirteenth century saw the church at its greatest extent and afterwards the declining settlement was mirrored by the progressive removal of structural elements. By the late fifteenth century the aisles had gone. The medieval chancel was shortened in the seventeenth century, and the only later addition was a vestry. The church continued in use, but by the nineteenth century it was used only by the inhabitants of the outlying settlement of Thixendale, and they built themselves a new church in 1879. Occasional services were held until after the last war, but in the end the church became ruinous, in which condition it is preserved today, having faithfully served the villagers for over a thousand years.

But what of the rest of the village – what can we say of its development? Traces of the peasant houses can be seen beside the linear depression or hollow way which marks the main street of the village. The houses are marked by low grassy walls, generally forming a rectangular outline. These are the foundations of stone structures, but the earliest dwellings – with the exception of the manor house – were built of timber. Chalk, normally quarried from the tofts themselves, was not used for building until after the late thirteenth century. Even then it seems that the houses were frequently rebuilt, possibly in each generation, suggesting rather flimsy construction.

Substantial variations have been found in the types of house. Some were certainly of the 'long house' type in which men and animals shared the same roof, with a cross passage and partition dividing the two functions. Other buildings had simpler two-roomed plans, however, suggesting differences of prosperity and occupational specialization. Examples of different house plans are laid out on the site, and useful reconstruction drawings indicate types of superstructure consonant with the excavated evidence. The manor house to the north-west of the church was of more substantial construction, with thick stone walls and an undercroft as befitted its higher status.

There is a mill pond and dam south of the church which apparently originated in the eighth century. The low boundary banks of the crofts can be seen all along the western side of the valley. The long narrow plots behind the houses would have been used by the peasants as gardens in which vegetables could be grown. Beyond, slight traces of the ridge and furrow in the open fields can be detected running at right angles to the crofts. With the woodland on the opposite side of the valley, the basic physical elements of the village are complete. Wharram Percy is a remarkable place to visit, for it is both a deserted village and a sort of open air laboratory. Work continues, watched by sheep grazing the house mounds just as they have done ever since the last villagers left.

112
PICKERING CHURCH, North Yorkshire

Wall-paintings and Castle

The church of St Peter and St Paul at Pickering contains some of the finest late medieval frescos in England. Upon entering the church through the south door, the wondering visitor leaves the busy market-place behind, and looks in amazement at the nave walls which glow with saints and biblical scenes. The twentieth century falls away for a moment and we are immersed in the age of faith.

St Christopher stands in a river containing cavorting creatures before a craggy landscape. He looks towards the Infant Christ on his shoulder and leans on his ragged staff. To the left a magnificent St George, the very image of medieval chivalry, clad in richly caparisoned plate armour astride his great destrier, plunges his lance into the Dragon of Darkness. Further east, St Edmund, King and Martyr of the old East Anglian kingdom, stands tied to a tree as the heathen Danes fire arrows into his body. The King still wears his crown, and the Danes appear as late medieval foot soldiers, but the message of the scene is clear enough.

Apart from the English saints, there are fascinatingly detailed scenes from the lives of John the Baptist, St Catherine and the Virgin Mary, and a series depicting the Seven Acts of Mercy. The execution of John the Baptist is graphically shown next to the banquet at which Salome receives

Map Reference Castle: SE 800845, Map 100
Church: SE 799840
15 miles (24 km) south-west of Scarborough on the A170. The church is just off the north side of the main street and the castle is at the end of the street which runs north from the church. The castle is in HBMCE guardianship, open standard hours and Sunday mornings in summer; there is an education room with displays.

The head of St John the Baptist is handed to Salome in this fifteenth-century dining scene.

his head on a charger. The diners are attired as fifteenth-century kings and courtiers, with a liveried servant offering up a lidded cup to a table crowded with metal utensils, and at which the diners use only knives as cutlery.

Boldness and clarity are the chief features of these paintings. In an age when few could read, such pictures were important in communicating the Christian message, and here the emphasis on English saints, including St Thomas of Canterbury above the scene of St Edmund, ensured that the message would be popular as well as spiritual. Even though the scenes were heavily restored in 1880, the bright colours and bold execution are fully medieval in their flavour.

Pickering Castle was established by the Conqueror himself, but its relative strategic insignificance is reflected by the absence of major work after the early thirteenth century. It is in essence a motte and bailey, fossilizing in stone the form of the primary earth and timber defences. A central shell keep crowns a prominent motte, with inner and outer wards, the former containing domestic accommodation and offices. It seems the castle became less a military focus than an administrative centre for the Honour of Pickering, and a favourite resort for hunting in the extensive forest of that name.

113

MARKENFIELD, North Yorkshire

Map Reference SE 295674, Map 99
Nearest Town Ripon
3 miles (5 km) south of Ripon off the A61, just north of the crossroads to Bishop Markton and Markington, is a bridle path on the west side of the road signposted 'Hell Wath Lane'. The house is ¾ mile (1 km) up the track. Privately owned and open April–Oct, Mon, 10–12.30, 2.15–5. In May only the exterior can be viewed on most days; there is an admission charge.

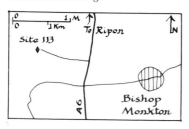

A fine hall house

John de Markingfield was given a licence to crenellate in 1310. Usually, this phrase means that the owner was allowed to build a castle, but soon after 1300 in the north the fashion grew for fortified manor houses instead. Markenfield is the best example of such a house, and still presents a charming combination of domesticity and military preparedness. Whether the decision to build a fortified house was repented after Bannockburn and the raids which followed it is unknown, but the fashion shows the increasingly peaceful expectations of the northern population.

The house is moated, and is L-shaped on plan. There have been some later alterations but the original arrangement of a first-floor hall in the main range facing the entrance is clear enough. The hall is lit by tall two-light windows with decorative tracery and was approached via an external stair; the gable of the porch can be seen to the left of the windows. Beneath the hall was the kitchen and other vaulted domestic offices. In the other arm of the L are a chapel and solar, but most of the windows in this section are later. In the angle between the ranges is a pinnacled stair turret, and the parapets are all embattled.

The tall two-light hall windows with the gable of the porch to the left.

114

THE YORKSHIRE ABBEYS, North Yorkshire

Fountains, Rievaulx and Jervaulx

The 'White Monks' or Cistercians were, as we explained in our *Norman Guide*, chiefly responsible for the economic exploitation of the Yorkshire uplands. In that book, we used Byland as an example of a well-preserved early plan, but we now turn to the other famous monasteries of Fountains, Rievaulx and Jervaulx to follow the story further. Before immersing ourselves in details, a word about the names of these monasteries. Fountains is straightforward enough, and refers to springs in the sides of the valley in which it lies. The others are similarly geographical, and reflect the difficulties of French founders trying to cope with the names of the valleys of the Rivers Rye and Ure respectively!

To take Fountains first, for it is both the finest example of a large Cistercian house and an incomparably beautiful site: it was founded when a small group of monks broke away from the old Benedictine foundation of St Mary's at York in 1132, choosing instead to follow the austere

Map Reference Fountains: SE 271683, Map 99
Rievaulx: SE 577849, Map 100
Jervaulx: SE 172857, Map 99
Nearest Town Ripon (Fountains, Jervaulx), Helmsley (Rievaulx)
Fountains is 2 miles (3 km) west of Ripon off the B6265 to Pateley Bridge. Owned by the National Trust and open every day except 24 and 25 Dec, Oct–March 10–4, April–end of June and Sept 10–7, July and Aug 10–8. Tel Ripon 4246.

Rievaulx: 2¼ miles (3.5 km) west of Helmsley on minor roads off the B1257. In HBMCE guardianship, open standard hours and Sunday mornings in summer.

Jervaulx: 15 miles (24 km) north-west of Ripon on the A6108. Private site open most days with honesty box.

Cistercian Order. Fountains was perfect; it was a remote level site amply supplied with water and building stone. The first years were hard, but in 1135 Hugh, Dean of York, joined the community and brought his considerable wealth with him. Local landowners such as the Mowbrays and Percys soon began to endow the new foundation and building began.

The community expanded rapidly, and in 1138–9 three daughter houses were established, the first of a total of eight, one of which was at Lysekloster in Norway. Progress was not even, however, and after the then Abbot opposed the King in his choice of an Archbishop of York, the candidate's supporters burnt the monastic buildings in 1147. A major phase of rebuilding and expansion took place between 1150 and 1302, mostly in the Cistercian Transitional style. This included the rebuilding and enlargement of the lay brothers' range on the west side of the cloister. An immense dormitory was constructed over an undercroft and the reredorter was built out over the River Skell.

The ruined latrine at the rear of the Abbot's house, with the east wall of the monks' refectory beyond.

We do not know the numbers of lay brothers at Fountains at this time, but it must have been comparable with if not greater than the five or six hundred at Rievaulx. There were in addition between fifty and a hundred monks. In all, including servants and others, there must have been around a thousand people occupying these buildings at the height of the monastery's fortunes in the thirteenth century. But many of the lay personnel would have been non-resident, looking after the granges and other interests of the house.

Fountains had very extensive endowments of land, mostly upland sheep pastures and fell. The Cistercians were agricultural pioneers and developed great skill in managing their often widely dispersed holdings. By the end of the thirteenth century Fountains was the largest producer of wool in the north and owned as many as 15,000 sheep; wool provided three-quarters of the monastery's income. There were in addition fisheries, particularly on Malham Tarn and Derwentwater; lead was mined at Greenhow Hill, iron came from Craven and Hutton Moor and millstones were made at Sawley and Crossland near Huddersfield. It is little wonder that the abbots of Fountains were often as much prized for their managerial skills as for their spirituality!

Building continued after 1203, including the Chapel of the Nine Altars, in the Early English Gothic style, signalling a departure from the strict austerity of the early years. During the second half of the century the economic difficulties which began to affect villages like Wharram Percy did not leave Fountains unscarred. The great famine of 1315–16 was followed by Scottish raids after Bannockburn which destroyed many granges. Lay brethren were in short supply, a difficulty compounded by the Black Death, and as a result many granges were leased out to lay owners. Fortunes rallied somewhat during the fourteenth century, but by then there were only thirty monks and 117 lay brothers. As late as the reign of Abbot Huby on the eve of the Dissolution reform was being attempted, but the monastery was finally dissolved in 1539.

Rievaulx and Jervaulx generally shared the fortunes of Fountains. Rievaulx in particular was a large and famous house and at its height had over 140 monks and 500 lay brothers, 'so that the church swarmed with them like a hive with bees'. The monastic buildings are well preserved and, like Fountains, were substantially complete by about 1200. Jervaulx was always a smaller house and is less complete today, but its ruins are kept in a careful state of benign neglect, which lends an agreeably Gothic air to the site. These three sites together illustrate one of the most impressive spiritual movements of medieval England. Their ruins have often been likened to 'towns', which in a sense they were, but their founders cherished a vision of divine order in the midst of this wild and beautiful countryside.

115
CASTLE BOLTON, North Yorkshire

Map Reference SD 034918, Map 98
Nearest Town Richmond
12 miles (19 km) south-west of
Richmond, signposted off the A684
in Wensleydale to Castle Bolton
and Aysgarth Falls. On minor roads
running along the edge of
Wensleydale the site of the castle
can be appreciated. The castle is in
private ownership and run as a
restaurant, open to the public with
gift shop.

Lord Scrope's apartments

This great castle, built in 1375–80, was the outward and visible sign of the prominence of Lord Scrope, Chancellor to Richard II and 1st Baron Scrope of Bolton. This castle was more than a status symbol, however; it was a serious military initiative, and the setting for the complicated affairs and lifestyle of a major late medieval magnate. For the castle had by this time become a more complex institution than in earlier times. It was now a residence as well as a refuge, and it had to accommodate all the retainers, soldiers and officers of the household which a man like Scrope would require for the maintenance of his dignity.

Bolton is an example of the northern courtyard type of castle in which the angle towers, by contrast with southern sites like Bodiam, are rectangular rather than round. The corner towers project slightly beyond the curtain walls, and the whole is symmetrical. The main entrance faces east down the village street; while this was not particularly strong, if an attacker did succeed in penetrating the outer wall he emerged into the central courtyard which was a daunting killing ground, with arrow loops on all sides. Around this courtyard are ranged suites of comfortable accommodation for as many as eight different households, as well as twelve chambers for functionaries such as priests and squires. This style of domestic accommodation can be likened to a modern block of flats, though here the kitchen and services were communal. These arrangements were an awkward compromise between the necessity for a garrison, stewards and other humbler folk and the desire on the part of the lord and his family for an element of privacy.

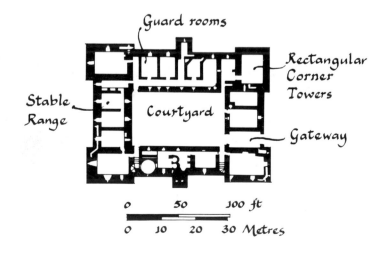

Ground-floor plan of the castle showing the central killing ground, well looped and guarded against assault.

The castle hangs off the north side of Wensleydale above the village, dominating the end of the attenuated village green. This village has a markedly rectangular layout with narrow fields running back behind the houses. The date of this planning is unknown, but it could well be contemporary with the castle itself. Just to the north of the castle is the parish church of St Oswald which was again probably built in the fourteenth century, and is first heard of in 1399. In all these activities, we see the hand of the great lord moulding the site of his stronghold to his own requirements.

116
MOUNT GRACE PRIORY, North Yorkshire

A community of hermits

Mount Grace is the best surviving English example of a Carthusian monastery. The Order was founded by St Bruno in the desolate valley of the Grande Chartreuse in south east France in 1084. It was an extremely austere order, and its setting high in the foothills of the Alps paralleled the privations of the third-century 'Desert Fathers' of Christian monasticism in the Egyptian desert.

The monks of the Order lived in separate house-like cells and, unlike the brothers of other Orders, did not observe the Divine Office each day in the church. Instead, they lived their lives in quiet contemplation, prayer and some physical labour, meeting together only on feast days and other special occasions. They were in essence hermits bound loosely together in a community.

Map Reference SE 453982, Map 99
Nearest Town Northallerton
7 miles (11 km) north-east of Northallerton, east of the A19 just ½ mile (0.8 km) south of junction with the A172. Well signposted, up narrow track with car park. Site is owned by the National Trust but is in HBMCE guardianship and is open standard hours. Tel Osmotherley 249.

The reconstructed 'house cell' at Mount Grace; its accommodation must have been generous by medieval standards, with a workshop above and domestic chamber beneath, all set in the midst of a garden

The monks wore rough hair shirts and coarse undyed habits. For three days a week they lived on bread and water, and on the other four they had vegetables which they cooked in their cells, some cheese and fish. Book writing and carpentry were the favoured labours of the brothers, and each kept a garden around his cell in which herbs and flowers were grown. Lay brothers looked after the practical affairs of the monastery under the direction of the Procurator, who was responsible for the administration.

Mount Grace was founded late in our period, in 1398, by Thomas Holland, Duke of Surrey and half-brother to Richard II. The sombre aspect of the Carthusians commended itself to a population still recovering from the horrors of the plague. The layout of the site is highly distinctive, and the sort of communal buildings normally associated with monastic life, such as the frater, dormitory and large church, are absent here. Instead, the inner court is surrounded by the small house-like cells of the monks, one of which has been reconstructed to show the layout of a workshop above and a domestic chamber beneath.

117
HARTLEPOOL CHURCH, TOWN WALLS AND PORT, Cleveland

Map Reference NZ 529336, Map 93 Take the A689 from Hartlepool centre and follow the signs to the Headland and St Hilda's Church. The church stands proudly on the promontory, which was the site of an important Saxon monastery. South-west of the church the medieval town wall and Sandwell Gate can be seen.

Hartlepool might at first sight seem an improbable place to bring the trusting visitor in search of medieval England, but it has a fascinating history. This was the site of a monastery founded in the 640s by Hieu, who was succeeded as abbess by St Hilda, who later founded the famous monastery at Whitby. Recently, archaeologists have discovered traces of Anglo-Saxon buildings beside the church, and much new light has been shed on the early development of this important site on a peninsula above the North Sea.

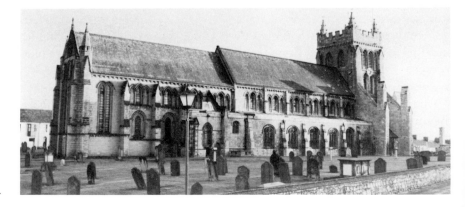

This great church in the Early English style was originally meant to have had transepts at the west end, as indicated by the protruding walls on the far right.

The late fourteenth-century gateway in the Sea Wall.

A town certainly existed at Hartlepool by the mid twelfth century, and in 1200 it was granted a charter by King John. At this time, it was owned by the powerful Bruce family, who built the spectacular church and were probably responsible for the earliest bank and ditch defences. Robert Bruce, a Norman noble, was the very same man who killed John Comyn in 1306 and had himself crowned King of Scots. Ironically, it was the war with England that followed which led to Hartlepool being devastated by the Scots under James Douglas in 1316, the inhabitants watching helplessly from their ships off shore. Edward I made Hartlepool a major supply base for his Scottish invasion, and the recent excavations have located banks of ovens in which bread for the army may have been baked.

Today, we find a town graced by a splendid church in the Early English Gothic style and girt with a handsome stone wall to the south. The nave has fine six-bay arcades, that to the south being slightly earlier; both have attached shafts and moulded circular capitals. The western bays of the chancel are original, as is the western tower decorated with tall blank arcading with shaft rings. Remarkably, the church was meant to have had a cruciform plan at the west end rather than the east, a feature reminiscent of Kelso and highly unusual in England.

Apart from this memorable church, the fourteenth-century Sea Wall to the south has a gateway to the Fish Sands where boats used to draw up on the shingly beach. It affords a fine view of the harbour with a lighthouse and a jetty; cargo ships and fishing smacks still use the port and it has an air of activity. The town wall crossed the headland, though most has now been removed.

118
WARTON, Lancashire

Map Reference SD 499723, Map 97
Nearest Town Lancaster
6 miles (9.5 km) north of Lancaster
on minor road west of the A6. In
the centre of the village, opposite
the church, behind the
early 19th-century rectory. In HBMCE
guardianship, open standard hours,
no custodian but a clear plan with
description are on display.

A medieval rectory

Opposite the church of St Oswald, behind the present rectory, are the ruins of its medieval precursor. Fourteenth-century evidence in the church is limited to the south aisle wall and other fragments, but it is to that period that the rectory ruins belong. They represent a fairly modest medieval house, the principal element of which was a ground-floor hall open to the roof. In the gable of the 'high' end is a quatrefoil light, and immediately to the west is a small block, now partly incorporated into the rear of the later rectory, which probably contained a chapel.

At the 'low' end of the hall are the customary entrances to the buttery and pantry, in this case flanking a central passage to a vanished kitchen. Over these service rooms was a chamber with a fireplace in the end wall and a smaller inner room. Only the lower parts of these rooms survive, together with a garderobe. The house would have afforded comfortable accommodation for a single man and his household, and we could imagine the medieval rectors of Warton sitting by the hall fire and pondering their sermons.

The hall lies to the left, and the doorway near the centre led into the 'low' end. To the right are the remains of the service block.

119

RUFFORD AND SAMLESBURY, Lancashire

Timber-framed halls

These two halls belong to the very end of our period – and might indeed have been built after 1485 – but they are essentially medieval houses and provide a good impression of the standard of living open to the very wealthy. Rufford was held by the Heskeths from the thirteenth century until 1936, when the then Lord Hesketh presented the house to the National Trust. It is built around three sides of a courtyard with the splendid timber-framed hall linking service rooms and chambers in the east wing and family rooms to the west. Much has been changed later, but the hall itself is practically unaltered.

The exterior is straightforward enough, with a large polygonal bay window lighting the upper end, and a doorway at the lower. The sides have two four-light windows and decorative timber quatrefoils. By contrast, the interior is elaborately, even riotously, decorated. The hammerbeam roof is of five bays with cambered collars, embattled hammer beams terminated by angels and huge armorial bosses. Four purlins divide the roof on either side into three tiers of quatrefoil wind braces with concave sided paterae at their centres. The screen, which divides the screens passage from the body of the hall, is movable, and is carved with primitive richness; it is, however, an addition of the early sixteenth century.

Samlesbury is similar to Rufford in that the hall is the earliest element of the remaining plan, which is also arranged round a courtyard. Despite later alteration, it is still an important example of the south Lancashire and Cheshire type of timber-framed hall. The roof is of four bays and has arch braces supporting cambered collar beams with square kingposts above. Diagonal wind braces, scalloped on one side, run between the purlins and

Map Reference Rufford: SD 463160, Map 108
Nearest Town Ormskirk
7 miles (11 km) north of Ormskirk on the east side of the A59, at the north end of the village. National Trust, open April–end Oct, daily (except Fri) 2–6.

Map Reference Samlesbury: SD 590300, Map 102
Nearest Town Preston
On the A677, 6 miles (9.5 km) east of Preston. Samlesbury Hall Trust, open Tues–Sun, 11.30–5 in summer, 11.30–4 in winter.

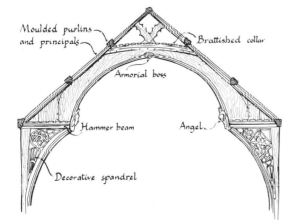

One of the highly decorated roof trusses at Rufford with pierced decorated spandrels, carved angels on the hammer beams and a boss to the apex.

the principal rafters. Unfortunately, the original appearance of the hall can only be deduced from nineteenth-century illustrations. They show carved doorways, a movable screen like the one at Rufford and an elaborate canopy at the higher end.

120
CHESHIRE AND GREATER MANCHESTER

Timber-framed houses

There is an amazing wealth of timber-framed houses in this area, natural enough in view of the fact that it was heavily wooded in our period and included the great forests of Delamere, Wirral and Macclesfield. Apart from high-status and defensive buildings like the greater abbeys, parish churches and castles, timber was widely used for houses and smaller churches. Timber frames were erected on low stone walls to preserve them from damp, and the panels filled with wattle and daub. The floor and roof timbers were notched, tenoned or pegged into the principal beams.

All we can do here is to indicate the best examples which are (or in the case of Baguley Hall, will be) publicly accessible. Baguley is a good place to start since it is one of the earliest examples, dating to the early fourteenth century. The original arched doorways survive, and the walls have heavy broad upright and horizontal timbers with braces in the form of cusped St Andrew's crosses. The wall above the screens passage is particularly impressive, with quatrefoils in its upper parts formed by cusped braces.

Smithills Hall was probably built by one of the Radclyffe family in the later fifteenth century and the hall is the earliest remaining part. The roof has quatrefoil wind braces, a motif which is continued in the framing of the east and west walls. The other walls were later rebuilt in stone. Nearby Hall i' t' Wood, one of the most famous and picturesque of all these buildings, has similar framing to that at Smithills, but incorporates a projecting upper floor.

Bramhall, Little Moreton and Aldington halls repeat the same basic pattern with sturdy frames and cusped braces. At Bramhall, the hall has an oriel window and wall-paintings, which remind us that the stark black and white appearance of these buildings is very much a nineteenth-century convention. Originally they would have been much more subtle, and were probably often coloured both inside and out. Little Moreton, another 'chocolate box' house, was originally H-shaped with the great hall linking two domestic ranges. It was remodelled in 1559, however, and we are left with only the 'skeleton' of the medieval house.

Finally, we turn to Aldington. The manor came into the possession of

Map Reference Baguley Hall
Baguley Hall in Greater Manchester is situated in the Wythenshaw district.

Map Reference Smithills Hall, Greater Manchester: SJ 700115, Map 109
Nearest Town Bolton
1½ miles (2.5 km) north-east of Bolton off the A58. Well signposted. Bolton Metropolitan Borough. Open April–Sept, Mon–Sat (except Thurs) 10–6, Sun 2–6; Oct–March, Mon–Sat (except Thurs) 10–5. Tel Bolton 41265.

Map Reference Hall i' t' Wood, Greater Manchester: SJ 722115, Map 109
Nearest Town Bolton
2 miles (3 km) north-east of Bolton town centre off the A58. Well signposted. Bolton Metropolitan Borough. Opening times as Smithills Hall. Tel Bolton 51159.

Map Reference Bramhall, Cheshire: SJ 890863, Map 109
Nearest Town Stockport
4 miles (6.5 km) south of Stockport, well signposted off the A5102. Metropolitan Borough of Stockport, open Jan–Nov, daily except Mon, 12–4 in winter, 12–5 in summer. Tel 061 485 3708.

the Leigh family in 1315; nothing remains of this period, but we know a house stood here and that it had a chapel licensed in 1398. The existing great hall was built by Thomas Leigh between 1480 and 1505, and is timber-framed throughout. It is of imposing dimensions and has a splendid hammer beam roof of the type seen at Rufford with angels and heraldry. The lower end of the hall has the customary three service doorways, but here they are enriched with carved tracery and strange beasts. At the higher end is the grandest timber canopy of honour in the region; dated 1505, it presumably set the final seal on this resplendent chamber.

Map Reference Little Moreton Hall, Cheshire: SJ 832589, Map 118
Nearest Town Congleton
4 miles (6.5 km) south-west of Congleton off the A34. Well signposted. National Trust, open March and Oct, Sat, Sun, 2–6; April–end Sept, 2–6 daily except Tues. Tel 02602 272018.

Map Reference Aldington Hall, Cheshire: SJ 905805, Map 109
Nearest Town Macclesfield
5 miles (8 km) north of Macclesfield on the A523. Privately owned. Open Good Friday–29 Sept, Sun and Bank Holidays. In Aug, Wed and Sat 2–5.30. Tel Prestbury 829206.

Bramhall retains a pleasantly domestic air and, if we ignore the Victorian 'black and whiteness', we could almost return on the instant to the fifteenth century.

121
NORTON PRIORY, Cheshire

Excavation and Museum

Norton Priory was founded in 1134 as a house of the Austin Canons, who followed the Rule of St Augustine of Hippo. The canons were popular with lay folk, and Norton attracted many gifts from local landowners. Indeed, the house became so wealthy that it was actually raised to the status of an abbey in the fifteenth century, which was unusual for an Augustinian foundation. But Norton was, in many ways, a rather undistinguished house; its buildings were fairly modest and not particularly well preserved. The site merits inclusion in this book, however, by virtue of the very imaginative interpretation of the site which the Norton Priory Museum Trust has effected. For under its auspices Norton provides a unique insight

Map Reference SJ 548830, Map 108
Nearest Town Runcorn
From the M56 Junction 12 the site is well signposted. Norton Priory Museum Trust. Open March–Oct, 12–6 weekends, 12–5 weekdays; Nov–Feb daily 12–4. Tel 09285 69895.

A section of one of the delightful fourteenth-century tiled pavements at Norton Priory.

into monastic life and also into many other facets of medieval society.

Excavation of the priory church and claustral buildings is well advanced, and still continues. In the museum is a great range of finds from the site, ranging from pottery to window glass and tombstones to tiles. All this is interesting enough, but at Norton the techniques used to produce many of these items are explained and displayed. A kiln, in which decorative floor tiles of the type seen here, at Hailes Abbey and elsewhere were fired, is actually on display, and experiments have been conducted into manufacturing techniques. This use of 'experimental archaeology' marks Norton out as a rewarding place to visit, and many of the technical questions which spring to mind when we look at abbeys and other major medieval buildings are answered here.

122
CHESTER, Cheshire

Map Reference SJ 405658, Map 117 Castle is in guardianship and open standard hours, good exhibition. The most notable medieval stone vaulted undercrofts are at Brookland, 12 Bridge Street; Brown's Restaurant, 28 Eastgate Street; and the Blue Bell Café, Northgate Street. The 15th-century Dee bridge was widened in 1826 and carries a modern road.

A great medieval city

Medieval Chester grew up on the site of the Roman legionary fortress called Deva. By the mid fourteenth century it was a prosperous port on the River Dee, but later there were problems with silting and trade declined. Apart from the Cathedral and churches, there are vaulted cellars, the covered first-floor walkways called the Rows, now largely Victorian, and the whole circuit of the medieval walls.

The walls are some two and a half miles in length and built of red sandstone; they rest partly on Roman foundations and were largely completed by the thirteenth century. Chester is the only completely walled town remaining in England. The Water Tower, added to the circuit in 1322–5, was designed to protect the harbour entrance. The Dee Bridge is slightly later, and represents an impressive feat of medieval engineering. The Castle was located in the south-west corner of the town, but most of the early work has been removed.

The late thirteenth century saw the peak of Chester's fortunes, for it was then used as a base for Edward I's campaigns as well as being a mercantile centre in its own right. It is from this period that the handsome cellars come, some twenty-five in all, which were under the houses of the more prominent merchants. The cellar at No 11 Watergate St is probably the best, and it may be as early as 1270.

The Cathedral precinct is an oasis of calm, retaining something of its former monastic air. For until 1541 this was a Benedictine abbey, and it was only later that Henry VIII raised it to cathedral status. The church is a complicated building and was heavily restored in the last century, partly on account of its soft red standstone. The best feature is undoubtedly the late-fourteenth-century choir stalls, which have poppyhead ends and elaborate canopies encrusted with crocketed pinnacles. The Dean's stall has a Tree of Jesse as well as a charming seated pilgrim. The Vice Dean's stall opposite has a Pelican in her Piety, a well-known theme, but more unusual is the Elephant and Castle about half-way along the north side.

The greatest treasures are the misericords. These vignettes of medieval life and thought are a fascinating collection, and well illustrate the very diverse themes at the command of the sculptors. They are a glorious mixture of the sacred and profane, the churchy and the secular. Only a few can be detailed here – there are over fifty altogether, although five are Victorian. Here may be found wrestlers, a quarrelsome couple, piglets searching for acorns, various knights including the famous one falling from his horse (possibly representing Pride), as well as depictions of Gluttony, the Coronation of the Virgin and a delightful study of the Flight of Alexander. Perhaps the best of all depicts two herons, wonderfully naturalistic and yet retaining that calm dignity which speaks so eloquently of the age which made them.

The late fourteenth-century elephant and castle bench end in the Cathedral.

123
LOWER PEOVER AND MARTON, Cheshire

Timber-framed churches

Timber-framed churches come as something of a surprise today but wooden churches were common in the Anglo-Saxon and Norman periods, and even during the Middle Ages they must have been quite usual in wooded parts of the country like Cheshire. St Oswald's at Peover is a building of great interest and considerable importance. It is possible that it originated in the thirteenth century, since there is a record of a deed of 1269 between the parishioners of Peover and the Prior of Norton agreeing to the foundation of a chapel and the appointment of a chaplain. In the light of recent work on barns in Essex and elsewhere, there is no reason why the rather crude octagonal pillars of the nave could not be of that date. Although restored, the interior is impressive with its octagonal arcades, mostly original, and arch braced roof.

More atmospheric is Marton. This little church was founded in about 1350 by Sir John Davenport of Bramhall, and was endowed in 1370 with land to maintain a priest. During the eighteenth century the chancel and side chapels were rebuilt in brick and the windows were replaced in 1850, but the nave and fine timber belfry are original. The contrast between the outside, which has something of the aspect of a cricket pavilion, and the

Map Reference Lower Peover: SJ 774743, Map 118
Marton: SJ 850668, Map 118
Nearest Town Macclesfield
Lower Peover is 2 miles (3 km) south-west of Knutsford. The church is just off the main road, up a lane called 'The Cobbles'; a rustic wooden sign points to the church.

Marton is 3 miles (4.5 km) north of Congleton on A34. Church has good car park.

Another timber-framed church can be seen at Warburton, SJ 7089, Map 109.

interior, which is a 'forest' of octagonal wooden pillars, arch braces and tie beams, can only be described as spectacular. No other timber church retains its medieval atmosphere half so well.

The fourteenth-century timberwork of Marton Church; note the octagonal pillars and arched braces to the trusses.

124
ASTBURY CHURCH, Cheshire

A remarkable roof
The Church of St Mary was planned in the fourteenth century, as the work in the aisles indicates, but most of the present structure was built in the late fifteenth. It presents a curious external aspect since it has an unusual three-storey porch and a detached tower and spire. The tower and recessed spire are important because they are precisely dated by the will of Roger Swettenham, to 1366. The interior is mainly Perpendicular, of seven bays, with no structural division between the nave and chancel.

But it is the roofs at Astbury which are the main reason for visiting the church. Cheshire is well blessed with good roofs – Barthomley, the nave at Malpas with its bosses and angels, and the late example of Northwich are memorable – but Astbury has the finest set in the county. The roofs over the south porch, the nave, chancel and aisles are splendid examples of the local style. They are divided into compartments by cambered beams and purlins forming eight square panels to each bay. All the principal members are carved with running mouchettes and the elaborate bosses carry monograms or Symbols of the Passion. In the south aisle are extraordinary pendent lanterns enriched with blind cusped tracery, crocketed pinnacles and foliage; they look like nothing so much as majestic Christmas decorations.

Map Reference SJ 846615, Map 118
Nearest Town Congleton
1 mile (1.6 km) south of Congleton on the A34, set in an attractive village square.

One of the extraordinary pendent 'lanterns' in the south aisle at Astbury Church.

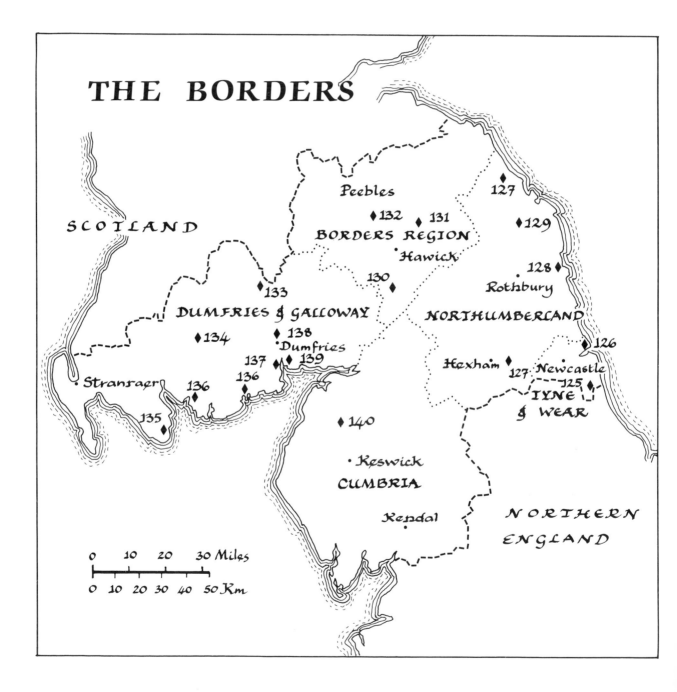

THE BORDERS

SCOTLAND

Peebles

♦ 132 ♦ 131

BORDERS REGION

•Hawick

♦ 127

♦ 129

130
♦

128 ♦

Rothbury

♦ 133

DUMFRIES & GALLOWAY

NORTHUMBERLAND

♦ 134

♦ 138
•Dumfries

137 ♦ 139
♦ ♦

Hexham

♦ 126

127 Newcastle

Stranraer

♦ 136

136
♦

♦ 127

125 ♦
TYNE
& WEAR

135
♦

♦ 140

•Keswick

CUMBRIA

Kendal
•

NORTHERN
ENGLAND

0   10   20   30 Miles

0   10   20   30   40   50 Km

THE BORDERS

Introduction

The Border during the Middle Ages became a progressively uneasy place in which to dwell. After the relative calm of the thirteenth century, Edward I attacked Berwick in 1296 and pressed deep into Scotland. At first the war went well enough, but Edward never quite succeeded in subjugating the Scots, and even the victory over William Wallace at Falkirk did not solve the problem. With the accession of Edward II in 1307 the Scots were pre-eminent once more, and after the Battle of Bannockburn in 1314 Scottish raiders ranged freely over the Border. They forced the northern English on to the defensive, and preyed upon their wealthy farms and settlements.

Gradually, over the fourteenth century, the Border line itself was forced southwards by the Scots until the English held only a chain of castles in south Scotland. Raiding continued on both sides, and by the mid fourteenth century the Scottish lowlands actually fared the worse. This uneasy political situation resulted in a distinctive legacy of monuments on both sides of the Border. The English and Scottish kings vied for the major citadels like Berwick and Carlisle, but also kept a careful eye on castle-building projects in this frontier zone. The Scots' construction of Hermitage Castle, controlling as it did the Liddesdale route across the Border, did not go unremarked, and that castle, together with other major fortresses like Caerlaverock, frequently changed hands.

But for every great magnate like the Percys at Warkworth and the Douglases at Threave, there were many more smaller lords and their families who had not the means to build substantial castles. Their answer was the fortified house or 'pele' tower, called after the Latin *pilum*, meaning a palisade. Southern Scotland has the thirteenth-century fortified house at Morton as well as the tower houses of Newark, Cardoness and Orchardton. In England is the small castle, really a slightly overblown tower house, at Hylton, the vicar's pele at Corbridge, the strange 'church pele' at Ancroft and the fortified church at Boltongate in Cumbria. These smaller fortifications are dramatic reminders of the perils of Border life during the later

Middle Ages, and in the case of the Corbridge pele at least it was still in use as late as the seventeenth century.

Amidst these difficulties the arts of peace did fitfully flourish, however. At Muirhouselaw in southern Scotland is a rare example of a small farmstead surrounded by a light moat which cannot have been intended for defence. There must have been many such homesteads, but few have survived. In England, farming is represented by a most unusual 'site', the herd of wild white cattle at Chillingham. These strange beasts are seemingly the direct descendants of the herd which is known to have been in the park here in the thirteenth century, and they thus provide a unique living link between past and present.

Religious life is well represented in this area, beginning with the ancient site at Whithorn with its memories of St Ninian, which remained an important pilgrimage centre throughout the Middle Ages. At Lincluden is probably the best of the late medieval Scottish collegiate churches, while Sweetheart is a fine though late Cistercian abbey, founded by the sorrowing Lady Devorgilla in memory of the 'sweet heart' of her husband. Across the Border, the splendid rock-cut hermitage at Warkworth, buried in trees beside the River Coquet, is a romantic attraction not to be missed. Otherwise, Tynemouth Priory probably sums up the Border as well as any other site: an uncomfortable balance between the conflicting requirements of defence and prayer. After the foundation of the castle there late in the thirteenth century, Tynemouth was a military as well as a spiritual bastion against the Scottish menace.

125

HYLTON CASTLE, Tyne and Wear

Map Reference NZ 358588, Map 88
Nearest Town Sunderland
3¾ miles (6 km) west of
Sunderland, just off the A1290,
signposted to the Hylton Castle
Housing Estate. It is set in its own
small park surrounded by trees, and
retains a calm air despite being
surrounded by the modern estate.
The castle is in HBMCE
guardianship and open standard
hours.

A tower house

The family of Hylton seems to have held the locality and castle from the mid twelfth century until the mid eighteenth. In about 1400 Sir William Hylton built the existing castle in the form of a strong tower house which was described as a 'gate house'. This description seems misleading, however, since this was always the dominant building on the site and there is little evidence of any ancillary structures or even of a real defensive circuit. The castle was clearly intended as the principal residence of the family, and it makes few concessions to defence in either its site or internal arrangements.

The castle was considerably altered in both the eighteenth and nineteenth centuries, and hence the details of the original fenestration are uncertain. There would obviously have been fewer windows than now, but

The imposing west façade of the castle.

apart from this difference the complicated battlements and extravagant armorial displays, designed to advertise the owner's baronial rank, are original. The array of heraldic shields on the main front is one of the castle's greatest glories. Apart from the Hylton arms, important Northumbrian families like the Percys and the Lumleys are represented, as well as the arms of Walter Skirlaw, Bishop of Durham. This was the outward and visible sign of Hylton's claim to be considered among the northern nobility.

Inside, the vaulted ground floor was used for storage and services as well as for the accommodation of at least one retainer. On the first floor was the great hall, with the solar chamber at one end and the service rooms, here reduced to two, at the other. To one side was the chapel, and a turning stair gave access to the upper chambers and the roof.

Near the castle are the ruins of St Catherine's Chapel, which was a dependency of Monkwearmouth church. The chapel is first mentioned in the twelfth century, but the existing fabric appears to belong to an early-fifteenth-century rebuilding. Late in the sixteenth century huge, canted two-storey bays were added to either side of the earlier chancel, in the manner of transepts. The nave has now disappeared, and an early-eighteenth-century doorway gives access to the chancel through the blocked chancel arch. The chapel and castle together provide a good impression of a smaller late medieval lord's home. We are fortunate that this site is accessible; many a tower house elsewhere is occupied just as comfortably now as when it was first built!

The arms of Sir William Washington, from one of the shields on the west front.

126

TYNEMOUTH PRIORY AND CASTLE, Tyne and Wear

Map Reference NZ 374695, Map 88 Not signposted, but stands on a promontory at the east end of the broad Front Street. The Priory is in HBMCE guardianship and open standard hours. It has an imposing setting and shares its site with a 20th-century coastguard station.

Even though we visited Tynemouth on a rainy and mist-bound day, the majesty of its site above the sea was manifest. Indeed, the mournful foghorn and tolling bell of the offshore buoy provided an atmospheric accompaniment to this memorable site. The exposed position has meant that the wind has heavily eroded the stone walls into fantastic shapes and, in view of the rugged nature of the place, it is no surprise that it was first settled in the seventh century as an austere monastic site. Even in the Percy chantry at the east end of the later church, the howling wind is a constant reminder of its location.

The monastery was refounded as a daughter house of the Benedictine monastery of St Albans in 1090 and the abbey church and claustral ranges were substantially completed with the early-thirteenth-century west front. By the end of that century more building was required; the natural defences of the site were considered inadequate in the face of the Scottish menace, and in 1296 the monks obtained a licence to crenellate from Edward I.

So from the late thirteenth century onwards Tynemouth became a temporal as well as a spiritual sanctuary. This function was continued after the Reformation by Henry VIII, and even as recently as the Second World War, when the site was again fortified to act as a coastal defence base for Tyneside. The most dramatic physical evidence of this military import-ance is the massive gatetower and barbican built by Prior John de Wheathamstede late in the fourteenth century. This 'castle' had been

The fifteenth-century vault of the Percy Chapel.

jointly funded by the priory itself, fattened by the offerings of pilgrims at its shrines of St Oswin and St Henry of Coquet, and the Crown, which once more recognized the value of this buttress against the Scots.

Tynemouth is thus a unique example of the confluence of ecclesiastical and military designs. The priory is set within a castle, and the enclosure is one of the largest fortified areas in England. From at least the fourteenth century the priory was required to maintain a standing garrison and we can well imagine the cost and unsuitableness of such an arrangement. It is fitting that the mighty Percy family chose this place to build a chantry chapel in the mid fifteenth century. This structure is small but surprisingly intricate, with a well-preserved vault painted to resemble the night sky, and having no fewer than thirty-three sculpted bosses wherein are mingled the arms of the Percys with Christ, the Virgin and the Twelve Apostles.

When visiting this forlorn and windswept chamber, the visitor might care to ponder the lament of a twelfth-century monk sent here from St Albans:

> . . . Spring and summer never come here. The north wind is always blowing, bringing with it cold and snow, or else storms in which the wind tosses the salt sea foam in masses over our buildings.

One of the bosses from the Percy vault depicting The Risen Christ holding the Banner of the Resurrection, with the kneeling figure of Mary Magdalene beside him.

127
CORBRIDGE AND ANCROFT, Northumberland

Towers on the Border

After England and Scotland came to open warfare in 1296, the Border between the kingdoms became a dangerous place indeed. Here in Northumberland, Edward I's ferocious attack on Berwick brought the rapid realization that the Scots would strike back. With the death of Edward and the disaster of Bannockburn in 1314, the Scots were ascendant and men of the Borders had to make what shift they could for their own defence.

Churches and their clergy were not always spared by invading forces, and some high prelates actually took part in battles at the head of their armed retainers. Thus the situation of Corbridge, on one of the main invasion routes into England, and Ancroft, which was isolated even further north, dictated prudent precautions. Both were provided with pele towers; these were rectangular or square structures, often protected with a palisade, called in Latin *pilum*, whence the term 'pele' is derived. These peles were the more modest equivalents of the great castles at Alnwick and Warkworth.

Map Reference Corbridge: NY 989644, Map 87
The Pele, in the churchyard in the centre of the town, is an information centre open 10–6 weekdays and 1–5 Sun.

Map Reference Ancroft: NY 999450, Map 75
Nearest Town Berwick-on-Tweed
5 miles (8 km) south of Berwick off the A1 on the B6525.

At Corbridge, the pele stands in the churchyard. It was built of large reused Roman stones in around 1300, and was used as a vicarage until the seventeenth century. Within fifty years of its construction, Corbridge had been burnt five times by Scottish armies. The tower has three storeys, the lowest, used for storage, having narrow slits in the walls and a small doorway to the east. The first floor has single larger windows in the side walls, matching the contemporary south doorway in the chancel of the church. The second floor has small rectangular lights, and above are reconstructed battlements. Defence was the overriding priority of the structure, and it must have been an exceedingly uncomfortable place in which to live.

Ancroft tower is highly unusual because it is actually built over the western end of the church. A twelfth-century corbel table extends beneath the tower walls, showing that it was originally part of the nave. The handsome south doorway was blocked by the east tower wall, and a spiral staircase was placed behind it. The ground floor is tunnel vaulted, and the deep splayed windows of the upper floor proclaim its defensive purpose. Even if such refuges could not ultimately prevail against an army, they provided security against less organized bands of marauders and thieves to which the Border was always prey.

Corbridge Pele, a stronghold within the churchyard.

128
WARKWORTH CASTLE, HERMITAGE AND TOWN,
Northumberland

The small town of Warkworth stands safely in a bend of the River Coquet, and the southern – landward – approach is guarded by a strong castle. This place was an important Border stronghold from at least the twelfth century, and it contains a group of medieval structures unparalleled elsewhere. The first of these must be the castle, which retains some Norman work in the walls of the outer ward, and which was successively strengthened throughout our period by the addition of towers and accommodation to its basic motte and bailey plan.

Warkworth is, however, most closely associated with the rise of the Percys, and it is to the third Percy lord, father of Harry Hotspur, that we owe the most magnificent addition to the castle. The elevation of Henry Percy to the earldom of Northumberland in 1377 led him to demolish the old Norman stone keep and to replace it with a tower house of the most advanced design, which may have influenced Tattershall and Raglan.

In plan, it is a square block with wings projecting from the centre of each side. The angles are chamfered, giving a decidedly un-medieval appearance, and at the centre is a lantern or light shaft which is a further advanced feature. The roominess of the plan permitted a grace of living seldom encountered in fortresses of the period. Apart from providing this lavish tower house, the Earl also revamped the lower hall in the Outer Court and began to construct a large chapel below the keep. This was destined to act as a college of chantry priests, but it was never finished, probably due to the reverses suffered by the family during the Wars of the Roses.

The town to the north with its long market-place was in effect contained within a huge outer bailey of the castle. At the north end stands a fine late-fourteenth-century fortified bridge with guard chambers. The parish church is basically of the twelfth century, and is an important example of a small but massive nave structure with a contemporary chancel vault. The lanes around the church retain their medieval scale, and in the fields to the west of the castle can be seen extensive traces of medieval ridge and furrow cultivation upon which the townspeople must have depended for their livelihood.

As if all this were not enough, Warkworth also boasts a most exotic hermitage which is reached from the castle by a river walk and a short boat trip. This is an ideal manner in which to approach such a secluded spot which is so permeated with that mysterious atmosphere of medievalism which fuelled the return to Camelot in the eighteenth and nineteenth

Map Reference Castle: NU 247057, Map 81
Hermitage: NU 242060
Nearest Town Alnwick
7½ miles (12 km) south of Alnwick on the A1068. The castle and hermitage are in guardianship. The castle is open standard hours, the hermitage in the summer season only. There is a good car park. From the castle, walk along the path by the River Coquet. The custodian will then row you across the river to the hermitage, a delightful short trip.

You can see well-preserved medieval ridge and furrow cultivation across the valley to the west of the castle.

The Emblems of the Crucifixion from a shield on the chapel wall.

A misty view of the castle towering above the River Coquet.

centuries. The Hermitage and Chapel of the Holy Trinity are hewn from the living rock, and were probably founded in the late fourteenth century. The living accommodation comprises a hall, solar and kitchen, all probably of the fourteenth century.

The first documentary reference is in 1487, when we learn that Thomas Barker was appointed chaplain for life to celebrate the mass and to receive in return a stipend of 66s 8d. What confessions and assignations took place here? Can we not imagine the young Hotspur bustling in here to make his peace with God before defying the Scots at Otterburn and Homildon Hill? But an indication of a more sombre purpose is indicated by the presence of the text from Psalm 42, v 3: 'My tears have been my meat day and night.' Two tales are told: one that a knight sought to expiate the accidental slaying of his brother, and the other that a knight mourned the loss of his sweetheart here. We will almost certainly never know the truth, but this little chapel, with its vault, stoup, altar and windows all cut from the rock, must be one of the most atmospheric sites in this book.

129

CHILLINGHAM, Northumberland

The wild white cattle

What, the trusting reader might well enquire, are cattle doing in a guide to medieval Britain? The reason is quite simple; there are records of these strange beasts going well back into the Middle Ages, and their presence at Chillingham is suspected from at least the thirteenth century. Therefore, since meat formed an important element in the diets of at least the upper echelons of medieval society, it seems desirable to look at the evidence available.

Many English breeds of cattle seem to owe their origins to pre-Roman Celtic strains, with the three black varieties – the Welsh Black, the Kerry and the Dexter – being among the most ancient. The Romans may have improved these breeds but it is noteworthy that Saxon cattle bones are from larger and more robust specimens than these early types of cattle. Also, the so-called 'coloured' breeds like the Lincoln Red, Sussex, Hereford, Devon and Red Poll all come from the southern areas of Britain, the areas of the Anglo-Saxon settlement. But we do not yet know how important these correlations are. Suffice to say that the cow was well established as a draught animal as well as a food source by the beginning of our period, and that monastic and other interests were at least as involved

Map Reference NU 062260, Map 75
Nearest Town Wooler
Take the B6348 from Wooler towards Bamburgh. At Chatton (5 miles, 8 km), turn south to Chillingham (1½ miles, 2.4 km) Follow the 'wild cattle' signs in Chillingham and turn left at the Church. The park is open April–Oct, weekdays, Sat, bank hols, 10–12, 2–5, Sun 2–5, closed Tues. Tel Chatton 250 for further information from the Park Warden. The park is well sheltered in the Till Valley. Also visit the church to see the monument to Sir Ralph Grey.

THE CHILLINGHAM BULL

A Bewick print of the Chillingham Bull.

in producing cattle as they were sheep. At the time of the Dissolution, for example, Fountains Abbey had 2,356 horned cattle and only 326 sheep.

But what of the White Cattle? There was from earliest recorded times a belief among husbandmen that white or pale coloured animals were less hardy than black or coloured varieties. Accordingly, they would probably not have been improved by breeding if anything better was to hand. Here at Chillingham, royal permission was granted during the thirteenth century to crenellate the castle and to create a park. This park apparently contained white cattle at that time, and has done so ever since. Thus the cattle which we see at Chillingham today are, as far as anyone knows, directly descended from those beasts of 700 years ago, and in seeing them, we are gaining some impression of the livestock of our period.

The cattle, which are now owned and managed by a charitable trust, roam completely wild in the park, and seem quite at home against their romantic backdrop of high flat-topped sandstone moors. In the winter of 1947 the herd was reduced to only thirteen head, and in 1967 foot and mouth disease got within two miles of the park pale. Yet they still survive, and let us hope that they will stand and stare for seven centuries more!

130

HERMITAGE CASTLE, Borders

Map Reference NY 497961, Map 79
Nearest Town Hawick
15 miles (24 km) south of Hawick on the B6399. The castle is just off the main road on the west side and is in SDD guardianship, open standard hours.

A Border fortress

The fastness of Hermitage enjoys a dark reputation for past deeds of murder and treachery, but when we visited it on a July evening it seemed peaceful enough, and it commands magnificent views of Liddesdale in which it stands. The Scots first built a castle here in 1242, to the great consternation of the English, for Liddesdale was a major corridor of communication and any threat to its neutrality was serious. No certain trace of that castle remains, but some of the earthworks around the later structure might derive from this first fortress.

At the core of the present castle is a small thick-walled tower house, probably built by the English family of the Dacres in the mid fourteenth century. This house probably came to grief during the Border wars of Richard II's reign, after the Battle of Chevy Chase. Later in the fourteenth century the Scottish Douglases made the earlier house the kernel of a large rectangular keep with a short wing attached to the south-west angle. About 1400 the castle was extended yet again to resemble more closely what we see today. Large square towers were added to three of the angles, and on the site of the earlier projecting west wing a larger service tower containing a bakehouse was built. Floor levels within the castle were

The mighty castle stands foursquare in Border country.

altered at various times, and in the sixteenth century gun loops were added, probably at the time the castle was taken back by the Scottish Crown owing to the treachery of its owners.

While the castle today presents a remarkably intact aspect, it is largely due to a well-meant but over-zealous restoration by the then Duke of Buccleuch in 1820. It was then that the flying arch on the east side, the gable and crenellated parapet were added. Notwithstanding this, the castle still gives an excellent impression of the pele tower writ large, which was the basic concept of the design. Here the Lord of Liddesdale could observe the comings and goings of the Border, and police it to a limited extent. Not the least important function of Hermitage was to act as a prison, and one of the first acts of the Douglases after capturing the castle in 1338 was to starve their rival, Sir Alexander Ramsey, to death here.

The greatest days of Hermitage were after the end of our period of course, for at the height of the mean and barbarous Border conflicts of the sixteenth century, which history has imbued with a wholly false glamour, Hermitage was in the eye of the storm. But a few hundred yards upstream of the castle lie the ruins of the Hermitage chapel, probably dating to the thirteenth century and which probably gave its name to the place. Although it seems to have been fortified later, something of the earlier tranquillity lingers over this place, and memories linger, too. The 'Cout of Keilder', probably Sir Richard Knout who died late in the thirteenth century, was buried here, reputedly a victim of Lord Soulis, Laird of Hermitage and black magician.

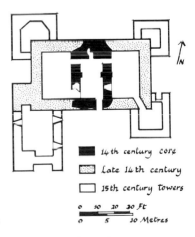

14th century core
Late 14th century
15th century towers

0 10 20 30 Ft
0   5   10 Metres

Phase plan of the castle.

131

MUIRHOUSELAW, Borders

Map Reference NT 631283, Map 74
Nearest Town St Boswells
The site is 3 miles (4.8 km) south-west of St Boswells. Take the A699 to Maxton and turn south-west down the minor road to Muirhouselaw. Go through the hamlet and look for the lodge cottage on the left. Ask for permission. Go to the short track and gateway just up the road and cross the field to see the site.

A moated homestead

This site provides a rare instance of a rural settlement which does not appear to have been defended. Few examples of this class of site remain, presumably due to later destruction or replanning. Muirhouselaw has a rectangular enclosure divided into two parts by a transverse ditch. It contains a pond and the foundations of at least two small rectangular buildings which could have been houses or byres.

On the ground the outer enclosure ditch is very clear, and not significantly banked on the inside, suggesting that defence was not the primary objective. Given the marshy nature of the place, drainage or protection from wild animals seems more probable. Beyond the ditch to the south and east extensive traces of ridge and furrow cultivation can be seen, which may well be contemporary with the enclosure. Thus we can reconstruct in our mind's eye a farmstead sheltered in the valley, surrounded by its arable fields with sheepwalks and pasture on the higher ground beyond.

The foundations of the buildings can be seen standing to a height of a foot or so and cattle have kicked away the turf to reveal the reddish stones of which they were built. This site is impossible to date accurately without excavation, but it is most probably of the thirteenth or fourteenth century. Sites like this must once have been very common, but we have only a handful to set against the tide of abbeys and castles which are the more familiar manifestations of medieval Scotland.

The cattle are standing on a mound marking one of the buildings, and the enclosure ditch can be seen in the background.

132
NEWARK CASTLE, Borders

A tower house

Newark is a good example of a small unadorned tower house, a miniature version of such great fortresses as Hermitage. Here the principal accommodation was on the first floor, above the stores and pit prison at ground level and beneath the roof stage which was reserved for defence. The small doorway at ground level was doubtless well barred, and the square walled enclosure, called a 'barmkin', would have accommodated barns and other buildings as well as providing a refuge for cattle at times of unrest. Newark was described as the 'new Werrk' in a charter of Archibald the Grim, Earl of Douglas, in 1423, so it was presumably built shortly before that date. The perils of Border life condemned many families to live in such uncomfortable circumstances.

The rectangular tower has three principal storeys reached by a turning stair in one corner. The ground floor is lit by small vertical slits and there are sparse windows to the upper floors. The two early entrances were on the north side, with a round-headed doorway on the first floor and an entrance, now with a seventeenth-century moulded stone surround, on the ground floor. In the west wall is a rectangular stone panel bearing the Arms of Scotland, which probably dates to the grant of Ettrick Forest and Newark, which lay within it, by James III to his Queen Margaret in 1473.

Map Reference NT 420294, Map 73
Nearest Town Selkirk
From Selkirk take the A708 west; at the hamlet called Broad Meadows is a bridge across the Yarrow Water, marked by a large sign. Just before the bridge, on the Selkirk side, are a lodge and a drive. The castle is ¾ mile (1.2 km) down the drive, through the forest. It is in guardianship and open at any reasonable time.

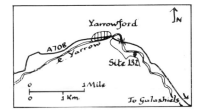

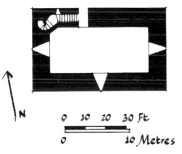

The simple plan of Newark Castle.

Newark Castle, a forlorn Border fortress.

133

MORTON CASTLE, Dumfries and Galloway

Map Reference NX 891992, Map 78
Nearest Town Dumfries
Take the A76(T) towards Sanquhar up the Nith Valley. At Canonbridge (16 miles, 25.6 km) turn right and right again, over a railway bridge. Then in Burn Brae turn left past the church and up a hill for ¾ mile (1.2 km). Turn left up an unmarked track for 1–1½ miles (2 km). Park by a gate with a green notice, 'Please leave no litter'. Walk across the field to the promontory above Loch Morton where the ruins of Morton Castle can be seen. In SDD guardianship, the castle is open at any reasonable time.

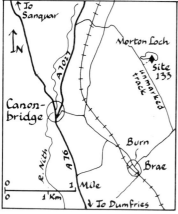

A defended house

Before the outbreak of the Wars of Independence late in the thirteenth century, Scotland had enjoyed relative peace for over a hundred years. One sign of those quieter times was the erection of fortified houses rather than castles, their builders trusting to a rule of law which was soon to be so drastically upset. Further north, Hailes Castle belongs to this same movement, and here at Morton the house stands idyllically on a headland jutting out into the tiny Morton Loch.

The house was placed broadside across the headland, in such a position as to take no real advantage of the defensive potentialities of the site. The headland never seems to have been cut off from the mainland by a ditch, although wall foundations are detectable. The landward side has an obliquely set gatehouse which afforded access to the first-floor hall. Although there is another round tower at the far end of this façade, the defensive value of the arrangements is vitiated by the generous mullioned and transomed windows on this side. They lit the hall, which was above an unvaulted undercroft lit by chamfered squarish windows. The hall had a screens passage by the entrance, and the doorway is well moulded. The whole effect is one of domesticity and comfort, an impression heightened by the ample windows.

So we must set Morton beside the greater Scottish castles, and let it stand with Hailes to remind us that not everything was darkness during the thirteenth century. The date of Morton seems quite late in that century,

Morton Castle is beautifully sited at the end of Morton loch.

and to judge from the fact that its defences were never strengthened it can never have been held against the English. Morton, like the vicar's pele at Corbridge, would have been sufficient to check a band of thieves or marauders but it could not have withstood a determined assault. It was a product of settled times, and many people must have looked upon this pleasant house with regret during the centuries of conflict which followed.

134
POLMADDY, Dumfries and Galloway

A deserted village

Polmaddy is a rare Scottish example of the sort of deserted village site familiar in England at Wharram Percy and elsewhere. Here the ruined houses stand in open grassland, their simple rectangular plans, divided into two or three units, clearly visible. On the flat land below the site, in the bend of the Polmaddy Burn, the long ridges of an early field system can be seen. It is a pleasant sheltered spot, an ideal site for a village.

The pilgrimage route from central Scotland to Whithorn crossed the burn at this point, and it was an important landmark on that route. We do not know precisely when Polmaddy was deserted, and some of the houses at least look as if they haven't been empty above a couple of centuries or so. But despite this difficulty, we include it as an example of shifting settlement patterns which left even quite substantial villages like this as ghostly places, forgetful of the presence of man.

Map Reference NS 590881, Map 77
Nearest Town New Galloway
Take the A713 northwards towards Ayr. Some 4 miles (6.4 km) north of Dalry is a turning left to the Dundeugh Forest, with a picnic parking place signposted up the track. Park at the picnic place and cross the raging burn by the green footbridge. Turn left across the slope and the earthworks of the village are spread out before you.

The walls of the ruined houses of Polmaddy village.

135

WHITHORN, Dumfries and Galloway

Map Reference Candida Casa:
NX 444403, Map 83
Nearest Town Newton Stewart
18 miles (29 km) south of Newton
Stewart on the A746. The church
and museum are in SDD
guardianship and open standard
hours.

Map Reference St Ninian's Chapel:
NX 479362, Map 83
About 3 miles (5 km) south-east of
Whithorn on a promontory beyond
the attractive harbour. A short walk
along the shore to the chapel.

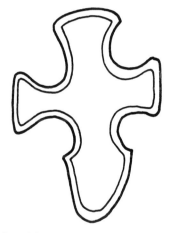

*One of the early crosses on the walls of
St Ninian's Cave.*

A pilgrimage centre

The Venerable Bede, writing in the eighth century, tells us of St Ninian, of how he had brought Christianity to the 'southern Picts' and built a stone church called in Latin Candida Casa, literally the 'white house' here at Whithorn. This description has fascinated historians ever since; was this true history or a fable of the origins of Christian Scotland? In 1871, dramatic confirmation of Bede's tale was provided by the discovery in Ninian's Cave nearby of a cross carved on the cave wall. This cross, and others found afterwards, are thought to be at least as old as the eighth century and quite possibly much earlier.

During the Middle Ages the truth of the Ninian story was never in serious doubt. This remote location on the south-west coast of Scotland was the goal of pilgrims from near and far. Ninian's grave and relics were venerated, and in 1427 King James I of Scotland gave royal protection to all visitors to the shrine, including Englishmen, provided they wore a pilgrim's badge, bore themselves as pilgrims and stayed in Scotland for no more than fifteen days. Traffic was evidently brisk, and the Premonstratensian priory, founded on the traditional site of St Ninian's church in 1177, regulated the traffic and preserved the saint's relics in a barrel-vaulted crypt which can still be seen on the site.

The cave and the little thirteenth-century chapel of St Ninian by it are the most direct links with the medieval history of Whithorn. The cave in particular is an atmospheric place. The offerings of modern pilgrims, often no more than a pebble inscribed with a cross or rough crucifix, keep the faith which stretches back over fifteen hundred years.

*The ruined nave of the
Premonstratensian priory built on the
site of the Candida Casa.*

136
ORCHARDTON AND CARDONESS TOWERS,
Dumfries and Galloway

These two tower houses were built during the fifteenth century, and they provide a good indication of how the owners of such buildings sought to ameliorate the rigours of their dwellings. Orchardton is the earlier, built in the mid fifteenth century, and unique because the tower here is round rather than the normal square or rectangular form. It was built by John Carrys, son of Alexander, the Provost of Lincluden collegiate church. The internal arrangements consisted of a ground-floor cellar, and – unusually – a first-floor chapel provided with a fireplace and piscina. A ruined range of buildings along the slope to the south presumably accommodated domestic offices. Orchardton is pleasantly situated, and served as a watchtower along this fair coast.

Map Reference Orchardton: NX 817551, Map 84
Nearest Town Castle Douglas 6 miles (9.6 km) south-east of Castle Douglas on a minor road south of the A711. In SDD guardianship and open at any reasonable time.

Map Reference Cardoness: NX 591553, Map 83
Nearest Town Gatehouse of Fleet 1 mile (1.6 km) south-west of Gatehouse of Fleet, the tower stands above the main A75 road. It is in SDD guardianship and open standard hours.

The distinctive circular tower at Orchardton.

Cardoness was built by the McCullochs late in the fifteenth century. They had been supporters of John Balliol and Edward I, but by the time of Flodden Field in 1513 Alexander, Laird of Cardoness, was killed with his king in Scotland's cause. Cardoness is not far from Threave and it shares with that castle the interesting feature of having been designed with artillery very much in mind. So we find here 'inverted keyhole' gunports of the late-fifteenth-century pattern as an integral part of the fabric. Likewise, as the report of a sixteenth-century English spy makes clear, the

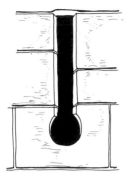

A gun loop at Cardoness.

castle was so sited that, 'there can noo ordinance nor gounes endomage yt of the sea, nor there canoo artyllare be taken to it upoun land'.

The tower is plain enough from the outside, with few windows, though there is a good sprinkling of gunports on the ground floor. The southern entrance was small with a stout oak door and an iron yett. The ground floor was divided into two cellars for storage and on the west side was a double prison, the upper having the rare facility of a garderobe, and the lower being of the more familiar pit variety. After this grim beginning, the hall on the first floor comes as something of a surprise. Here and in the bedchambers above are fireplaces with clustered columns and moulded capitals, finely wrought stone cupboards and a garderobe. An interesting detail is that the fireplaces are each provided with salt boxes, to keep that valuable commodity dry. These rooms were as comfortable as the troubled times of their construction could afford.

137

SWEETHEART ABBEY, Dumfries and Galloway

Map Reference NX 965663, Map 84
Nearest Town Dumfries
On the A710, 7 miles (11.3 km) south of Dumfries. On flat land beside the river. In SDD guardianship and open standard hours.

And the pious Lady Devorgilla

The abbey church, resplendent in its orange red sandstone, is a fine sight indeed. A noble monastery, it must already have been something of a monument to times past when it was built late in the thirteenth century, and it also has a notable foundation story.

It concerns the Balliols of Barnard Castle in England. The improbably named Devorgilla, wife of one John Balliol and mother of the puppet king of that name, had the royal blood of Scotland flowing in her veins. Her husband was one of the Regents of Scotland and the couple were devoted to one another. When her husband died, she had his heart embalmed and set in a silver casket which she hung round her neck. It accompanied her to her own grave before the high altar of the abbey which she had founded in 1273, and which the monks named Dulce Code, 'Sweet Heart', in commemoration of this great love. The site of her grave is now covered by a stone donated by Balliol College, Oxford, which she also founded.

Unhappily, the foundation of Sweetheart neatly coincided with the outbreak of hostilities between England and Scotland, and the new abbey was on the line of march between the two kingdoms. Afterwards, the abbey required a new patron, and it was 'refounded' by Archibald the Grim, Earl of Douglas and founder of the collegiate church at Lincluden. As a result of these reverses the original fabric of the church shows some evidence of repair, but the most dramatic evidence is the precinct itself. This contained an area of over twelve hectares, and was originally

The ruined nave and crossing of Sweetheart Abbey.

An effigy of Devorgilla holding the casket which contained her husband's heart.

enclosed by a wall with two gateways and on the southern side by a water-filled ditch. While it was not a readily defensible enclosure, its walls were a formidable barrier, and would have saved the monastery from all save a determined attack. This unusual provision is the most eloquent testimony to the difficult strategic position which Sweetheart unwittingly occupied.

The principal survival at Sweetheart is the church, which is remarkable in its conformity to the strict canons of simple Cistercian planning. The church was of the simplest in all save the presbytery which is enlivened by the use of fine traceried windows in the Gothic geometric style, but this and the grudging crossing tower are the only lapses from the Order's austerity. The church is well preserved, however, and the view up the nave with its moulded shafts to the five lights of the east window is very satisfying. In the south transept chapel lies the decorated coffin of John, the first Abbot, who swore fealty to Edward I, and the reconstructed tomb of Devorgilla shows her still holding her husband's heart after 700 years.

138
LINCLUDEN COLLEGIATE CHURCH,
Dumfries and Galloway

Lincluden belongs with Dunglass and Seton among that group of churches founded late in the Middle Ages by Scottish lords for the benefit of their souls. Here, however, we have a display of architectural decoration of a rare quality in early medieval Scotland, a tribute to the wealth of the Earl of Douglas who built it. As originally founded by Archibald the Grim in

Map Reference NX 966779, Map 78
Nearest Town Dumfries
The site is signposted in Dumfries, off the roundabout on the A76 Kilmarnock Road. It is in guardianship and open standard hours, but is closed on Thurs afternoons and Fri.

The tomb of the Princess Margaret in the choir of Lincluden Church.

1389, the college had eight secular priests, and masses were still being said here late in the sixteenth century. We can well imagine that this Archibald had need of prayers, for he had previously ejected a community of nuns in order to establish his church!

Although ruined, the choir, built early in the fifteenth century, is one of the richest ecclesiastical interiors in Scotland. It contains the tomb of Princess Margaret, who died in 1456 and who had married the founder's son. The tomb chest is decorated with heraldic shields set in cusped blank arcades and supports a fine effigy above which is a cusped and foliated arch with an ogee finial, all set in a panel of further cusped arches. The richly traceried windows may be the work of the French mason John Morow, who produced similar work at Melrose. Otherwise the sedilia and piscina are richly carved and canopied and some of the carved wooden stalls from this splendid choir are preserved in the Museum of Antiquities in Edinburgh.

The interest of Lincluden attaches to its masterful handling of the architectural elements and decoration in a manner which is neither French nor English but Scottish, and which marks the beginning of a separate style. It is a pity that the quality and restraint of the Lincluden choir were not continued at Roslin Chapel!

139

CAERLAVEROCK CASTLE, Dumfries and Galloway

The unclaimed fortress

It is a somewhat embarrassing fact that nobody can say for certain whether the Scots or English built the splendid castle at Caerlaverock! That such a mighty monument should want for so vital a piece of documentation is a source of wonder, but at the time of its construction, not long before 1300, the political situation was so complex and fast-moving that it probably isn't far from the truth to say that nobody had much time to record such matters for posterity!

The location of the castle does seem to favour an English initiative, however, and it probably acted as a bridgehead for a full-scale invasion. By 1300 it had fallen into Scottish hands, but whether it was actually finished by then is unknown. The year 1300 is an important date because Edward I had a siege here in person which was commemorated in a contemporary French poem. But it seems strange that, if Edward was indeed besieging a castle which he had earlier lost, the antagonistic French should make no mention of it.

Once regained, Caerlaverock was in English hands until 1312 when the constable, Sir Eustace Maxwell, suddenly declared for Robert Bruce. He slighted the castle in line with the Bruce's policy of denying strongholds to the enemy, but the castle was apparently reconstructed by the English before 1347. The later history of the castle is also complex, not least because there is a second castle lurking in the marshes just beyond the existing defences. It has been suggested that this was actually the early-

Map Reference NY 026656, Map 84
Nearest Town Dumfries
7 miles (11.2 km) south-east of Dumfries on the B725. A dramatic setting looking across the Solway Firth. In SDD guardianship, open standard hours, with a small site museum.

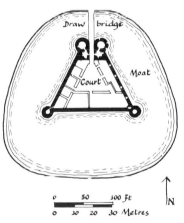

The triangular plan of Caerlaverock Castle.

The mighty round gate towers of Caerlaverock Castle, bristling with machicolations.

thirteenth-century castle, and that the existing ruins are altogether later, but the triangular plan and twin gate towers of the existing castle agree closely with the French acount of the siege.

Whatever the truth of these opinions, Caerlaverock stands as one of the most picturesquely sited of all Britain's castles, and one of the most architecturally satisfying. It is built as a regular triangle with round towers at each angle, the hallmarks of a late-thirteenth-century plan. But inside comes the greatest surprise of all, for the castle was transformed during the seventeenth century when a suite of rooms was constructed within the medieval shell which wanted for nothing in elegance and grace.

140
BOLTONGATE, Cumbria

Map Reference NY 229408, Map 89
Nearest Town Aspatria
Take the B5299 to Boltongate (6 miles, 9.6 km). The village is 1½ miles (2.4 km) east off the A595 Carlisle to Cockermouth road. The church is in the centre of the village.

A defended church

The Church of All Saints is very much a 'Borders' church, for it contains a feature unique in England but common enough in Scotland. The nave is roofed with a fine pointed stone vault of the sort seem in the collegiate church at Dunglass and, most elaborately of all, at Roslin Chapel. These vaults, which were first built in Scotland during the fifteenth century, were probably in part an answer to repeated destruction of churches by fire; a stone vault, unless deliberately ruined, would withstand fire quite well. This was the same period at which the provision of vaults in tower house became common, and doubtless their builders were as concerned for their own protection as for that of the church!

The peculiarities of this church do not end with the roof, however. Externally, the neat Perpendicular Gothic arrangement is varied by the provision of a gallery or 'fighting platform' around the upper parts of the nave. This carries on across the west end, and the bellcote has been awkwardly recessed to allow its uninterrupted passage. It seems likely that these defensive arrangements at Boltongate were analagous with those seen at the other end of the Border at Ancroft. This impression is heightened by the existence of corbels in the nave walls which may have supported a timber floor beneath the vault, an arrangement paralleled in some Scottish castles.

So Boltongate stands as evidence of the troubled conditions of the late-fifteenth-century Border. The stone vaulting technique itself was ultimately of Burgundian inspiration, coming first to Scotland via Cistercian Melrose and thence perhaps by its daughter house at Holm Cultram which held land in the parish.

The stark vaulted interior of All Saints Church, Boltongate.

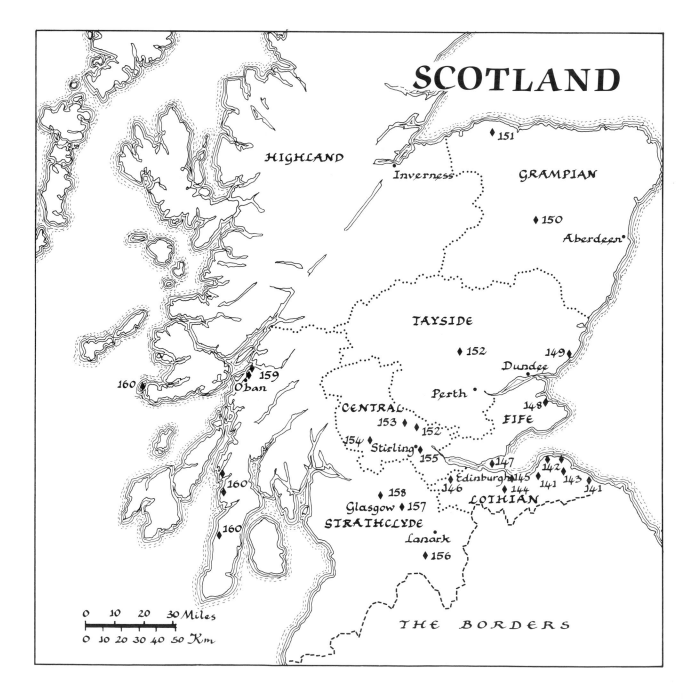

SCOTLAND

HIGHLAND

Inverness

GRAMPIAN

♦ 151

♦ 150

Aberdeen

TAYSIDE

♦ 152

149 ♦

Dundee

Perth

148 ♦

159 ♦
Oban

160

CENTRAL

153 ♦
♦ 152

154 ♦ Stirling ♦

155 ♦

FIFE

147 ♦

142 ♦
Edinburgh ♦ 145 ♦

160

146 ♦   141 ♦   143 ♦
144 ♦   141 ♦

158 ♦

LOTHIAN

Glasgow ♦ 157

160 ♦

STRATHCLYDE

Lanark

♦ 156

0   10   20   30 Miles
0 10 20 30 40 50 Km

THE BORDERS

SCOTLAND

Introduction

The story of medieval Scotland began quietly enough, with the early progress made by King David and the Canmore dynasty being extended by Alexander II and III, who brought the Western Isles under the sway of the Scottish Crown. Alexander III's accidental death in 1286 gave Edward I of England the chance first to arbitrate in, and then to dispute, the matter of Scotland's overlordship. In 1296 he invaded Scotland and established firm control, leaving the governance of the realm in the hands of an English council. But the famed William Wallace upset Edward's plans, and his rebellion forced a second invasion in 1298 which resulted in the English victory at Falkirk.

Yet still resistance was continued, this time under the leadership of Robert the Bruce. Edward, worn out by campaigning, died on his way to Scotland in 1305. His son, Edward II, was forced by Robert Bruce's successes to take the field once more in a disastrous campaign, culminating in the Battle of Bannockburn which appears in this book. Troubles at home and abroad prevented further English aggression, and after Edward II's deposition Robert Bruce was formally recognized as King of Scots by the Treaty of Northampton in 1328. His triumph was short-lived, however, for he died the following year, but Scotland's independence, although later challenged by Edward II, had been established.

Against this background of conflict, which was mirrored by internal rivalries and disturbances, it is scarcely surprising that castles are the major medieval Scottish legacy. Many of the earlier castles are impressive fortalices which, like Kildrummy, Bothwell and Dirleton, were in the forefront of military architectural innovation. At Hailes, however, is an early fortified house, built before the chaos of the later thirteenth century, a reminder of more peaceable times.

Later military developments are well represented too, of course. Tantallon castle demonstrates the late medieval preoccupation with height and grandeur, while at Doune we see a lavish fortress reflecting in its design the uncertainties of late medieval feudal loyalties. A further Scottish speciality was the 'tower house', well represented by the core of

Craigmillar near Edinburgh and Dunollie near Oban. These are the northern counterparts of the fine Galloway tower houses at Orchardton and Cardoness.

But not all Scottish monuments arose out of wars and strife. The Church made great strides under the Canmores, and of the five cathedrals included here three were established during the twelfth century. It is sad that these churches were so ill used in later times, though each retains clear evidence of workmanship which at St Andrews and Elgin in particular attained a standard comparable with the best contemporary English work. Most of the fittings of these churches were ruthlessly stripped out during the Reformation, but in the woodwork at Dunblane and the wall-paintings at Dunkeld we have rare survivals of interior details.

Incholm, Arbroath and Holy Rood (Edinburgh) represented the medieval monasteries, and together they afford glimpses of both ends of the scale of opulence. Incholm was a somewhat obscure house occupying a site hallowed by the early Celtic church. Its buildings are modest and serve to remind us of the austerities of monastic life. Arbroath and Holy Rood, by contrast, were much more resplendent foundations and retain substantial remains of their important early Gothic churches. At Arbroath is a fine lodging which attests the later significance of the house and its abbot. A religious foundation of a very different sort is the Preceptory of the Knights Hospitaller at Torphichen. This was one of three such houses in Scotland, and preserves an intriguing planned church as well as some of its dependent buildings.

As to the lesser churches, St Bride's Kirk at Douglas stands almost alone as an example of a parish church, and even it is only really included here for its historically important collection of Douglas monuments. A distinctive attribute of late medieval Scotland was its fine collection of collegiate churches, monuments to man's insecurity in the face of the Eternal. Of these, Dunglass and Seton are perhaps the best, but the chapel at Roslin remains in the memory by virtue of its exuberant and somewhat bewildering scheme of decoration. At St Andrews is the Kirk of the Holy Trinity, a major town church, as was St Giles Cathedral at Edinburgh before it became a cathedral after the Reformation.

When we look beyond church and state to the everyday legacy of medieval Scotland we find that it is poor indeed, with little to sustain the visitor. St Andrews provides some impression of a town of the period, and in addition to its churches has some altered houses, traces of its defences and a street pattern which is a medieval inheritance. The University also has some medieval buildings, and the town is probably the best Scottish survival. Otherwise, apart from the canons' houses at Glasgow and the abbot's lodging at Arbroath, houses are rare, and at the Peel of Gartfarren we find the transitory traces of a rural settlement, the date and history of which cannot be precisely told. We must hope that further fieldwork and research will swell this evidence in the future.

Last of all in this brief survey of Scottish medieval monuments, we must consider the splendid carved crosses and gravestones of the West Highland School. These objects, normally carved from hard and unyielding stones, are a reminder of the remoteness of much of Scotland, a far-flung kingdom in which diverse cultures confronted one another. The West Highland stones are sober and dignified memorials and seem as remote today as the Pictish stones which were already ancient when they were made. They remind us that most of the 'Scottish' sites in this book come from the south of that great land, and that over much of it life remained little changed throughout the Middle Ages.

141
DUNGLASS AND SETON COLLEGIATE CHURCHES,
Lothian

Late medieval Scotland was distinguished by the foundation of considerable numbers of 'collegiate' churches. The purpose of these foundations was to provide a suitable setting for groups or 'colleges' of priests to say masses for the repose of the founder's soul. During the turbulent times of the fifteenth century in particular, men had good cause to dwell upon their mortality and certain of the earlier types of provision for the departed had fallen out of fashion. Whereas their forefathers had founded or endowed monasteries, or later friaries, there was widespread discontent with these institutions and instead a more personal provision was made.

A man of modest means would leave money for masses to be said in his memory in the parish church. If he had the money, he might pay a priest to do this each day, possibly in a separate aisle or chapel added to the church for the purpose. But if the man was very wealthy, then he might build a special church with a college of priests attached to it. The collegiate church of St Mary at Dunglass is one of the earliest examples of such an arrangement in Scotland.

The college may have been founded as early as 1423 but was not confirmed by charter until 1450. The founder was Sir Alexander Hume, and he provided for three priests, the superior to have the title of Provost, and there were four boys to sing in the choir. Bread and wine for the daily masses, together with service books and lights, were all included in the foundation charter. Thus a small community came into being, living off the income of the property donated for the purpose, and all

Map Reference Dunglass: NT 418751, Map 67
Nearest Town Dunbar
Take the A1 south-east, 1 mile (1.6 km) north of Cocksburnpath turn right down an unmarked road. Go under the railway bridge and enter Dunglass Estate opposite, past a lodge and gate piers. Up the Hall drive, the church can be seen on a slight incline. In SDD guardianship, it is open at any reasonable time.

Map Reference Seton: NT 418751, Map 66
Nearest Town Tranent
1½ miles (3.5 km) north of Tranent. Signposted off the A198 Musselburgh to Longriddy road. In SDD guardianship, open standard hours but closed on Tues afternoons and Wed.

The collegiate church at Dunglass with its curious ashlar 'tiles'.

because of a wealthy man who lived in mortal dread of the hereafter.

As to the church, it originally consisted of a nave and smaller choir, with a northern chamber which might have been either a tomb chapel or, more probably, a sacristy. Soon afterwards a central tower and transepts were added to the basic plan and the present structure with its eyecatching stone-flagged roof resulted. Internally, the church is austere with ornament being limited to the gablettes over the sedilia and the chancel arch capitals. The sombre impression, so fitted to the weighty charge of the priests using the church, is emphasized by the high stone roof vault. We could only conjecture that being a collegiate priest must have been an extremely depressing experience.

Unlike Dunglass, Seton was not conceived as a unified structure but evolved gradually. The simple parish church had an undifferentiated nave and chancel, and to this a chapel and sacristy were added. In around 1470 George, 1st Lord Seton, obtained a licence from Pope Paul II to found a college and he rebuilt the choir with a fine polygonal apse and a vaulted roof. The windows were decorated with flowing tracery on the English pattern, and the whole impression is agreeably rich in the manner of Lincluden. The feeling here is one of lightness and grace as compared with Dunglass, and despite the curious aspect of the unfinished central spire Seton is an unusually satisfying example of medieval Scottish architecture.

142
DIRLETON AND TANTALLON CASTLES, Lothian

These two castles together illustrate the increasing sophistication of Scottish military architecture during the Middle Ages. The first castle at Dirleton, described in the sixteenth century as the 'pleasantest house in Scotland', was built by the de Vaux family who were invited to Scotland by King David I. The strong natural defences were augmented by earth and timber ramparts, but it was not until the late thirteenth century that the castle took on its present form.

John de Vaux was steward to Margaret, Queen of Alexander II, and her ancestral home was Coucy in France. The castle at Coucy, with its large round keep having immensely thick walls and vaulted stone floors, was the model for Bothwell and Dirleton. Here were built five round towers, three at the south-west and one each on the southern angles. They were linked by curtain walls of fine ashlar and, although compact, the castle presented a most imposing aspect. The original cramped accommodation was later extended by the Halyburtons during the fourteenth and fifteenth centuries by the addition of a hall and solar range along the east side.

At Tantallon, built in the 1370s by the 1st Earl Douglas who had earlier fought on the French side at Poitiers, we can trace the next stage in major castle building. This was an emphasis on height and boldness which found its expression here in a splendid show front of a strong central gateway with flanking towers, all linked together by a massive curtain wall. The site was one of great natural strength, with a sheer drop to the Firth of Forth behind, thus affording an opportunity for lavish display on the landward side.

Map Reference Dirleton: NT 516839, Map 66
Nearest Town North Berwick
Take the A198 west. Dirleton is the first village, bypassed by the main road, and on the north side. The castle is in the village of Dirleton, is in guardianship, and open standard hours. The site has beautiful gardens famed throughout Lothian.

Map Reference Tantallon: NT 596850, Map 67
Nearest Town North Berwick
2½ miles (6 km) east of North Berwick off the A198. Also signposted off the A1 on the cliff edge with views out to the sea and the Bass Rock. The site is in guardianship and open standard hours, but is closed on Tues and alternate Weds in winter.

A dizzying view from Tantallon Castle down to the Firth of Forth showing the later artillery emplacements.

Although 'modernized' for artillery during the sixteenth century, the arrangements of the earlier castle are easily comprehended. Behind the great land wall was a relatively modest hall range on the north side of the promontory which was extended in about 1400. To the rear of the site was a sea gate which was well looped against attack and afforded some security of supply in time of siege. The great fore tower in the middle of the defences was extended and provided with a barbican in the sixteenth century, but the junction between the old and new work is tolerably clear. Although not on the scale of such English fortresses as Warwick and Windsor, there is the same intention here to advertise the prestige of its owners, the mighty Douglases.

143
HAILES CASTLE, Lothian

Map Reference NT 574757, Map 67
Nearest Town Haddington
The castle is on the minor road, on the south side of the River Tyne, between Haddington and East Linton, 5 miles (8 km) east of Haddington. The site is in guardianship and open standard hours. It is also signposted off the A1.

A fortified house

Although Hailes is called a 'castle', it is really more akin to a fortified house of the type familiar in England at Stokesay and elsewhere. It is small and its defences, although serious enough, are not elaborate, being confined to an outer wall eight feet thick and a somewhat precipitous site above the rushing waters of the Tyne. The early house, built during the more peaceful times of the earlier thirteenth century, consisted of a tower containing living accommodation and a hall block, the fragmentary remains of which survive on the east side of the courtyard. During the

The south side of Hailes Castle.

fourteenth century the original enceinte was extended to the west and a second tower added. Finally, in the fifteenth century, a second hall was built between the two earlier towers.

A noteworthy feature of the site are the two pit prisons; prisons of this type occur at other castles such as Tantallon and were something of a Scottish speciality. The prisons here at Hailes are memorably grim, however. The hapless prisoner was lowered into the dank subterranean chamber on a rope, and was left until his captors decided to return. With no sanitary provision and no light, one can well imagine the vileness of any protracted incarceration in such a place. These 'black holes of Caledonia' must have provided a powerful deterrent to any who thought to annoy the Hepburns, lairds of Hailes.

144
ROSLIN CHAPEL, Lothian

A carved jungle

The chapel at Roslin is a most puzzling structure but, in essence, it is yet another of the late medieval collegiate churches like Dunglass and Seton, which became common in Scotland. These churches were built by their founders in order to ensure that their souls were prayed for after death. So far so good, but the Roslin Chapel is uniquely exuberant in its decoration, and is all the more unexpected when we look at the canon of late medieval building in Scotland. It is true that there is decoration at Lincluden, as there is at Seton, but it is only here at Roslin that such a display of sculptural fireworks was attempted.

There is nothing known of the life of the founder, William Sinclair, 3rd Earl of Orkney, to account for this dramatically individual statement nor, despite suggestions by later historians, is there any direct evidence for the presence of foreign craftsmen. The chapel is an enigma, a thing out of time and out of place; it was built, according to the inscription on the cornice, in 1450, although work probably started earlier. As to whether the effects achieved are successful, the visitor must decide. For our part, we felt it to be altogether too overheated, in the manner of a glasshouse filled with luxuriant jungle plants which had been allowed by their neglectful owner to run riot.

The existing structure is only the choir of the proposed church. It is aisled, and there is a sunken sacristy to the east and a nineteenth-century vestry at the west end. The five-bay divisions of the structure are marked by buttresses provided with 'flying' arches which have no structural function, and which therefore must be accounted part of the designer's caprice.

Map Reference NT 274630, Map 66
Nearest Town Edinburgh
On the A701 Penicuik to Edinburgh road, take the B7003 or B7006 east to Roslin. The chapel is signposted. It is in private ownership and there is a charge for entry.

The Apprentice pillar at Roslin.

Intricate foliage on a lintel over the aisle.

Inside, the piers are bundles of sixteen shafts rising to richly carved capitals and moulded arches having bands of foliage. At the east end on the south side is the fantastically decorated 'Prentice's Pillar', so called from the oft repeated but entirely unproved tale that it was carved by an apprentice who was later murdered by his jealous master. The nave roof is demonstrably of Scottish origin, since it is a stone vault of the sort seen at Dunglass and elsewhere. But here it is encrusted with stars, fleurons and squares divided by ribs which are fantastically hung with pendent cresting including vegetable sprouts and fleur-de-lis.

In the four eastern chapels are further carvings of the Dance of Death and the Three Living and the Three Dead, among other suitable themes. The Portuguese and Spanish parallels for this amazing structure are all later: Roslin stands alone as a bizarre and strangely disturbing monument to the morbid fear of death and its consequences which afflicted late medieval Scotland.

145
EDINBURGH AND CRAIGMILLAR CASTLE, Lothian

Map Reference Holyrood Abbey: NT 285710, Map 66
Nearest Town Edinburgh
The abbey ruins can be seen on a visit to the palace. As dates may vary, tel 031-556 7371 for information.

Map Reference Craigmillar: Map 66
Nearest Town Edinburgh
The castle sits on a high crag beside Arthur's Seat and has sweeping views of the sea and the Firth of Forth. It is 2½ miles (4 km) south-east of the centre of the city, signposted off the A68. It is in SDD guardianship and open standard hours but closed on Thurs afternoons and Fri.

Little survives of the thriving medieval town of Edinburgh apart from some rather inaccessible bits of masonry in the castle and the late medieval St Giles Cathedral. The church was rebuilt after its destruction by the English in 1385, and was made a cathedral in post-Reformation times. There is a vaulted nave of five bays flanked by double aisles, a crossing tower, short transepts and an aisled choir of four bays. Its present form results from numerous guild and other chapels being added to the original cruciform plan. The Victorian exterior largely hides the earlier work, but it is well worth visiting as the historic focus of Edinburgh.

On the east side of the city, beyond the walls, lies the Palace of Holyroodhouse, the Queen's official residence in Scotland. This place, redolent with memories of dark deeds like the murder of David Rizzio and haunting occasions such as Prince Charles Edward's ball before the tragedy of Culloden Field, was originally the Augustinian Abbey of the Holy Rood founded by King David in 1128. The great nave, even in its present state, is one of the grandest medieval monuments in Scotland. It was finished early in the thirteenth century, and its massive arcade piers with clustered shafts, paired triforium lights and high vaulted stone roof can stand comparison with the best English work. This was the burial place of Scottish kings, and although it was later despoiled it still evokes echoes of majesty and power.

Fine detailing and exotic tracery at Holyrood Abbey.

Three miles south east of the city is another important medieval monument, Craigmillar Castle. This castle neatly illustrates the development of a tower house, in this instance of the late fourteenth century, into something more nearly approaching a castle *per se*. The original L-shaped tower was well appointed with two vaulted stone floors, with a memorable fireplace in the first-floor hall. During the fifteenth century, the earlier cramped accommodation was relieved by the erection of a three-sided courtyard lined with buildings. This development lent the complex a more regular plan, and bears comparison with such English castles as Herstmonceux and Bodiam, except that the function of the 'keep' gatehouse was here fulfilled by the earlier tower. But in all else, in the regularity of plan, the projecting angle towers and the careful balance of domesticity and defence, we can detect the same inspiration at work.

146

TORPHICHEN PRECEPTORY AND SANCTUARY,
Lothian

Map Reference NT 596925, Map 65
Nearest Town Linlithgow
From Linlithgow take the A706 south-west. After 4 miles (6.4 km) go down the B792 to Torphichen. The preceptory is in the village and is signposted. It is in SDD guardianship and open standard hours.

This was the site of a preceptory of the Knights of St John of Jerusalem, often called the Knights Hospitaller, whose chief duty was to guard and sustain pilgrims to the Holy Sepulchre. The Knights of the Order took monastic vows, lived according to the Rule of St Augustine and wore black habits blazoned with a white cross. The Order became very powerful, and had 'tongues' or communities in many countries. The Tongue of England had its headquarters at St John's Gate, Clerkenwell, London.

The Knights had subordinate estate houses called commanderies headed by Preceptors who were responsible for the maintenance of the Rule. In Scotland, there were three houses of the Order and Torphichen was the first, a royal foundation by David I some time between 1144 and 1153. Parts of the existing buildings, such as the western crossing arch, are of the twelfth century, but much was altered later.

The surviving masonry belongs to the central part of the Hospitallers' church, with the cloisters being represented only by their foundations. The church was considerably restored by Sir Andrew Meldrum, who was preceptor in the 1430s, and an inscription on the north transept vault records his work. The church has a simple unaisled plan, but is unusual in having a suite of rooms over the ground-floor compartments. These were doubtless where ceremonies associated with the Order took place.

A further interesting aspect of the Torphichen site is the evidence that it retains for the 'Privilege of St John'. This high-sounding title relates to the right of Sanctuary which the Hospitallers enjoyed, and could extend to

The sanctuary stone in the Churchyard at Torphichen.

others. Sanctuary was of benefit to persons accused of crimes but who had not been convicted of them. It enabled them to escape the dangers of summary execution of the law posed by the 'hue and cry' and other primitive regulatory methods. At Torphichen, it appears that the area of Sanctuary was defined by four boundary stones with a fifth stone at the centre, which is still visible in the churchyard. The area was approximately three miles in diameter, and the remaining north and south stones retain their crosses. This is an interesting survival of an important aspect of medieval society which, because it arose from the privileged legal position enjoyed by the Church, was one of the many bones of contention between Church and Crown.

147
INCHOLM ABBEY, Fife

Map Reference NT 190826, Map 66
Nearest Town Inverkeithing
From the Forth Road Bridge take
the A92 east to Aberdour (5 miles,
8 km). The ferry leaves from the
West Sands at the foot of Shore
Road. Sailings are daily 10.30,
11.30, 1.30, 2.30, 3.20 between
June and mid-Sept. Sailings also
occur in April, May and late Sept.
For further information contact
Dougal Barnie, tel. 0383 860335.
The abbey is in guardianship, and is
closed on Wed afternoons and
Thurs in winter. Tel 031-221 1332
for more information.

An island sanctuary

The abbey dedicated to St Columba at Incholm was founded in 1123 by
King Alexander I as a thank offering for being saved from drowning. This
island, called the 'Iona of East Scotland', was however a Celtic Christian
site of some importance long before the Augustinian abbey was founded.
The western parts of the twelfth-century church remain, but in the
fifteenth century an entirely new church was laid out to the east of the
earlier building which, unlike its predecessor, was provided with transepts.
An unusual survival in the church is a small section of thirteenth-century
painted plaster depicting the burial procession of a canon.

Perhaps the greatest interest of Incholm attaches to its claustral buildings. These are an unusually complete set and include a fine octagonal
chapter house, a feature unusual enough in Scotland, but here combined
with an upper warming room in a most innovative composition. The
chapter house itself has a ribbed vault springing from slender wall shafts
which meet in a pierced carved ceiling boss through which a lantern could
be raised and lowered from the warming house above. Perhaps this
eccentric arrangement was in some way concerned with the provision of a
light to guide shipping in the treacherous waters around the island.

A further unusual feature is the way in which the cloister walks are not
provided with lean-to roofs but instead form the ground floors of the
surrounding ranges, a technique more usually encountered at friaries like
the Whitefriars at Coventry. At Incholm, it contrives to give the cloister a
rather stark aspect, an impression relieved only by the chapter house. Here

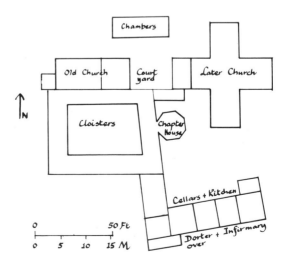

*A simplified plan of the abbey at
Incholm.*

Scotland · 245

at Incholm we gain a clear impression of the rigours of monastic life, but the setting of the site on an island in the Firth of Forth is delightful. It also proved very practical during the fourteenth century, for the monks of the island appear to have escaped the rigours of the Black Death!

148
ST ANDREWS CASTLE, CATHEDRAL AND TOWN, Fife

The origins of St Andrews are inexorably bound up with Scotland's patron saint and the arrival of certain of his relics here, brought by the Greek monk St Regulus, or 'St Rule' as he was sometimes called. Legend fixes Regulus's arrival in the fourth century, but history would place it in the eighth, during the reign of Angus I. It is, however, indisputable that St Andrews became the premier cathedral of Scotland, and that it was a structure of the highest excellence. Before the establishment of the cathedral–priory in 1144, there was an existing settlement of monks called Culdees on the stormswept headland beside the North Sea. These monks, guardians of St Andrew's relics, built the Church of St Rule which appeared in our *Norman Guide*.

The Culdees were, however, 'secular' monks, which is to say that they could marry and live a good deal less rigorous life than the Augustinians who came here in 1144. The two parties never came to open conflict, but the Culdees were gradually suppressed until, in the fourteenth century, they finally disappeared. The Augustinians built a great church here, one of the largest in Britain; it was begun in 1160, and the choir was completed by 1238 when Bishop Malvoisin was buried there. A great storm blew down the west end, and the church was shortened by two bays when it was replaced in about 1280. Also in the thirteenth century the existing claustral ranges were added, including the square chapter house which was later extended eastwards. The warming house, which was restored during the nineteenth century, now houses the site museum which contains many important sculptures and other objects.

Apart from the cathedral priory, St Andrews also became a burgh in the twelfth century, and it waxed rich on the proceeds of trade with the Low Countries. The street pattern of the town is largely medieval, and the scale of the buildings within the walls gives a good impression of its early appearance. South Street contains some buildings with medieval fabric, and behind No 42 can be seen two round arches with simple capitals. The Town Kirk of the Holy Trinity is a good though much restored early-fifteenth-century building with the same massive round piers as can be seen at Dunkeld Cathedral.

Map Reference NO 514167, Map 59 The Cathedral, museum and castle are in SDD guardianship and are open standard hours. Holy Trinity Church is in South Street and St Salvator's College is in North Street. Some of the houses in South Street have medieval fabric.

The precinct gateway at St Andrews.

In addition to its urban and ecclesiastical functions, St Andrews also became a university town in 1411. St Salvator's College retains its fine front of 1450 with a central tower flanked by residential buildings to the west and the college church to the east. Although altered and restored, the church contains the delicate founder's tomb of 1460, and three college maces of the same period; a remarkable legacy of nearly 500 years of scholarship. The Kirk of St Leonard, now part of that college, dates to the fifteenth century, though it is much altered.

The final major medieval element of the town is the castle of the Bishops of St Andrews. This is on a headland north-west of the abbey ruins. The first castle was erected by Bishop Roger in about 1200; some of its finely dressed ashlar can be seen in the later Fore Tower, and the early-thirteenth-century square keep remains. The castle was taken by the English in 1336 but was regained by Sir Andrew Moray the following year. Later, the castle was the site of some extremely ghoulish executions, including the martyrdom of Paul Crew of Bohemia, a physician. He was burnt to death in 1432 with a large brass ball fixed in his mouth, 'lest the power of his preaching might make converts among the multitude'!

149
ARBROATH ABBEY, Tayside

This was one of the wealthiest Scottish religious houses and is celebrated because it was here that in 1320 the Declaration of Arbroath was sealed by the Barons and community of the Realm. That letter followed the defeat of Edward II's army at Bannockburn, and was addressed to Pope John XXII; it asked that he should recognize Robert Bruce as King of Scots, and that his life sentence of excommunication should be lifted. Recently, scholars have thrown some doubt upon the significance of the Arbroath letter, which was probably drawn up by the then abbot, Bernard de Linton. But tradition does not doubt these matters, and the Declaration of Arbroath stands as a landmark in Scottish opposition to English ambitions.

But the story of Arbroath Abbey had begun long before these stirring events. This house of the Order of Tiron was founded in 1178 by King William the Lion. It is unusually dedicated to St Thomas of Canterbury, due to the miraculous conjunction between Henry II's bitter repentance for the murder of Becket and William's capture during a raid on Alnwick Castle. William had actually known Thomas well during his stay at the English court, and the apparent opposition of that saint to his warlike intentions had a profound effect.

What remains at Arbroath today are the bones of a major early Gothic church which was not substantially altered after its completion and dedication in 1233 – this despite seaborne English attack in 1350 and a fire, ascribed by the then abbot to the intervention of the Devil, in 1380. The ruins are impressive, and the scheme of great round pillars with engaged shafts and triplets of windows to the two upper stages can still be appreciated. Apart from the church, the abbot's lodging is an important survival of a domestic building which, by the time of the abbey's suppression during the sixteenth century, had grown into an imposing set of rooms arranged around a hall and bedchamber.

During the fifteenth century the abbot was raised to the status of a bishop: this enhancement was reflected by the privilege of self-government granted by James I. The 'Regality' of Arbroath thus became a state within a state and had its own legal officer, called a Baillie, and its own court. This position was lucrative, and the family of Ogilvie regarded it as their perquisite. The claim was challenged by the Lindsays, and after the ensuing Battle of Arbroath in 1446 more lords joined the founder beneath the floor of the abbey church.

Arbroath was thus a cockpit of Scottish history as well as a place of prayer and contemplation. A further bizarre twist was added in 1951 when the Stone of Destiny was found after its audacious theft from Westminster Abbey!

*Map Reference NO 644414, Map 54
The abbey is in SDD guardianship and open standard hours.*

The seal of Arbroath depicting St Thomas à Becket's martyrdom.

150
KILDRUMMY CASTLE, Grampian

Map Reference NJ 455164, Map 37
Nearest Town Ballater
Take the A97 for 23 miles (36.8 km). The castle is west of the A97 road. It is in SDD guardianship and open standard hours.

'Noblest castle of the north'

Kildrummy, like Bothwell, was designed as a courtyard castle with a circular keep, angle towers and a gatehouse. On the side of the courtyard furthest from the gate were a hall, kitchen and chapel block. The combination here of French and English styles with a curtain wall and a great tower or donjon gives Kildrummy special interest. A further advanced feature is the heavily defended gatehouse, but this was probably an addition to the original plan.

It appears that the designer of the castle was Gilbert de Moravia, Bishop of Caithness, who was also responsible for the cathedral at Dornoch. However, it seems that the gatehouse at Kildrummy may have been added later by Edward I's mason Master James of St George, who took such an active part in Edward's Welsh castle building. This is because Kildrummy fell to the English after a siege in 1306, and we know that it was afterwards repaired. Given the close similarities between the gatehouse here and that at Harlech, for which Master James is known to have been responsible, the presumption that it was an addition to the earlier plan seems irrefutable.

The castle belonged to the Earls of Mar, who were related by marriage to Robert the Bruce. It was this relationship which resulted in Kildrummy becoming a notable cockpit during the Wars of Independence, and why the Bruce sent his queen here after the defeat at Methven. So it was that the English came to Kildrummy, and although the Bruce's wife escaped from the siege his younger brother Sir Nigel and his comrades fell victim to the English besiegers. The castle was actually betrayed by a blacksmith called Osborne who set it on fire. It is related that he was rewarded by the English with 'as much gold as he could carry', which was poured down his throat!

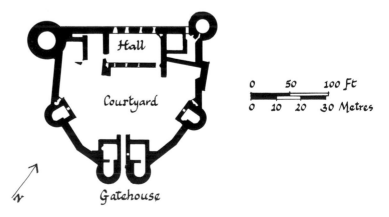

The regular plan of Kildrummy Castle.

151
ELGIN CATHEDRAL, Grampian

'The ornament of the realm'

The cathedral at Elgin was probably begun before the official establishment of the See of Moray here in 1224. The original church was modest enough, with an aisled nave, transepts and a square-ended aisleless choir. The west end did have twin towers, however, and there was a third tower above the crossing. A fire in 1270 extensively damaged this structure, and the nave was afterwards broadened by the addition of outer aisles to give a plan unique in Scotland. The eastern and western ends were also elaborated, and one of only three octagonal chapter houses in Scotland was added to the north side.

This was, apart from St Andrews, the finest medieval cathedral in Scotland, and in the tiers of windows in the east end of the presbytery and its wheel window we find more than an echo of contemporary work at

Map Reference NJ 223630, Map 28
The Cathedral is on the east side of the town, at the east end of Cooper Park. It is in SDD guardianship and open standard hours.

The twin towers at the west end of Elgin Cathedral. (Photo courtesy Peter Burton.)

A statue of Bishop Innes (1407–14) originally placed on the central tower but now in the south aisle.

Lincoln and other major English churches. Given this high quality of workmanship, it is even more tragic that the cathedral was preyed upon by the 'Wolf of Badenoch'. Alexander Stewart, Earl of Buchan, quarrelled with Bishop Alexander Bur, who excommunicated him. In May 1390 he, 'with his wyld Wykked Heland-men burned . . . the noble and highly adored Church of Moray with all the books, Charters and other valuable things of the country therein kept'.

So it was that a second massive programme of reconstruction was embarked upon, but this was directed towards the repair of the earlier structure rather than to its elaboration. The chapter house interior had to be remade, the western nave piers renewed, and the doors and windows of the magnificent west portal all date from after the Wolf's raid. This destruction was shocking enough, but the later story of the cathedral is even more unhappy. A fight called the 'Bloody Vespers' actually took place within the cathedral in 1555, and thereafter moral and physical decay took hold of the canons and their once beautiful church.

The history of Elgin is thus an affecting one, and we must use as much imagination as we can to conjure from its ruins the vision of a church which had been, 'the ornament of the realm, the glory of the kingdom, the delight of foreigners and stranger guests', as Bishop Bur lamented after the Wolf of Badenoch's raid.

152

THE CATHEDRALS OF DUNBLANE AND DUNKELD,
Central and Tayside

Map Reference Dunblane, Central: NN 782015, Map 57
The Cathedral is in guardianship and open standard hours. It is signposted off the A9.

Map Reference Dunkeld, Tayside: NO 025425, Map 53
The Cathedral is at the end of Cathedral Street. It is in SDD guardianship and open standard hours. In the close is the Cathedral Museum, open June–Sept. 10.30–12.30, 2.30–4.30, Mon-Sat.

The Diocese of Dunblane came into existence after the election of Bishop Clement in 1233; before this the bishop's 'cathedra' (seat) was probably at nearby Muthill, which appears in our Norman Guide. Dunblane Cathedral is substantially as built by Clement, but on the south side of the nave is a twelfth-century Romanesque tower which survives from an earlier church on the site. The Cathedral is of modest size and proportion with aisles to the nave only. On the north side of the choir is a long chamber, probably originally divided by a wooden screen. To the right of the doorway to the chamber is the effigy of a bishop, almost certainly the tomb of Clement the founder.

The nave is the most ambitious part of the church and has arcades of moulded and pointed arches with clustered shafted pillars. Above are clerestorey windows, again with shafts and moulded heads. The choir was refitted earlier this century, but at the west end of the church are preserved three of the late-fifteenth-century canons' stalls with carved misericords.

The west doorway and flanking trefoiled niches of Dunblane Cathedral.

These tipping seats, a common enough sight in major medieval churches, were provided to support the canons during long periods of standing during services. They are handsomely carved, and provide a rare glimpse of Scottish medieval ecclesiastical woodwork.

Dunkeld Cathedral stands on an ancient site beside the famous River Tay. The earliest part of the existing church is the unaisled choir, which was first built in the thirteenth century but remodelled by Bishop Sinclair before 1337. It is the nave which claims our attention, however. This was begun in 1406 by Bishop Cardeny whose abraded tomb lies in the south aisle replete with a fine crocketed ogee canopy and effigy. At first sight the nave looks decidedly Romanesque, with substantial drum pillars and restrained mouldings. The arcades are pointed and moulded, however, and in the middle stage are remarkable cusped semi-circular lights. This use of drum pillars is paralleled in the Kirk of the Holy Trinity at St Andrews, and was not apparently a reversion to earlier styles but an attempt to follow the contemporary fashions of the Low Countries where similar piers are known.

The Scottish thistle on a misericord of the Chisholm stalls at Dunblane.

Finally, in the fourteenth-century west tower are two wall-paintings depicting biblical themes. These rarities complement the choir stalls at Dunblane and together they provide a dim impression of the former glories of these cathedral churches. Bishop Lauder, who completed the nave, donated a reredos depicting the twenty-four miracles of St Columba, a heavy silver pyx hung above the altar, and on the pillars to either side were figures of angels. But all this finery was borne away on the later tide of iconoclasm; we are left with grey walls and memories.

153
DOUNE CASTLE, Central

Map Reference NN 731011, Map 57
Nearest Town Dunblane
Doune is 3 miles (4.8 km) west of
Dunblane on the A820. The castle
is in SDD guardianship and open
standard hours, but is closed all
winter.

*The dramatic site of Doune Castle
above the River Teith.*

Key to the highlands

The castle at Doune was established late in the fourteenth century to
control the key strategic route from Edinburgh to the western fortresses at
Dunstaffnage and Inverlochy. It was then that the Scottish kings turned
their attention to the subjugation of the Lord of the Isles, and its builder,
Robert Stewart, was not only the Regent of Scotland but also Duke of
Albany. This title implied an overlordship of the whole of Highland
Scotland, and Doune was to be the caput of his vast domain. Albany's
dominion over the Highlands was by no means assured, however, and long
after the construction of Doune battles were still being fought to decide the
issue.

Doune remains as an important early castle, with a great square
gatehouse tower containing the lord's accommodation and a separate set of

buildings containing the retainers' hall and offices. This separation of accommodation, which is also seen at English sites like Bodiam, reflects the parlous days of the later Middle Ages when the allegiance of the soldiery could not necessarily be guaranteed, and the requirements of rank and status also required the separation of the classes. The small doorway which now links the retainers' hall with the lord's accommodation is thus a later insertion, since its presence would otherwise have vitiated these attempts at segregation.

The lord's hall in the tower had a solar above with a small chapel set in the thickness of the outer wall. The entrance to this accommodation was up a separate staircase and in addition, the lord's chamber had a 'bolt hole' in the floor through which a rapid exit could be made. These arrangements clearly reflect the uncertain expectations of the castle's builder!

Particularly noteworthy at Doune is the imposing entrance, which was covered by an outer door, a portcullis and an iron 'yett' gate, a speciality of Scotland. The Doune yett is well preserved, and the manner in which it was carefully forged from iron bars is a triumph of the smith's art. Beyond is a long gate passage leading to the inner court; it is one of the most impressive castle entrances in Scotland. In the retainers' hall is a brave display of banners reflecting the many noble families who have links with Doune. Mary Queen of Scots came here, as did a number of high ranking prisoners when the castle was used as a prison by the Jacobites during the '45 rebellion.

154
THE PEEL OF GARTFARREN, Central

A medieval farm site

As the visitor to medieval Scotland cannot have failed to notice, the visible remains of the period incline to castles, cathedrals and churches with domesticity and the secular arts of peace being but poorly represented. In part, of course, this is due to the unsettled political conditions which affected Scotland at times during our period, but it is also seemingly a product of the nature of rural settlement here. Whereas in many parts of England nucleated villages were common in the Middle Ages, in Scotland matters seem to have been rather differently arranged.

Instead of a village-based settlement pattern, we find instead the concept of the 'group farm' which comprised a small cluster of houses and ancillary buildings. These units were known as 'fermtouns' in the Lowlands and normally as 'clachans' in the Highlands. They were occupied by tenants, normally three to eight in number, and held an uncertain number

Map Reference NS 535954, Map 57
Nearest Town Callander
From Callander take the A81 south towards Glasgow for 14 miles (22.4 km). The Peel is 1 mile (1.6 km) north of the B835 turning, on the left-hand side of the road, about 100 yards off the road in rough grazing. There is limited room to park beside the road and care should be taken.

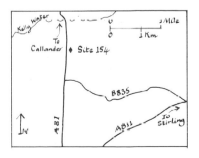

The ditch of the Peel of Gartfarren.

of cottars, who occupied cottages on the farm and laboured at a fixed rate when required. If such a settlement had a church, then it would be known as a 'kirkton', or if a mill, 'millton'. But such features were comparatively rare, and most would not have been so distinguished.

This interpretation is a product of projecting backwards the known later pattern of settlement; it is not certainly known that group farms existed in medieval Scotland, for we have neither excavated sites nor unequivocal documentary evidence. It is however generally thought that the group farm was the basic unit in many areas, and that an economy based on stock rearing and small-scale arable cultivation was the rule.

Here at Gartfarren, we have a site which might represent a 'fermtoun'. It is unusual because it is enclosed by a square banked and ditched enclosure, possibly to prevent cattle from straying, and the foundations of at least one rectangular house can be traced on the ground in the north-east corner. There would have been other buildings, but they would probably have been flimsily constructed of wood, and hence have left no trace above ground today. We cannot date this site, nor the extensive field system visible across the main road to the south, but it is probable that both are medieval, and that they together provide a tantalizing glimpse of rural settlement in medieval Scotland.

155
THE BATTLE OF BANNOCKBURN, Central

After the death of Edward I, 'Hammer of the Scots', on campaign at Burgh-by-Sands (Cumbria) in 1307, his weak and vacillating son Edward II ascended a parlous throne. Troubles at home with his nobles partly dictated an attempt to draw attention away towards the north, and in 1314 he rode into Scotland with a large and well-equipped army. Robert the Bruce had reduced the English presence to garrisons in the castles of Berwick, Bothwell and Stirling. All the other castles, including Edinburgh itself, had fallen by ruse or rout. Edward marched to the relief of Stirling, and it was just to the south of that town that his host was trapped by the Bruce on marshy ground near the Bannock Burn.

An attempt by Gilbert de Clare, Earl of Gloucester, and the 'Great Van' of the English army to dislodge the Scots from a strong position astride the Falkirk road was repulsed, and Edward resolved to outflank the enemy. He marched north-eastwards across the Burn and camped for the night. In the event his deployment was disastrous, for he had blundered into a trap. His chosen camp site, called the Carse, offered too narrow a front for the army to advance and it was bounded on three sides by the Bannock Burn, thus further hindering his deployment.

So it was that on the morning of 24 June 1314 the Scots closed the trap by advancing into the neck of the Carse and valiantly resisting the renewed onslaught of the Earl of Gloucester. This reverse was grave indeed for the English, but it turned into disaster when the shattered divisions fell back, effectively preventing the following ranks from engaging the enemy. The Scots, who used closely packed groups of spearmen called 'schiltrons', which had earlier proved their worth at Stirling Bridge and Falkirk, stood firm against the confused English attack.

The English advance having been thus broken, it was the moment for the three Scottish premier divisions under Bruce, Moray and Douglas to drive forward into the disorganized English army. The spearmen pressed relentlessly and the English archers, whose covering fire had proved so effective at Falkirk, were driven from the field by Bruce's light horse. The English wavered, and when Edward retired from the field the reverse became a rout.

How many of Edward's 20,000 men were killed is uncertain, but casualties were particularly heavy in the high-ranking force of cavalry and 500 were ransomed. In the words of one chronicler, 'Bannockburn betwixt the braes was so charged with horses and men that men might pass dry over it upon drowned horses and men.' Robert Bruce showed himself a brilliant tactician and a determined leader. Edward, by contrast, left the field a

Map Reference NS 812923, Map 57
Nearest Town Stirling
The National Trust has an information centre which is signposted off the M9 motorway at Junction 9. This is open daily April–Sept. Every 20 minutes there is an audio-visual presentation lasting 12 minutes, also a tourist information centre and a model of Stirling and the battlefield. The actual site of the battle is built over, although the Bannock Burn is still there. There is a monument on the spot where Robert the Bruce planted his standard, just near the Centre. See also the 15th-century bridge at Stirling.

The monument on the battlefield to Robert Bruce.

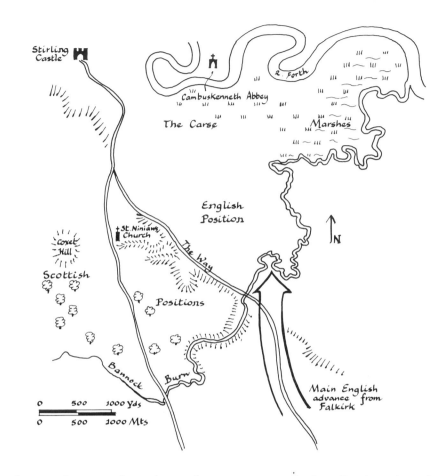

A simplified location plan showing the positions of the two armies.

disgraced man and vainly sought sanctuary in Stirling Castle only to be told that it must itself soon fall. He returned to England where, though his personal courage was never in doubt, his lack of military skill, coupled with his delight in the company of young men, sowed the seeds of his ruin.

At Bannockburn today is a rather sanitized visitor centre with audio-visual commentary, models of the field and copious information, retailing and restaurant services. It is frankly difficult in this atmosphere to invoke the gravity of this site on which such a heroic conflict took place. But beyond the gleaming portals, beside the monument, stands the splendid statue of the Bruce in his warlike caparison, mounted on his destrier. On the plinth are inscribed the immortal words of the Declaration of Arbroath which still summon up the blood:

Not for glory, riches or honours do we fight,
but for freedom alone, which no man loses but with his life . . .
Amen.

156

DOUGLAS, Strathclyde

St Bride's kirk

Although architecturally undistinguished, the chancel of St Bride's Church is one of the most evocative shrines of Scottish history. Time has dealt harshly with this parish church for it was once, by Scottish standards at least, quite impressive, having had an aisled nave which was a rarity among churches of its class. This feature, like the wealth of monuments on the site, is a tribute to the power and prestige of the Douglas family.

Apart from its monuments, this church has also played a more direct part in historical events, for it was here on Palm Sunday 1307, during the Wars of Independence, that the Black Douglas fell upon the English garrison as they left their morning devotions. The English commander was killed along with his men, and the Douglas castle, the site of which can still be seen in the nearby park, was utterly destroyed in line with the Bruce's 'scorched earth' policy.

Perhaps the most famous tomb in the church is that of 'Good Sir James' Douglas, who supervised the Palm Sunday slaughter and won lasting fame for himself in the desperate exploit of the Bruce's heart. King Robert I entrusted Douglas with the task of carrying his heart to the Holy Land after his death. Douglas hung the heart in a silver locket round his neck and set off. He got as far as Spain, where the King of Castile prevailed upon him to assist him in a fight against the Moors. He was mortally wounded and,

Map Reference NS 835311, Map 72
Douglas is west of the A74 Glasgow to Carlisle road on the A70. The church is on the north side of the village behind the square. Obtain the key from the keyholder; the church is in SDD guardianship.

The ruined nave of St Bride's Church, Douglas.

knowing that he could not go on, he flung the heart at the infidel host and cried, 'Go first, as thou wert wont to go!' and thus the Bruce led his final charge. The heart was fortunately rescued and placed before the high altar at Melrose Abbey. It was after this stirring episode that the original Douglas arms of silver with three silver stars on a blue chief (an upper horizontal stripe) were altered to incorporate the red heart of the Bruce.

157
BOTHWELL CASTLE, Strathclyde

Map Reference NS 688593, Map 64
Nearest Town Glasgow
On the south-east side of Glasgow near Uddington. It is signposted off the main road at Uddington and can be found down Castle Avenue with a short walk to the actual site. It is in guardianship and open standard hours, closed on Thurs afternoons and Fri in winter. It has a beautiful setting overlooking the Clyde.

A drawbridge slot in the north-eastern tower.

This powerful fortress in a bend of the River Clyde was built by Walter de Moravia (Moray) late in the thirteenth century. It embodied all the latest technology of castle-building, and finds its echo not only in the Edwardian castles of north Wales but also at Coucy in France. As originally planned, it had a massive circular donjon keep with its own separate moat and drawbridge. Before this was a huge kite-shaped bailey, the northern entrance of which was protected by closely set drum towers.

As Bothwell occupied an important strategic position, it changed hands several times during the Wars of Independence and was slighted by the Scots on at least two occasions. But the most noteworthy episode occurred in 1301 when Edward I took personal charge of a siege here. He ordered the construction of a tall tower called a 'belfry' at Glasgow and it was brought here on thirty waggons. This tower had a drawbridge at the top which dropped onto the wall head, allowing the besiegers to swarm into the fortress. Edward had 6,800 men at this siege, including engineers, masons and twenty-three miners from the Forest of Dean. The castle surrendered after three weeks, but it was besieged again on at least one other occasion.

Interestingly, the castle as first conceived was apparently beyond the resources of its builder. It appears that the defences of the great north ward never rose above the foundations which can still be traced in the grass. This is hardly surprising, for the cost of the original works, executed as they were in the finest polished ashlar, must have been prohibitive. This is not the only constructional enigma, for we know that the castle was deliberately destroyed on two occasions, once after Bannockburn and again after a brief English reoccupation under Edward III in 1336. This last episode led to the present inner ward acquiring its rectangular shape and the Douglases, who then owned the castle, added the fine machicolated tower to the south-east angle of the inner court. Bothwell is one of the finest examples of secular architecture in Scotland, and the finish of the thirteenth-century parts in particular could hold their own against any building in England or France.

158
GLASGOW, Strathclyde

Cathedral and houses

Glasgow Cathedral is the best preserved of Scotland's major medieval churches, and it is a remarkable tribute to the people of the city that they stoutly insisted on retaining the building. The diocese was established at Glasgow by King David I on an ancient site associated with the sixth-century bishop St Kentigern, otherwise known as St Mungo. The city arms commemorate the legend of the saint, since there is a robin, the head of which is said to have been miraculously restored, and a salmon with a ring in its mouth, which marks another of the saint's miracles. Although of

Map Reference NS 603656, Map 64
The Cathedral is not well signposted in the city. It is on the north-east side of the city centre. From George's Square go east along George Street, into Duke Street and left up John Knox Street. The Cathedral is in a small square with some parking available. It is in SDD guardianship but is also used for services. Open April–Sept, 10–7, and Oct–March 10–5.30. In the square also is Provand's Lordship which is run by the Museums Dept and Glasgow City Council and is open to the public. Provan Hall, on the outskirts of Glasgow, 6 miles (9.6 km) east of the centre, is not open to the public although it is owned by the National Trust for Scotland.

Glasgow Cathedral.

Stiff leaf carving on a capital near St Kentigern's tomb in the crypt of Glasgow Cathedral.

different constructional periods, the Cathedral presents a remarkably uniform appearance. It is an aisled rectangle on plan, the nave divided from the choir by a stone pulpitum, the only surviving example in Scotland.

It was in about 1240 that Bishop William de Bondington began to build his magnificent choir which, owing to the lie of the land, was supported on an undercroft. This was not only the site of St Mungo's shrine but also the setting for a virtuoso display of stone carving unsurpassed in Scotland. The stiff leaf capitals are tightly curled and deeply undercut, birds and other creatures lurk in the foliage and the whole effect is very English and on a par with Lincoln. Above the shrine rose Bondington's great choir which has wide moulded arches, paired triforium lights with pierced quatrefoil panels and triple clerestorey windows. The side windows have plate tracery and the sumptuousness of this interior is highly memorable.

The nave belongs to the later thirteenth century, and building continued into the fourteenth. This work is not so accomplished, but the eight large bays are highly unusual in having triforium and clerestorey bays linked under tall arches with clustered shafts. During the later fifteenth century Robert Blackadder, first Archbishop of Glasgow, began an addition to the south transept. Only the undercroft was completed, however, which is now called the Blackadder aisle. This has good roof bosses depicting armorial escutcheons and, in one instance, *memento mori*.

Apart from its splendid Cathedral, Glasgow also affords the rare opportunity to visit two medieval houses which belonged to the Canons of Banlanark. They were both apparently built in about 1470; Provand's Lordship in Castle Street was the town residence whilst Provan Hall just outside the city was the rural retreat. There are few surviving medieval houses in Scotland and both these are severely plain, which may be as much a reflection of their builder's taste as of the prevailing fashion. Provan Hall is a small rectangular hall house with a circular stair turret attached to one corner. The hall has a vaulted undercroft containing the original kitchen, and the stair tower is well looped for handguns, showing that the canon who built the house had an eye to his security!

Map Reference Dunstaffnage: NM 882344, Map 49
Nearest Town Oban
Dunstaffnage is 3 miles (4.8 km) north-west of Oban, signposted off the A85 at Dunbeg. It is in SDD guardianship and open standard hours, but closed Thurs afternoons and Fri in winter.

159

DUNSTAFFNAGE AND DUNOLLIE CASTLES, Strathclyde

Dunstaffnage is one of a small group of curtain wall castles in the West Highlands the others being Kisimull in Barra, Mingarry in Ardnamurchan and Tioram in Moidart. All are sited on rocky coastal outcrops, and their defences are arranged to fit their irregular sites. The castles cannot be closely dated but the first half of the thirteenth century seems architecturally and historically plausible, for it was then that Alexander II effectively extended his sway westwards to the Atlantic. If this is accepted, Dunstaffnage would probably have been built by Duncan McDougall, Lord of Lorn, or his successor Ewen. The curtain walls are of unusual strength and thickness, and Dunstaffnage varies from the others in the group by having projecting circular towers at three angles of its roughly quadrangular plan. In the courtyard are two ranges of buildings along the east and west sides, with the hall, now demolished, probably having been to the east.

Not far to the west of the castle stand the ruins of a chapel also probably built by Duncan McDougall. In plan, the chapel is a simple rectangle but interest attaches to the accomplished work of the paired side windows of the chancel. Although still of rounded form, the rear arches are decorated with continuous roll mouldings and dogtoothing. The use of free-standing shafts indicates that McDougall compensated for his reduced independence in the face of the King's advance by building a chapel of unusual quality.

Dunollie Castle, by contrast, is a fifteenth-century tower house of the familiar pattern set in a small square courtyard. The tower is square on plan and has a vaulted cellar reached by stairs in the southern angle beneath the two principal rooms. Unusually, the cellar roof retains impressions of the wickerwork shuttering used to support it during construction, a technique used in Anglo-Saxon England and later in Ireland. This was also a stronghold of the McDougalls, and commanded the important anchorage to the south which later became the town of Oban.

Map Reference Dunollie: NM 852314, Map 49
Nearest Town Oban
North-west of Oban, 1 mile (1.6 km) on the minor road to Garnavan. On a rocky outcrop in Oban Bay.

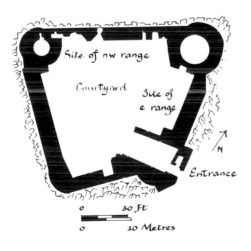

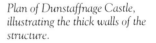

Plan of Dunstaffnage Castle, illustrating the thick walls of the structure.

160
WEST HIGHLAND SCHOOL OF CARVING, Strathclyde

Map Reference Iona: NM 284240, Map 48
Regular ferry service from the western tip of the Ross of Mull at Fionnphort. The island is owned by the National Trust for Scotland. There are 2 collections of medieval grave slabs on the island, one at St Ronan's Church by the Nunnery and the other at the Abbey Museum. Between the Nunnery and the Abbey is Macheans Cross, a late-15th-century sculpture.

Map Reference Kintyre: NR 695445, Map 62
Nearest Town Tarbert
At the Church of Killean, on the Mull of Kintyre, on the A83 20 miles (32 km) south of Tarbert. Medieval tombstones are in the north aisle of the ruined church.

Map Reference Campbeltown Cross, Campbeltown, Kintyre: NR 720204, Map 68
At the centre of a roundabout at the north-east end of the Main Street stands a late-14th-century disc-headed cross.

Map Reference Saddell Abbey: NR 784320, Map 68
Nearest Town Campbeltown
On the B842 9 miles (14.4 km) north of Campbeltown, the ruined abbey contains a collection of stones of the Kintyre and Loch Awe Schools.

Map Reference Kilmartin: NR 858935, Map 55
Nearest Town Lochgilphead
9 miles (14.4 km) north of Lochgilphead on the A816. The church contains a collection of carved slabs of the Loch Awe and Iona School in a former mausoleum; in SDD guardianship.

Carved crosses and gravestones
One of the most intriguing and distinctive products of late medieval Scottish society are the stone crosses and graveslabs of the West Highlands. Most seem to belong to the fourteenth and fifteenth centuries, and were apparently made at a variety of centres of which Iona is the most famous. Over 600 of these monuments are known or recorded, a figure which represents an uncertain proportion of the original output. While the carvings are all found within the boundaries of the medieval dioceses of the Isles and Argyll, they relate most closely to the area of authority of the Lords of the Isles, who were also patrons of the Abbey at Iona.

Iona, indeed, might be the key to this sculpture. The carvings there are probably the earliest of the four geographical groups identified by Steer and Bannerman in their book on the subject. This would be fitting, of course, in view of Iona's primary role in the history of Christianity in Scotland. But this correspondence should not encourage the easy conclusion that these later carvings were in any save the loosest sense a continuation of earlier Celtic traditions; the West Highland School was an independent development.

Whatever the origins of the School, they must be sought in later medieval Scottish society and, to judge from the persons of rank, wealth and status which the stones commemorate, in its upper echelons. Perhaps this Scottish tradition was the counterpart of the nearly contemporary movement in England towards funerary effigies, but if it was, why is the distribution so localized? These and many other questions should tease the visitor when these fascinating monuments are searched out in their often romantic and secluded settings. What follows is a brief summary of the principal groups, together with an indication of the decorative motifs used.

The Iona workshop was probably the earliest, and used a distinctive three-lobed motif used either singly, in opposed pairs, or with tendrils or roundels. Sometimes there are swords, galleys or panels of interlace. In the churchyard at Iona itself are fine relief slabs of soldiers and churchmen, providing a unique 'portrait gallery' of the fourteenth and fifteenth centuries. Details of vestments and armaments are faithfully reproduced, and the effigy of Bricius MacKinnon is particularly fine.

The Kintyre workshop made extensive use of foliate motifs, though trilobes also occur. The lobes here are of the same size, however, and the carving is less skilful with some overcrowding. Swords, often with decorated pommels, fish and animals occur, as do galleys with furled sails. This group may have been associated with the Abbey of Saddel in Kintyre.

The third group, which is less homogenous, has been termed the Loch Awe School. These are the least proficient of the West Highland carvings, and may have been executed by journeyman masons travelling about the region. The decoration is less structured, and the foliage flaccid. Panels bearing long central swords or depicting warriors are known.

Even more amorphous is the Loch Sween School, principally identifiable by the divergence of its motifs from those already described. This is a late development of the art, and is original in its composition and subject matter. Swords on these monuments are of the claymore type, which was unknown before 1500. A further late indication is the use of a stone of this type to commemorate the Prioress Anna, who died in 1543 and was buried at Iona.

Map Reference Keills Chapel: NR 691805, Map 61, and Kilmory Chapel: NR 702751
Nearest Town Lochgilphead
From Lochgilphead take the A816 north and after 1½ miles (2.4 km) turn left down the B8025 towards Loch Sween. Keills Chapel is at the end of this road (15 miles, 24 km). Kilmory Chapel is on the west side between Loch Sween and Loch Coalisport on the shore down a minor turning left off the B road past Castle Sween, 13 miles (20.8 km) down the minor road. Both chapels have been roofed in by the SDD and contain collections of medieval stones, mostly from the Loch Sween School.

A fifteenth-century slab of a soldier at Kileran, in the Iona School tradition.

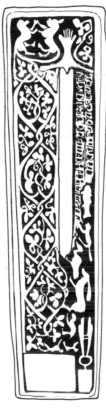

Another slab from Kileran, of the Kintyre School of carving. The inscription reads, 'John the son of Ewan had this stone made for himself and for his father'.

List of Medieval Kings

1216–72	Henry III	1413–22	Henry V
1272–1307	Edward I	1422–61	Henry VI
1307–27	Edward II	1461–83	Edward IV
1327–77	Edward III	1483	Edward V
1377–99	Richard II	1483–85	Richard III
1399–1413	Henry IV		

Glossary

ABACUS (plural 'abaci') The flat slab used on the top of a capital.

ADVOWSON The right of the patron of a church to nominate a new parson.

ADZE Tool used in masonry which resembled an axe with an arched blade at right angles to the handle.

AISLE, AISLED HALL In a church, an aisle is a space parallel to and divided from the main nave, choir or transept. In secular architecture, it describes a building in which the main rectangular space is flanked by parallel aisles.

AMBULATORY An aisle enclosing an apse or straight-ended sanctuary, often used for processional purposes.

APSE A semi-circular termination of a chapel or chancel.

ARCADE, BLANK ARCADE An arcade is a row of arches on pillars or columns. A 'blank' arcade is one in which the arches are left solid, and normally refers to decoration on walls.

ASHLAR Masonry constructed of squared hewn stones.

AUGUSTINIAN ORDER Popularly known as 'Black Canons' from the colour of their habits, they were an order of priests organized on monastic lines.

AUMBRY Recess or cupboard used for sacred vessels in a chancel.

BALLFLOWER Decoration consisting of a globular flower of three petals enclosing a small ball; characteristic of the early 14th century.

BARBICAN An outward extension of a gateway.

BASTION Projecting part of a fortification.

BATTER The inclined face of a wall, normally at the base.

BATTLEMENT Indented parapet of defensive wall made up of merlons (raised parts) and embrasures (the gaps between).

BELFRY Bell tower, attached or separate; bell space in a church tower.

BENEDICTINE ORDER The 'Black Monks' of the Order founded in 529 by St Benedict of Subiaco. The Rule of St Benedict formed the basis of practically the whole of later monasticism in medieval Europe.

BESTIARY Medieval moralizing treatise on beasts, often illustrated and which provided the inspiration for much medieval decoration.

BOSS An ornamental knob or projection covering the intersection of ribs in a vault, often carved.

BUTTRESS A mass of masonry projecting from or built against a wall to give added strength.

CAMERA A private withdrawing room.

CAPITAL The head or crowning feature of a column.

CARTHUSIAN ORDER Order of monks founded by St Bruno in 1086; this was the most austere order and emphasized the virtues of contemplation and personal austerity.

CHANCEL The east end of a church where the main altar is placed; reserved for clergy and choir.

CHANTRY CHAPEL Chapel attached to or inside a church given for the saying of masses for the soul of the founder and other specified persons.

CHAPTER HOUSE Room in a monastery where the business of the community was transacted and where a chapter of the Monastic Rule was read each day.

CHEVET The east end of a church provided with radiating chapels.

CISTERCIAN ORDER A 'reformed' Order founded in 1098 at Citeaux in Burgundy, a stricter offshoot of the Benedictines.

CLAUSTRAL Of the cloister, monastic buildings.

CLERESTOREY The upper stage of the main walls of a church above the aisle roofs, pierced by windows.

CLUNIAC ORDER Founded at Cluny in Burgundy early in the 10th century, the Order became famous for its elaborate liturgy and ceremonial and for its patronage of the arts.

CORBEL Block of stone projecting from a wall, normally supporting a roof.

CROCKET Decorative cresting put on the sloping sides of spires or gables.

CRUCIFORM Cross-shaped.

CRUCK Large curved timber supporting both walls and roof.

CRYPT Underground room beneath a church, often used for burials and the display of relics.

CURTAIN WALL A wall which connects two towers of a fortification; so called because it 'hangs' between the (taller) towers.

DAIS Raised platform at the end of a hall for a high table, throne, etc.

DECORATED Division of English Gothic architecture covering the first half of the 14th century.

DOG-TOOTH Typical Early English Gothic ornament in the form of a projecting pyramidal star.

DRIP MOULD Projection above a window or door which keeps rain from the parts below; also called a 'hood mould'.

DRUM PILLAR Large cylindrical columns, particularly used in late medieval Scottish churches.

EARLY ENGLISH The architectural style which succeeded Romanesque and which featured pointed arches, lancet windows and simple tracery.

EASTER SEPULCHRE A dresser-shaped recess, normally in the north wall of a chancel, used in the elaborate Easter ceremonial, often highly decorated.

EXTRADOS The external face of an arch.

FINIAL Ornament finishing off the apex of a roof gable.

FLUSHWORK Decorative use of flint and freestone, especially in East Anglia.

FREESTONE Any stone that cuts well in all directions and especially fine-grained limestone or sandstone.

FRESCO Method of painting a picture in watercolour on a wall or ceiling before the plaster is dry.

GABLETTE A decorative motif or feature in the form of a small gable.

GILBERTINE ORDER A double Order of monks and nuns founded during the 12th century by St Gilbert of Sempringham.

GOTHIC The pointed-arch style prevalent in western Europe from the 12th to the 16th century.

ICONOGRAPHY Illustration of a subject by drawings or figures.

IMPOST Bracket set into a wall upon which the end of an arch rests.

KEEP Great tower or donjon, the main element of a castle.

KNIGHTS HOSPITALLER Order of military monks founded c. 1048.

KNIGHTS TEMPLAR A military order originally formed to protect pilgrims to the Holy Land, suppressed in 1312.

LABEL STOP An ornamental or figural boss at the beginning and end of a drip mould.

LAVATORIUM A place for washing hands before meals in a monastery.

LAY BROTHER A man who has taken the habit and vows of a religious order but is employed in manual labour and is excused other duties.

LOZENGE A diamond shape.

LYNCHETS Long parallel terraces commonly found on hill slopes and formed by the extension of ploughing on to marginal land.

MACHICOLATIONS Openings supported on corbels at the top of a wall for dropping stones, etc., on besiegers.

MEDALLION Decorative panel in the shape of a medal.

MINSTER The mother church (not necessarily a cathedral or monastery) serving an area eventually divided up into parishes.

MISERICORD Shelving projection on underside of hinged seat in choir stall, serving when the seat was turned up to support person standing.

MOTTE AND BAILEY Castle comprising a mound of earth or turf (motte) and a defended open courtyard (bailey).

NAVE The western arm of a church, which normally forms the main body of the structure.

NIMBUS Bright cloud or halo over the head of a saint.

OGEE Arch with a double continuous curve, concave below and convex above.

PARVISE Room over a church porch.

PERPENDICULAR Division of Gothic architecture covering the period from c. 1350 onwards; so called from its emphasis on verticality.

PIANO NOBILE Principal storey of a house with the reception rooms; usually on the first floor.

PILASTER Shallow rectangular column projecting only slightly from a wall.

PISCINA Basin for washing the communion or mass vessels, provided with a drain; normally in or against the south wall of the chancel near the altar.

PRECINCT Space around a church or monastery enclosed by a wall.

PRESBYTERY The part of the church lying east of the choir; it is the part where the altar is placed.

PRIORY Monastic house whose head is a prior or prioress, not an abbot or abbess.

QUATREFOIL Symmetrical four-lobed shape.

RAMPART Stone wall or wall of earth surrounding a castle or other fortress.

REBUS A visual pun, normally on a personal name.

RELIC Revered object associated with a saint. This could either be a piece of clothing or some similar item, or else a fragment of a saint's body.

ROGATIONTIDE Days of prayer and fasting in the early summer associated especially with prayers for the harvest.

ROOD LOFT A gallery above a rood screen dividing nave and chancel.

SANCTUARY Area around the main altar of a church.

SCREENS PASSAGE Passage at the 'low' end of a domestic hall between the entrances to the service rooms and the screen which closed off the hall itself.

SEDILIA Seats for the priests, usually three in number, on the south side of the chancel of a church.

SOLAR Upper living-room of a medieval house.

SPRINGING Level at which an arch rises from its supports.

STRING COURSE Projecting horizontal band or moulding set in the surface of a wall.

TENEMENT A piece of land held by one owner; many such legal entities have survived almost unaltered from medieval times, thus providing a distinctive plan element in an otherwise modern arrangement, e.g. long, narrow tenements survive in the centres of many old market towns.

TIE BEAM Beam connecting the two slopes of a roof at the height of the wall tops to prevent the roof from spreading.

TRANSEPT The transverse arms of a cross-shaped church, normally between the nave and chancel.

TRANSITIONAL Term used to describe the buildings showing the change between the round-arched Romanesque style and the thinner-walled pointed-arch style of Early English Gothic, c. 1180–1200.

TREFOIL Symmetrical three-lobed shape.

TRUMEAU Pillar dividing a large doorway.

TYMPANUM Space between the lintel of a door and the arch above it; often decorated.

VAULT An arched ceiling or roof in stone; can be barrel, groined or ribbed.

VERNACULAR Native or indigenous architecture using local styles or materials.

VOUSSOIR A wedge-shaped stone used in the head of an arch.

Index

Note. page numbers for main entry are given in italics